The Millennial Kingdom

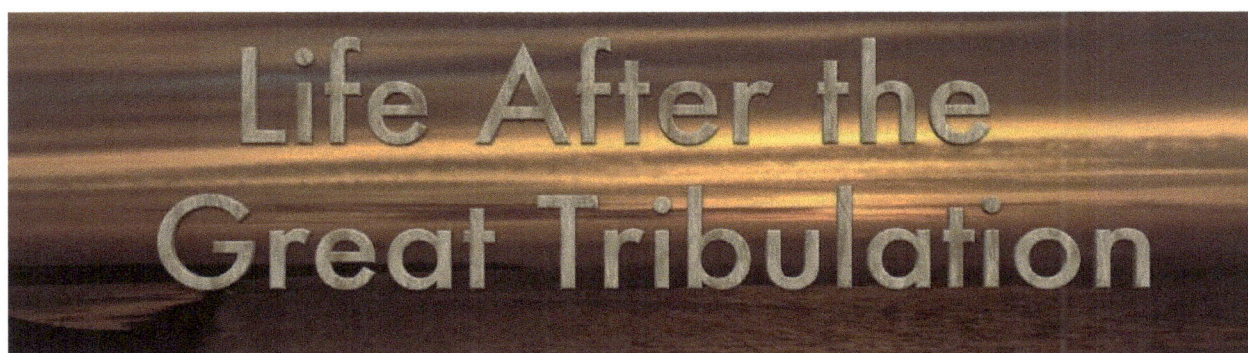

Life After the Great Tribulation

Don T. Phillips

"The Millenial Kingdom — Life After the Great Tribulation, by Don T. Phillips. ISBN 978-1-951985-45-5.

Published 2020 by Virtualbookworm.com Publishing Inc., P.O. Box 9949, College Station, TX 77842, US. ©2020 Don T. Phillips.

Preface

The *Millennial Kingdom* is a 1000 year period of time which will take place after the *Age of Grace* or the *Church Age* will have completed its appointed time. Since Jesus Christ died on the Cross of Calvary around 30 AD, there have been almost 2000 years that have elapsed since He established a New Covenant that was based upon faith and grace. When Jesus Christ was resurrected from the dead and ascended to His Father in heaven, the *ecclesia* (called out and chosen) in Christ started to form the *body of Christ*, which is the full body of all New Testament believers. Under the Old Covenant, salvation and eternal life were offered exclusively to the Jews, who were chosen by God to be His own holy people. The Nation of Israel (Jews) were called through Abraham and his progeny. They were to be a peculiar people...a holy people ...who God had chosen for Himself out of the earth. However, the blessings and salvation which were offered to Israel were *conditional* upon certain laws and commandments being observed.

Now therefore, if ye will obey my voice indeed, and keep my covenant, then ye shall be a **peculiar** *treasure unto me above all people: for all the earth is mine*   Exodus 19:5

When God rescued His people from slavery in Egypt, He gave them a set of statutes (the 10 commandments and 713 social, dietary and civil laws) to follow. The law was a *taskmaster* whose purpose was to show man that he could never live up to god's standards. The law was never meant to save anyone, but was intended to teach man that it was impossible to find salvation under the law. James said clearly that if anyone living by the law broke only one commandment of the law that the entire law had been broken (James 2:10). Breaking God's law was a sin, and the *wages of sin is death* (Romans 6:23). The opposite of death is life, and in the fullness of time God sent His only Son to redeem man from all sins and to offer eternal life by faith and grace. All of the Old Testament saints were saved in the same way as any New Testament saint....By faith in a Messiah that would be sent to redeem them from sin. Abraham is a prime example of an Old Testament man who was justified by faith, apart from the Law (which, when Abraham lived, was not even given yet): *Abraham believed God, and it was credited to him as righteousness*. If the law had been given to guarantee eternal life, then righteousness and salvation would have been by the law. But all had sinned and fallen short so that a redeemer had to have been sent from God that what live a sinless life and offer salvation and forgiveness of sin through His perfect life. The law was simply a tutor and taskmaster to bring us to the realization that we must be justified by faith in Him who knew no sin

Christ came and instituted a *New Covenant* which was not based upon the law but on *faith and grace*. There is a body of New covenant believers that teach a doctrine called *Replacement Theology*. Replacement Theology teaches that the Church has replaced Israel and the Jews in

God's eternal plan of salvation. This theology maintains that Israel is no longer God's chosen people and that only the Church (Body of Christ) has a place in God's plan or in the future. This is categorically false doctrine. The Jews have not been cast aside by God. Jesus Christ came and shed His precious blood for the sins of the *world*. Salvation is offered freely to both Jews and Gentiles. The New Covenant offers only one way that salvation can be attained...believe upon the Lord Jesus Christ with all your heart and mind. Jesus told the Jews during His earthly ministry: *I am the way, the truth, and the life: no man cometh unto the Father, but by me* (John 14:6). In Christ, there is no distinction between a Jew and Gentile (Romans 10:12). Yes, the Jews are God's chosen people, and through them came the Jewish Messiah and our Lord and Savior Jesus Christ. This promised *seed of Abraham* (singular) was to bless and redeem all the nations of the earth. It is only through Jesus that Jews—or anyone else—can find God's forgiveness.

God has made unconditional, covenant promises to Israel and the Jews that *cannot* be broken. One of the most important covenants that God made with Israel is the promise that Israel and the 12 tribes spawned from Abraham, Joseph and Jacob would one day inherit a land of promise and that they would dwell there in peace and prosperity. Even though Israel possessed the land after the exodus from Egypt, and they are reclaiming the land of promise today, Israel and the Jews have never conquered and inherited the land that was promised to Abraham, Moses and King David. The realization and fulfillment of this promise is the most important theme of the Millennial Kingdom. Another prophetic promise that god made to Israel is that one day King David will be restored to rule and reign over a 12 tribe, united kingdom. This will also be fulfilled in the Millennial Kingdom. Promises were not only made to the Jews and Israel that must come to pass, but promises were also made to the New Covenant saints that will one day complete the body of Christ. Two of the most important are that every Christian will be rewarded in the Millennial Kingdom for righteous works in the flesh while each was alive upon this earth. Those rewards will be determined at the *Bema Seat Judgment* following the *Battle of Armageddon*, and at the *Judgment of the Na*tions or the Judgment of the Sheep and Goats. All the Old Testament believers, the New Testament church, and Tribulation martyrs will receive their glorified bodies and return with Christ to reign as kings and priests for one thousand years (Exodus 19:6; Daniel 7:13-14; Zechariah 14:5-9; 1 Peter 2:5, 9; Jude 14-15; Revelation 1:6; 5:10; 20:6).

The promise and expectations of the 1000 year Millennial Kingdom are sometimes obscure, hidden and difficult to place in their proper perspective. Many prophecies and descriptions are found *hidden* in the Old Testament...particularly in the books of Joel, Daniel, Zachariah, Isaiah, Hosea and Ezekiel. In the New Testament practically every book has overtones of the Millennial Kingdom, but most particularly in Matthew, Mark, Luke and John and of course the prophetic Book of Revelation.

This book was written to unveil the mysteries of the Millennial Kingdom in a language and presentation that the average Christian can comprehend and understand. No matter how a person interprets the rapture of the church and what the Wrath of Satan and the Wrath of God means to a born-again Christian, every Christian will have an active role in the Millennial Kingdom. Hence, this book should be of interest to everyone who expects to be with Jesus Christ forever. A (hopefully) integrated, comprehensive and a biblically-supported discussion of the Kingdom is presented in 8 Chapters. When conjectures appear without definitive scriptural support are offered...The conclusion is presented as such. Scriptural references are liberally provided for future study.

Chapter 1 The Fullness of Time

This Chapter will present the 7 *Dispensations* of time which define God's timeline from Adam to eternity. The 8 main covenants that have been made between God and Man will then be placed into this timeline and which will be fulfilled in the Millennial Kingdom. The Theological beliefs which are commonly taught concerning the actual existence of the Millennial Kingdom will be summarized, and then the role of both the Jews and Gentiles in the Kingdom will be presented.

Chapter 2 The Millennial Kingdom

The Millennial Kingdom will bring about radical changes on the earth. Israel will be transformed into a fertile and peaceful land which will be farmed and harvested by Jewish inhabitants. The animal kingdom will be transformed such that the lamb will lie down with the lamb and children can play with cobras. These and other changes will be discussed. Christ will rule over 12 tribes of Israel with King David. Both Jews and gentiles, believers and unbelievers will live in nations around the world.

Chapter 3 Rule and Reign in the Millennial Kingdom

The Land of Promise as defined by God in Genesis 15-17. It is composed of Current Israel and parts of other surrounding countries. The land will be populated by 12 tribes of Israel. Christ will rule in a Theocracy over the whole world, and King David will be resurrected and rule over the 12 tribes. New and Old Testament saints will also rule and reign over cities and towns. Special responsibilities will be given to the 12 disciples and those who have been martyred serving Christ.

Chapter 4 Kingdom Inhabitants

The Millennial Kingdom will be populated initially by Jews from the 12 tribes of Israel and from a remnant chosen in the Judgment of the Sheep and Goats. These are all real people in earthly bodies. Over the next 1000 years there will be many believers, unbelievers, Jews and Gentiles who will scatter across the earth. Of particular interest is a group of 144,000 Jews from 12 tribes of Israel who will inherit the promised land.

Chapter 5 The Land of Israel

There were two divisions of the promised land. The 1st was after the 40 year exodus from Egypt. Joshua led Israel across the Jordan river and engaged the Gentiles that inhabited the land. Joshua was very successful, but never did conquer all of the land that was promised and never cleansed the land of idol worship. The 2nd division of the land will be in the Millennial

Kingdom and will fully realize the promise of God. Of particular interest is a 13th section of land that will be given to Jesus Christ which includes Jerusalem Christ will build His Holy Palace and His throne room just north of Jerusalem, and He will rule and reign at this site for 1000 years. A Holy Temple will be built in which sacrifices to Jesus Christ and to God will be offered. In remembrance of the accomplished work of Jesus Christ on the Cross of Calvary. The Feasts of Passover, Firstfruits, Unleavened Bread and Tabernacles will be observed.

Chapter 6   The Three Invasions of Israel

The Millennial Kingdom will be framed by 3 major invasions of Jerusalem. The 1st invasion will be 3.5 years before the Great Tribulation ends (The Jerusalem Campaign): The 2nd invasion will take place just as the Tribulation period ends and the Millennial Kingdom begins (The Armageddon Campaign): and there will be a final invasion of Jerusalem which will end the Millennial Kingdom (Satan's Last Stand). Each of these 3 invasions will be described in some detail.

Chapter 7 Judgments: Rewards and Condemnation

There will be three different judgments which will impact the Millennial Kingdom. The 1st is The *Bema Seat Judgment* for rewards. It will be held just after the Battle of Armageddon. Only those who have accepted Christ as their Lord and savior will be there. The 2nd is the *Judgment of the Sheep and Goats*. This will be held following the Bema Seat Judgment and will involve all of those who have survived the great Tribulation. The Sheep will be rewarded and will inhabit the Millennial Kingdom, and the Goats will be condemned and cast into the Lake of Burning Fire. The 3rd judgment is the *Great White Throne*. It is a judgment of unbelievers from all ages and those believers that have come out of the Millennial Kingdom... alive or dead.

Chapter 8   The New Jerusalem and Eternity

After the 1000 year Millennial Kingdom has run its course, it will be time for eternity to begin. There are five major issues which will be addressed.

- What will happen to this earth?
- What will happen to Satan and sin?
- Who will enter into eternity?
- Where will eternity be spent?
- Where will God and Jesus Christ call home?

The detailed features of the Millennial Kingdom are mostly hidden in the Old Testament, with other prophecies found in the canon of New Testament scriptures....particularly the Book of Revelation. The average Christian is either unaware or has never studied the 1000 year Millennial Kingdom. It might come as a surprise, but every born-again Christian will have a place in this Kingdom to Come. Join me in an exciting journey through the pages of the Holy Scriptures and be amazed at the wonders of this Kingdom.

Dedication

This book is dedicated to the Gideon Organization

Table of Contents

Chapter 1

God's Plan for the Fullness of Time

There is a wonderful age coming soon which is referred to as the *Millennial Kingdom*. It is the culmination of God's plan for man, which began in the Garden of Eden when He created Adam and Eve. The original plan of God was for man to live in peace and harmony with nature and the animal world. Adam and Eve were to live in the garden paradise of Eden where they were: *to be fruitful, and multiply, and replenish the earth, and subdue it: and have dominion over the fish of the sea, and over the fowl of the air, and over every living thing that moved upon the earth* (Genesis 1:28). The earth was to be ruled by God as a *theocracy*, and He would walk and talk with Adam and Eve in the cool of the evening (Genesis 3:8). In this perfect, ideal environment Adam and His descendents were to live forever. Only one law of God was not to be broken:

[**16**] *Of every tree of the garden thou mayest freely eat:*
[**17**] *But of the tree of the knowledge of good and evil, thou shalt not eat of it: for in the day that thou eatest thereof thou shalt surely die*   Genesis 2: 16-17

We all know the story....That old liar, Lucifer, tempted Eve and she fell from grace. It was the same old story, Eve thought that she knew more than God did and that she would not surely die if she ate of the fruit from the *Tree of Knowledge of Good and Evil*. It is the same today: Man in his sinful nature refuses to obey the will of God. He refuses to believe in faith that the time spent in this world is only a fleeting moment in eternity, and that there is an omnipotent and omniscient God who created the heavens, the earth and all that is in it. Sinful man cannot comprehend that within every mortal body is a soul that will live forever, and that eternity will be spent in only one of two places: Either with a loving and compassionate God whose only Son died for our sins, and offers every man or woman eternal life by believing in Him.... or in a place of eternal torments and agony called the *Lake of Burning Fire* (Revelation 21:8). There are those who claim to believe that Jesus Christ offers eternal life to all who will believe that He died for our sins on Calvary, and that He is the son of God but they change or ignore the clear teaching of the Holy Bible because of "political correctness". Such a "Christian" claims that the Bible is an updated book and can be ignored or reinterpreted. Just like Eve, they believe Satan and not the everlasting word of God. *God will not be mocked and He will not be deceived.* So Adam and Eve were driven from the Garden of Eden and sin ruled the world from that point on. God knew that His original plan for mankind was doomed to failure, and since time began He had known that Jesus Christ His only Son would be sent down from heaven to die for the sins of mankind; past, present and future, on the Cross of Calvary. Every Christian should be aware of God's progressive plan to redeem mankind. The plan of God involves 7 *Dispensations of Time*. The word *dispensation* should not confuse or bewilder any Christian today. A *Dispensation of Time* is simply a finite period of time over which God has dealt or will deal with men in a distinct way to fulfill His redemptive plan. This is such an important basic concept that the 7 dispensations of time will be briefly reviewed.

The graphic shown on the following page will frame our discussion. Most Christians will recognize Dispensation 5 (Dispensation of the Law) and Dispensation 6 (The Dispensation of Grace). Dispensations are sometimes called *ages*. We are currently living in the Dispensation of the New Covenant which is also called the *Church Age* or the *Dispensation of Grace*. The Dispensation of the Law and the Dispensation of Grace are separated by the Cross of Calvary. When Adam and Eve rebelled against God and committed the first sin, the consequence was *death* (Genesis 2:17). The Lord clothed their bodies in skin (Genesis 3:21) and drove them from the Garden (Genesis 3:23). When Adam left the Garden of Eden he began to die, and he lived 930 years (Genesis 5:5). So death reigned in the world until Christ Conquered death by His resurrection from the grave.

[14] *Nevertheless death reigned from Adam to Moses, even over them that had not sinned after the similitude of Adam's transgression, who is the figure of him that was to come.*

[17] *For if by one man's offence death reigned by one; much more they which receive abundance of grace and of the gift of righteousness shall reign in life by one, Jesus Christ.)*

[21] *That as sin hath reigned unto death, even so might grace reign through righteousness unto eternal life by Jesus Christ our Lord*   Romans 5: 14,17,21

When Christ died on the Cross of Calvary and shed His blood for the remission of sin, the *Age of the Law* was finished and a new *Age of Grace* began. We can now boldly stand *justified* before God, redeemed from sin by His only Son. This *Dispensation of Grace* will continue until the full body of Christ has been formed in Him. Sometime soon...at a time that only God knows....He will turn to His son Jesus Christ and tell Him: *GO*......It is time to gather all the *ecclesia* to you and then reclaim the world that Adam and Eve once reigned. At the first advent of Christ He came as a suffering servant to reconcile all men to God. When He will return a second time He will appear in all of His majesty and glory as a conquering king....the Lord of Lords and the King of Kings !

When this Age of Grace comes to an end at the second advent of Christ, the 7th and last Dispensation will begin, which is the 1000 year **Millennial Kingdom**. We will now briefly review these 7 dispensations. For a complete discussion and exposition of each age, see Phillips, *The Eternal Plan of God*.

The Seven Dispensations of God

A *dispensation* is defined as a certain *period of time* during which God deals with people in a particular way. The Greek word for dispensation is *oikonomia*, and in the Bible it is used to mean a *manner, method, or particular arrangement of dealing with a group of people that God has chosen.* Calling a dispensation primarily a period of time will not bear up under close scrutiny of the scriptures. Usually the length of time is not emphasized or even mentioned; it is the manner in which God is dealing with mankind over a particular period time which distinguishes one dispensation from another. The word **dispensation** is found four times in the scriptures, all in the New Testament writings of the apostle Paul (I Corinthians 9:17, Ephesians 1:10, Ephesians 3:2, Colossians 1:25). Each verse makes it clear that God has always dealt with man according to specific promises, commands, relationship or laws. In Ephesians 3:2, Paul reveals to the Gentiles that God is now redeeming man by *grace* and not by *works*. Grace is defined to operate not over a specific period of time, but across all time both before and after the cross. It is not a work-based doctrine but a faith-based doctrine. The salvation of mankind has always been based upon *faith* in His Son, Jesus Christ, and is a free gift. The Old Testament saints from Adam to the 1st advent of Jesus Christ only knew that forgiveness of sins and redemption would someday come by a prophesied redeemer; New Covenant saints now know that the *anointed* or *appointed* one was *Jesus Christ*. Salvation by faith has *always* been the only way that mankind could be redeemed from sin. In reality, it was not free at all but a great price was paid by Jesus Christ for the redemption of all mankind on the cross of Calvary.

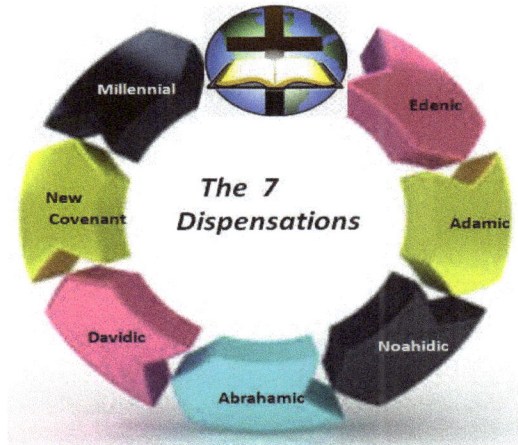

The *Dispensation of Grace* can be contrasted with the *Dispensation of the Law,* where the relationship between man and God was based upon observing God's written laws. Under the Law, obedience was not an option but was demanded by God. Obey the laws and live; break them and die (Galatians 3:10-13). The Law only condemned and was put in place to show people that it was impossible to live under God's standards. James wrote that if one breaks only one law, he has broken them all.

For whosoever shall keep the whole law, and yet offend in one point, he is guilty of all
James 2:10

For all have sinned, and come short of the glory of God   Romans 3:23

The opposite of *death* is *life*, and Jesus Christ came not to abolish the law but to replace the law with a New Covenant that is based upon salvation by faith and grace. In the *Dispensation of the New Covenant,* the law is still holy and good because it was given to man by God, who is pure and good.... but it no longer condemns man to eternal death. Christ said: *I am the way, the truth and the life*. It is not that the Law was unjust : salvation by grace does not negate the law, but makes it possible for all who believe in Jesus Christ as their savior to live and not die under eternal condemnation.

For the law having a shadow of good things to come, and not the very image of the things, can never with those sacrifices which they offered year by year continually make the comers thereunto perfect.   Hebrews 10:1

God uses dispensations to deal with man in different manners, under different circumstances, to teach and reveal Himself and His eternal plans. When God reveals himself to man, the revelation may be at a specific point in time; but because it is the nature and character of God that is being revealed it is usually bound to that particular point in time or necessarily limited to the dispensation in which it is revealed

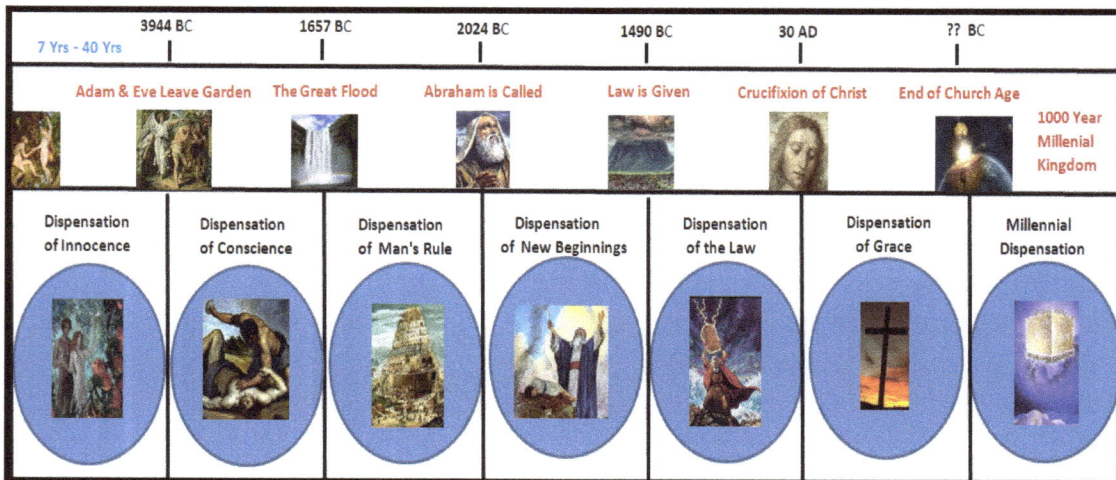

3944 BC	1657 BC	2024 BC	1490 BC	30 AD	?? BC
7 Yrs - 40 Yrs					
Adam & Eve Leave Garden	The Great Flood	Abraham is Called	Law is Given	Crucifixion of Christ	End of Church Age
					1000 Year Millenial Kingdom
Dispensation of Innocence	Dispensation of Conscience	Dispensation of Man's Rule	Dispensation of New Beginnings	Dispensation of the Law	Dispensation of Grace	Millennial Dispensation

4

The history of man can be divided into seven different distinct periods of time called *Dispensations*. The previous graphic provides an overview of the seven different dispensations that will span the existence of mankind upon this earth. God is currently in the 6th dispensation of time, and it has been almost 6000 years since Adam and Eve were created.

Dispensation of Innocence

The *Disposition of Innocence* began with the creation of Adam and Eve and continued until they sinned against God and were cast out of the Garden of Eden. The duration of this period of time is unknown. It has been proposed as one week, less than one year, seven years and even 40 years long by various biblical scholars. The end of the Dispensation of Innocence clearly demonstrates what can happen to man if they do not obey a sovereign and Holy God and follow their own will and conscience. When Adam and Eve were cast out of the Garden of Eden, they left a perfect, sinless place. They were given dominion over all of the earth and were sustained by all manners of fruit which grew in the Garden. They were only required to till and keep the Garden of Eden in which they lived, and to replenish the earth with their offspring. The concept of sin was not known at all. God had only one command or law, and that was that Adam or Eve could not partake (eat) of the fruit of the *Tree of Good and Evil*. When Lucifer came and tempted them to eat the fruit of the *Knowledge of Good and Evil*, he told Eve a lie which she believed. Satan convinced Eve that if she ate the fruit, she would not die but knowing good from evil she would then be like God. Eve's problem was the same as men and women have today; she thought that she knew more than God. We should not be strictly critical of Eve, Adam ate the fruit also. So both Adam and Eve sinned by eating the fruit and for that sin they were expunged from the Garden of Eden. They would have lived forever and walked with God in the cool of the evening, but from the moment that they both sinned they began to die. Adam lived for 930 years after he and Eve were cast out of the Garden.

Disposition of Conscience

The *Dispensation of Conscience* lasted about 1,656 years from the time that Adam and Eve were evicted from the Garden of Eden until the Great Flood (Genesis 3:8–8:22). This dispensation of time had no written laws and the behavior of man was dictated by his own will and conscience. This does not imply that man did not know good from evil or was not aware that man did not know sin. The heart and mind of man clearly understood what was right from wrong. Discernment and truth was inherited from Adam when he ate from the tree of knowledge which differentiated good from evil. However: *When there is no written law then how could sin be defined* ? (Romans 4:15). The apostle Paul addressed this question when he spoke of the Gentiles, who were not under the law of Moses

[14] For when the Gentiles, which have not the law, do by nature the things contained in the law, these, having not the law, are a law unto themselves:
[15] Which shew the work of the law written in their hearts, their conscience also bearing witness, and their thoughts the mean while accusing or else excusing one another
Romans 2: 14-15

Every man and woman is inherently aware of good and evil. Each posses a clear standard by which individual actions can be judged. This understanding and knowledge is called *conscience.* conscience might be the most sensitive aspect of human nature. It is the instinctive knowledge of right from wrong.

Adam was alive during most of this dispensation. He and Eve began to populate the world and live in it. Many things changed because they sinned. Houses had to be built.....gardens had to be planted and cultivated....and the animal kingdom was now at enmity against all mankind. In the Garden of Eden, Adam and Eve were vegetarians. Now they could eat meat but no blood. Adam undoubtedly told his offspring and their children the consequences of sin, but they would not listen. They went their own way and did not obey the Lord. There was no written law, but the scriptures clearly reveal that after Adam and Eve fell, evil and sin was understood without any written law. This is made plain when Cain slew Abel. When God found what he had done, Cain responded by saying: *Am I my brother's keeper?* He knew that he was and he knew that he had sinned when he killed his own brother out of jealously. *How did God respond?* He banished Cain from his presence forever and drove him into the wilderness. One cannot mock God or sin against God without suffering the consequences. Things only got progressively worse until God had enough. The earth was filled with violence, corruption and sin; and so God told Noah to build an *ark*. After 120 years He would destroy the world with a great flood: *The wages of sin is death.* The only righteous people who would be spared from death were Noah, his 3 sons and their wives...eight in all. After the great flood, the world had been purged from all sin and was ready to begin anew. *Would things now be different?* Unfortunately, sin still existed in every man ....the sin nature had been imputed to all of these 8 people by Adam and would be passed on to all who would be born by man and women.

Dispensation of Man's Rule

The *Dispensation of Man's Rule* has also been called the *Dispensation of Human Government.* It lasted about 425 years and began when Noah and his family left the Ark after God had brought a great flood upon the whole earth. God looked at His creation and found that only Noah, his three sons and all their wives were worthy of saving. It is true that all mankind sprang from Adam and Eve, but it is equally true that people on the earth today also sprang from Noah and his family. Man was once again to re-populate the earth, and they ruled themselves without any written laws. They were ruled by their heart, their own conscience and the inherent conflict between good and evil. When man was left to follow his conscience after Adam and Eve was expelled from the Garden of Eden, they failed miserably. They would not learn to live in righteousness. There is a strange paradox concerning what defined sin before the law was given to Moses. Paul wrote:

Blessed is the man to whom the Lord will not impute sin   Romans 4:8

Because the law worketh wrath: for where no law is, there is no transgression   Romans 4:15

If there was no law before Moses, then how could those people before the law was given be held accountable? There may not have been a written law, but we know for sure that sin existed before the law.

[**13**] *For until the law sin was in the world: but sin is not imputed when there is no law.*
[**14**] *Nevertheless death reigned from Adam to Moses, even over them that had not sinned after the similitude of Adam's transgression, who is the figure of him that was to come*
Romans 5: 13-14

This is a very difficult passage of scripture. The *law* which Paul references in Romans 5:13 was the Law given to Moses at Mt. Sinai. Paul concludes that even before the law had been written down, sin was already in the world: *Sin reigned between Adam and Moses*. He then paradoxically states that if there is no law then sin cannot be imputed. His conclusion is not only universal but logical. One cannot break a law when there is no law! But, Adam sinned against God when there was no written law so the conclusion is that Adam had broken a law against God that was not written down. Even if man did not sin *after the similitude of Adam*...they did not eat of the forbidden fruit.... the *wages of sin are death* and *death still reigned*. This is an astounding truth to anyone today who thinks that they can be saved without breaking any of the 10 commandments. Christ stated during His earthly ministry that: **all have sinned, and come short of the glory of God** (Romans 3:23). Hence, there are only two possible conclusions: (1) Men before the law was written on tablets of stone sinned because their conscience and their actions were contrary to any law...written or unwritten. *Who would deny that before the 10 commandments were written down on stone, murder is a sin*? When Cain slew Abel there was no written law, but He clearly understood that he had both lied to God and that he had sinned against his brother (2) Strictly interpreting Romans 3:23, sin is a consequence of violating God's laws. Since sin *was* present (Romans 5:14).....then not only did conscience reveal sin to man, but God must have revealed to them actions which would constitute sin. Either way....there is one immutable and eternal truth that can be learned: Any person who had committed a sin between Adam and the cross knew that sin must be forgiven if they were to stand before God and inherit eternal life. Those who trusted God and followed after his precepts and holiness believed in faith that God would provide a way to redeem man from the consequences of sin. All of the Old Covenant *saints* died in faith that a redeemer would arise who would take away their sins. This was prophesied even before the great flood (Genesis 3:15). It is reasonable to assume that all who lived before the law was given to Israel and Moses would know that a redeemer would arise. The 10 commandments are sometimes called the Law of Moses, but make no mistake about it....the law was given to Moses by God. It should be properly called *the Law of God as given to the people by Moses*. The key concept is that every person from Adam to the end of the Church Age would be saved in exactly the same way....*by faith*.

Dispensation of New Beginnings

The *Dispensation of Man's Rule* ended when Abraham was called out of Ur in the land of the Chaldees. At that time, God would start a *new* dispensation called the *Disposition of New Beginnings*. This new dispensation established Israel as God's chosen people, and it lasted 430 years between when Abraham was called out of the Chaldees to when God liberated Israel from Egyptian bondage and gave the written law to Israel at Mount Sinai. The *Dispensation of New Beginnings* was 430 years long, and it was divided into two distinct periods of time: (1) The *Age of Promise*, and (2) The *Age of Bondage*.

The Age of Promise lasted exactly 215 years. It began when God called Abram out of Ur of the Chaldees and ended when Abraham took his family to Egypt. God made several covenant promises with Abram and then changed his name to *Abraham* (Genesis 7:15), which means "Father of many nations". A new beginning with a new patriarch who had been given a new name. During this period of time Abraham, Lot his brother, and the new Nation of Israel grew and prospered. They lived in a land with new covenant promises called the *Land of Canaan.* This continued until God caused a natural disaster to occur which was to test the faith of His new nation. Abraham was a great man of faith (Hebrews 11:8) but just like all mortal men his faith gave way to doubt, In an act of not believing God to sustain and protect His chosen people, Abraham left the land of promise and took his families to Egypt. During the period of time that Abraham and his family lived in Canaan, God dealt with Israel as a *theocracy*. He was the divine ruler who directly communicated with man to reveal His sovereign will. When the Children of Israel left Canaan they were divinely protected for several years by Joseph, and then they became slaves making bricks and cutting rocks for the great pyramids. The sub-age of *Promise* had given way to the sub-age of *Bondage*. Promise and prosperity had given way to servitude and slavery.

The Age of Bondage also lasted exactly 215 years. Because of unbelief and failure to accept God as their theocratic ruler in Canaan, the Children of Israel became the property of the Egyptian Pharaoh. Israel spent 215 years in Egypt in slavery under several Egyptian Pharaohs. Finally, God in His mercy heard their cries and sent His servant, *Moses,* to lead them out of bondage. Moses was a very unusual man: As a young child He was adopted into Egyptian royalty and served the Pharaoh for 40 years. After he killed an Egyptian, he fled Egypt and became a lowly sheppard in the Land of Mideon. As He was tending sheep, God appeared to him and called him back to Egypt to free His people from bondage. The

Dispensation of *New Beginnings* ended after Moses led the Nation of Israel out of Egypt, crossed over the Red Sea, and was given the Law was given by God to the people at Mount Sinai.

Dispensation of The Law

The *Dispensation of the Law* lasted approximately 1520 years. It began at Mt. Sinai in 1490 BC when Moses and the people were given the 10 Commandments, and ended when Christ suffered and died on the Cross of Calvary in 30 AD. The Dispensation of the Law is often called the *Old Covenant*. When it ended, it was superseded and replaced by the *New Covenant*. The Dispensation of the Law had one major feature: God gave Israel a set of 10 commandments through Moses at Mount Sinai after they had crossed the Red Sea and emerged as a free nation. The 10 Commandments...which are generally referred to as *The Law*.... were given to govern their religious and moral character, and through time another 613 commandments were given to govern their social, dietary and religious life. The Law could never save anyone; it was a *taskmaster* which brought man to the full realization that no one could live as righteous as God commanded, and sin resulted in death and condemnation.

Dispensation of Grace

The New Covenant ushered in a new period of time called the *Dispensation of Grace*. The Dispensation of Grace is still in effect today, and will continue until the 2nd advent of Christ. Our Lord and Savior Jesus Christ came not to destroy the Law but to fulfill the law. His sacrificial death as the perfect Lamb of God on the Cross of Calvary ended the Dispensation of the Law. Redemption from sin, salvation, and the gift of eternal life was now based upon faith and appropriated by grace. Salvation by faith and grace began what we now call the *New Covenant*. The Dispensation of Grace started in 30 AD and will continue until Jesus Christ returns as a conquering king at His 2nd advent. This is generally identified as taking place on the Feast of Yom Kippur. Note that this belief does not predict the time and date of the 2nd advent of Christ. It does not even predict the day since the Feast of Yom Kippur can fall on a different day in different years.

The Millennial Dispensation

The seventh and final *Millennial Dispensation* will begin after the great Tribulation ends and the *Battle of Armageddon* is fought at the end of the Church Age. The 1000 year *Millennial Kingdom* will begin after the *Battle of Armageddon* is fought outside of Jerusalem; after the *Bema Seat Judgment* of all believers for rewards; and after the *Judgment of the Nations* (See Chapter 7. The Millennial Dispensation will last 1,000 years and is commonly referred to as the *Millennial Kingdom*. The word *Millennial* never appears in scripture, but has been constructed from two Latin words; *Mille* which means *thousand* and *annul* which means *year*. The beginning of the Millennial Kingdom will initiate a 1000 period of time during which Jesus Christ will rule and reign *on this earth* from His palace and throne in Jerusalem. His Kingdom will be worldwide but it will begin with a Jewish remnant from each of the 12 tribes of Israel who will finally inherit and live on the land that God promised to Abraham long ago. The 1,000-year millennial kingdom will end in the creation of new heavens and a new earth. This earth as we now know it will be purged by fire and restored to an Edenic state: Eternity will then begin.

It is impossible to understand the Millennial Kingdom without understanding its purpose in God's plan for both the people and the earth that He has created. *The Church* Age and the *Great Tribulation* has come to an end. Every saint had earlier been raised from the grave or *raptured* out of an evil world. After the *Wrath of God* is poured out on a sinful world (the 7 Bowl (Vial) Judgments (Revelation 16:1), Satan and his army will be defeated at the Battle of Armageddon: The Antichrist and the False Prophet will be cast into the *Lake of Burning Fire*, and Satan will be bound and cast into the *Bottomless Pit*. After the Battle of Armageddon, the Bema Seat Judgment for reward of all the saints and the Judgment of the Nations will then be held (See Chapter 7). *Why doesn't eternity start at this time? What is the purpose of the 1000 year Millennial Kingdom? What role will the Nation of Israel and the redeemed saints play in this new Kingdom of God?* we will answer these and many other questions in subsequent Chapters, but before this can be accomplished one needs to understand God and His Covenant Relationship with Israel. The covenant that God made with Abraham and Israel are central to understanding the role and purpose for Israel and the 1000 year Millennial Kingdom. For completeness, we will briefly discuss the major covenant relationships which God has established with man.

Covenants of God

There are 8 major covenants which God has made with man. These covenants are spread over the 7 different dispensations already briefly discussed. These seven *Dispensations* divide the full council of God's word and His plan for mankind into seven distinct periods of time. However, the seven Dispensations are not of the same duration and they do not overlap with one another. Each Dispensation starts with a distinct event after which God will deal with man in a particularly different way. Equally important is the concept of a *Covenant Relationship*

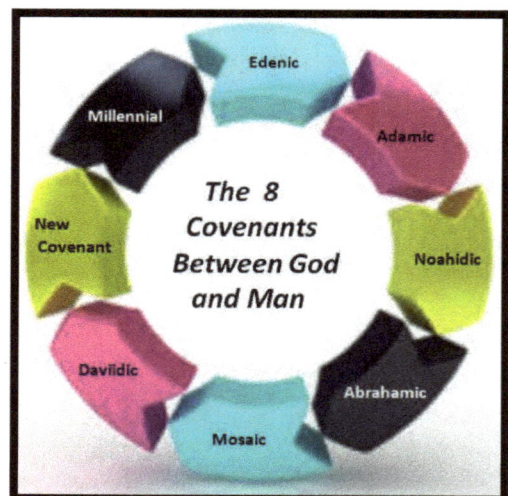

The 8 Covenants Between God and Man

Edenic
Adamic
Noahidic
Abrahamic
Mosaic
Davidic
New Covenant
Millennial

between God and mankind. A **covenant is a sacred agreement between God and a person or a set of people.** The Greek word for covenant can also mean *promise*.

When God makes a covenant promise with mankind, there are always specific conditions and agreements between the two parties. Man's relationship to God has always been largely based upon covenantal promises. The study of *Biblical Covenants* is central to understanding how God has dealt with man and the sin issue throughout the seven dispensations. Different dispensations always operate under specific covenant relationships with God, but not all dispensations are defined by covenants. Specific covenants between God and man can start and end *anywhere* across the spectrum of the seven dispensations and usually exist through more than one dispensation. Understanding the way covenants operate within and between the seven different dispensations will reveal to man how to *rightly divide the word of God.* Covenants between God and man fall into two mutually exclusive and independent categories. They are either (1) *Conditional,* or (2) *Unconditional.*

Conditional Covenants

A *conditional covenant* usually depends on the faithfulness of one or more parties, and the covenant is invalidated if either party should break the conditions of the covenant. Whenever a conditional covenant is made between God and man, if the covenant promises are made null and void,the trespass is *always* by man and not by God. This is sometimes misunderstood: God will never invalidate or change the conditions of an *unconditional covenant* made by Him, but He is justified in annulling a *conditional* covenant if man fails to keep the conditions of the covenant. The classic example of a conditional covenant between God and man was the one that God made to Adam and Eve in the Garden of Eden. The Lord made the Garden of Eden for Adam and Eve to live in forever. He gave them dominion over all of the creatures that He had made, and provided for everything that they might need. They were to commune with God and live forever by eating of the Tree of Life. God *promised* Adam and Eve that this would go on forever. There was only one Law that could not be broken.

But of the tree of the knowledge of good and evil, thou shalt not eat of it: for in the day that thou eatest thereof thou shalt surely die   Genesis 2:17

Adam and Eve violated their covenant with God and ate of the *tree of the knowledge of good and evil* which rendered their covenant with God null and void.

When Israel reached Mount Sinai 47 days after leaving Egypt, Moses went up on the mountain and met with God.

11

[3] *And Moses went up unto God, and the LORD called unto him out of the mountain, saying, Thus shalt thou say to the house of Jacob, and tell the children of Israel;*
[4] *Ye have seen what I did unto the Egyptians, and how I bare you on eagles' wings, and brought you unto myself.*
[5] *Now therefore, **if ye will obey my voice** indeed, and **keep my covenant**, then ye shall be a peculiar treasure unto me above all people: for all the earth is mine:*
[6] *And ye shall be unto me a kingdom of priests, and an holy nation. These are the words which thou shalt speak unto the children of Israel*
[8] ***And all the people answered together, and said, All that the LORD hath spoken we will do***
Exodus 19: 3-6

Sadly, within days the people were worshipping idols of gold. They soon lost their *treasure* by getting worse and worse. Finally, God had all 12 tribes taken into captivity and the City of Jerusalem was burned and ransacked. This is why their land of promise is still largely in foreign hands today.

Unconditional Covenants

An *unconditional covenant* is one that is not dependent on the faithfulness of either party, but remains valid from its point of initiation until it is fulfilled. Unconditional covenants are unilateral between God and man. The interesting thing about an unconditional covenant between God and man is that no matter how unfaithful or disobedient man might be, the covenant (promise) will always be fulfilled because God is faithful and true and cannot lie. What God promises unconditionally, He will fulfill. We will see that unconditional covenants initiated by God to Abraham over 3500 years ago continue to be in effect from the moment that God stated His promises until the promises come true, no matter how much time might elapse. There may or may not be conditions to be met by man when God makes an unconditional covenant. Violation of any conditions may delay the fulfillment of the covenant, but will not cancel the promise(s) of God. Covenants in the Bible between God and man are always originated by God and are an act of His holiness and grace. Since God is faithful and true (Jeremiah 42:5), He cannot lie and cannot sin. *Conditional covenants* between God and man *always* terminate because of the unfaithfulness and the sinful nature of man. *Unconditional Covenants* between God and man may be delayed, but will always be fulfilled. There were eight main covenants made between God and man throughout Biblical history.

- **The Edenic Covenant**
- **The Adamic Covenant**
- **The Noahidic Covenant**
- **The Abrahamic Covenant**
- **The Mosaic or Old Covenant**
- **The Davidic Covenant**
- **The Covenant of Grace or the New Covenant**
- **The Millennial or Kingdom Covenant**

The following diagram illustrates the timing and relationship between each of the seven different dispensations and the eight covenants which were made between God and man. The key event which triggers each dispensation is also given, along with the approximate date that each of the seven dispensations begin and end. Except for the *Davidic Covenant*, the year in which each covenant is given corresponds to a dispensation start date. However, the duration of each covenant might span one or more dispensations...... particularly if the covenant is unconditional.

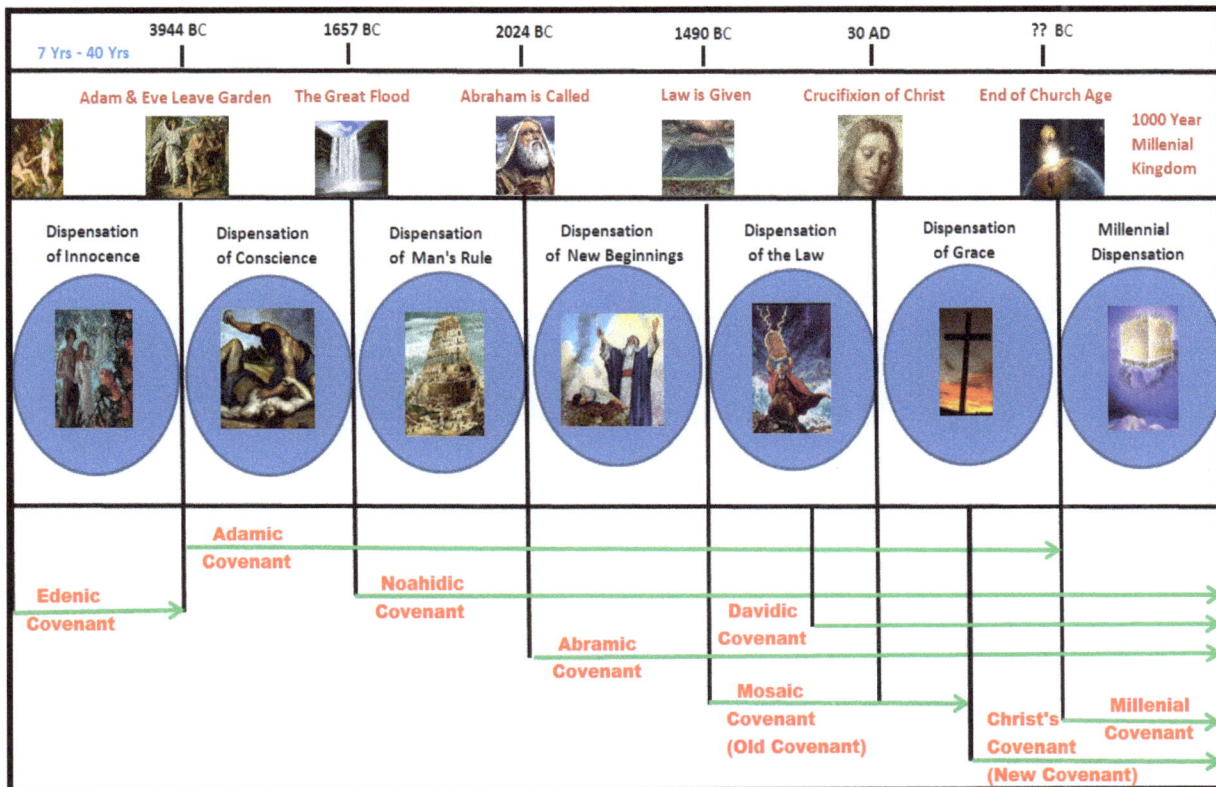

3944 BC	1657 BC	2024 BC	1490 BC	30 AD	?? BC
7 Yrs - 40 Yrs					

Adam & Eve Leave Garden	The Great Flood	Abraham is Called	Law is Given	Crucifixion of Christ	End of Church Age	1000 Year Millenial Kingdom

Dispensation of Innocence	Dispensation of Conscience	Dispensation of Man's Rule	Dispensation of New Beginnings	Dispensation of the Law	Dispensation of Grace	Millennial Dispensation

Edenic Covenant

Adamic Covenant

Noahidic Covenant

Abramic Covenant

Davidic Covenant

Mosaic Covenant (Old Covenant)

Christ's Covenant (New Covenant)

Millenial Covenant

The Eight Covenants Between God and Man

Adamic Covenant (Genesis 1:26-30, 2:16-17)

The Adamic Covenant was unlike the other covenants that were established between God and man. The Adamic Covenant was more like a set of rules that Adam and Eve had to follow as they lived in the Garden of Eden. God established a set of restrictions that had to be followed as they experienced an intimate relationship with Him. We call these commandments *covenants* consistent with biblical literature, and to emphasize that God cannot tolerate sin or disobedience. The omnipotent God exists at an entirely different plane than mankind. The Adamic Covenant included the command to multiply and to populate the earth with their offspring. However, the most important restriction was to never eat from the tree of the knowledge of good and evil. This *covenant* contained a terrible penalty for disobedience; if violated, both Adam and Eve would *surely die*.

13

Noahidic Covenant (Genesis 9:11)

The first use of the word covenant in the scriptures occurs in Genesis 6:18. The actual covenant was given in Genesis 9:11. The Noahidic Covenant was spoken to Noah following the departure of Noah, his family, and all of the animals from the ark: *I* (will) *establish my covenant with you, that never again shall all flesh be cut off by the waters of the flood, and never again shall there be a flood to destroy the earth.* This covenant included a sign of God's faithfulness to keep His word; a rainbow would appear in the sky when it rained. This covenant was *unconditional* and did not depend upon the faithfulness of either Noah or his descendants.

Abrahamic Covenant. (Genesis 15, II Samuel 11:7-16, II Chronicles 17:10-14)

This *covenant*, first made to Abraham in Genesis 12: 1-3 was reinforced and expanded across Genesis 1 to Genesis 22. It was an extensive and far-reaching covenant between Abram (Abraham) and all of his offspring. We will not discuss this in great detail, but it contained *four* fundamental promises: (1) God pronounced a blessing upon Abram, to make his name great and to make his seed into a great nation, (2) The covenant promised that Abram's blessing would be extended to many people and nations. A blessing would fall upon all those who blessed Abraham and a curse would fall upon those who cursed him, (3) God vowed to bless the entire world through Abram's seed; the fulfillment of this part of the covenant is through Jesus Christ, who was of Abraham's family line, through Sarah, Isaac, Jacob and Leah from which Judah was born and eventually Jesus Christ (4) The fourth basic covenant was that Abram's seed would be given what is now called the *Land of Canaan* as a *perpetual inheritance.* When God finished declaring all of the promises of His covenant with Abram, He caused him to fall into a deep sleep. He then took some animals and birds, killed them, placed them in a parallel path, sprinkled their blood over the path and then passed between the animals. This was a *blood oath* in which He swore by Himself (unilaterally) that all of His promises would be fulfilled. He then changed the name of Abram to Abraham to ratify the covenant. This was an *unconditional covenant* known as the *Abramic Covenant.* Later, God gave Abraham the rite of *circumcision* as the specific sign of the Abrahamic Covenant (Genesis 17:9–14). It is important that one part of this unconditional covenant with Abraham was a *land covenant.* The Abrahamic Covenant included the promise of land which they would one day inhabit(Genesis 12:1). It was a specific piece of land called the Promised Land or the Land of Milk and Honey. The boundaries included all of the land between the Euphrates River to the north, the Egyptian River to the south, the Mediterranean Sea to the West and the Dead Sea to the East. The unconditional promise was later clearly specified to include a portion of the land for each of the 12 tribes of Israel. We will see that this promise is fundamental to understanding why the Millennial Kingdom has to be a 1000 year period of time during which the 12 tribes of Israel will live in peace and prosperity on the land which was promised to Abraham, and later reiterated in promises to Moses and King David. The Abrahamic Covenant was repeated in Deuteronomy 30: 1–10 and to Joshua and the 12 tribes of Israel before they crossed the River Jordan..

It must be recognized that when Israel crossed the River Jordan after the 40 year exodus from Egypt, Israel did conquer and live upon a portion of this land called the *Land of Canaan.* But they apostatized, did not trust God to vanquish all of their enemies in conquering the land, and failed to conquer all the land promised to them at that time. Israel has *never* inherited all of the land promised to Abraham, Moses and King David.... but they will. This is the main purpose of the Millennial Kingdom and it will come to pass. The portions of land assigned to each tribe and the dimensions of each piece are given in Ezekiel 40-45 and will be discussed in Chapter 3. God is not going to renege on His promise. Centuries after Abraham died, the children of Israel took possession of most of the land under Joshua's leadership (Joshua 21:43). However, at no point in history has Israel controlled all of the land God had promised to them. There remains, therefore, a final fulfillment of the *Abrahamic Covenant* that will see Israel occupying their God-given homeland to the fullest extent. The fulfillment will be more than a matter of geography; it will also be a time of holiness and restoration (Ezekiel 20: 40–44 and 36:1—37:28).

The Mosaic Covenant (Exodus 20-Deuteronomy 28)

The *Mosaic Covenant* is sometimes called the *Old Covenant*. This covenant is found scattered between Exodus 20 and Deuteronomy 28. It promised the Israelites a blessing for obedience and a curse for disobedience. Much of the Old Testament chronicles the fulfillment of cycles of judgment for sin and blessings when God's people lost faith, repented and returned to God. The Mosaic Covenant is sometimes called the Sinai Covenant because it was first spoken at Mount Sinai after Israel had been saved from death by the pursuing Pharaoh and his army by the waters of the Red Sea. The Mosaic Covenant was a *conditional covenant* between God and Israel. God made a covenant with Israel that if they would obey His laws and separate themselves from the Gentile world that He would bless and protect them (Exodus 19: 5-8). The Mosaic covenant was different from the Abramic Covenant: The Mosaic covenant was *conditional* and depended upon whether or not the Nation of Israel would obey God. The blessings and fulfillment of God's promises rested upon how Israel would responded to the commands of God. There were basically 3 Covenant promises made to Israel by God.

If Israel would obey all of the laws and commands that God set before them:

> 1.0 The Jews would be God's chosen people and He would bless them above all other nations.
> 2.0 The nation of Israel would be a Kingdom of Priests
> 3.0 Israel would be a holy nation
> 4.0 Any nation or people that would bless Israel would be blessed, and any nation that would curse Israel would be cursed
> > Exodus 19: 3-6

When God made His covenant with Israel at Mount Sinai the people all loudly proclaimed: *All that the Lord has spoken we will do* (Exodus 19:8). The multiple parts of these 3 basic promises are found in Deuteronomy 28.

The Davidic Covenant (II Samuel 7:8-16).

The *Davidic Covenant* is actually a reassurance and expansion of the Abrahamic and the Mosaic Covenant. This *unconditional covenant* was given to King David, and reinforced the land Covenant given to Abraham and his seed. This is sometimes called the *Palestinian Covenant*. Neither is quite correct since the Davidic Covenant involved more than just the land of Palestine, and the original land Covenant which was given to Abraham was much larger than the land which was conquered and settled by Israel after Joshua crossed the Jordan River. Inherent in the covenant promise of God was that if Israel would not obey Him and follow His laws, God would allow other nations to conquer Israel and carry them into captivity. When King Solomon died, his united kingdom was ripped into two parts: One was the Northern Kingdom and the other was the Southern Kingdom. After about 200 years the Northern Kingdom was completely conquered and taken into captivity by Assyria. Only 200 years later, the Southern Kingdom was conquered and taken into captivity for 70 years by Nebuchadnezzar and the Babylonian Empire. Ten of the 12 tribes of Israel from the Northern Kingdom were previously taken into captivity by the Assyrians and were never heard from again. We call these the *Lost 10 tribes of Israel*. All 12 tribes *will* be united again and eventually be restored to *all* the land of promise in the Millennial Kingdom. This covenant will not be fulfilled until after the *fullness of the Gentiles* has been completed.

For I would not, brethren, that ye should be ignorant of this mystery, lest ye should be wise in your own conceits; that blindness in part is happened to Israel, until the fullness of the Gentiles be come in   Romans 11:25

After the *fullness of the Gentiles has come in*, the Jews as a nation will turn to Jesus Christ as their promised Messiah. This will happen at the end of the great tribulation period described by the Apostle John in the Book of Revelation.

And so all Israel shall be saved: as it is written, There shall come out of Zion the Deliverer, and shall turn away ungodliness from Jacob   Romans 11:26

The Covenant of Grace (Jeremiah 31: 31-34, Matthew 26:28)

The Covenant of Grace is often called the *New Covenant*. This covenant was ratified by Jesus Christ, the Son of God, at the Lord's Last Supper (Luke 22:20). Within 12 hours He would be sacrificed on the cross of Calvary and through His sacrificial death He would take away the sins of the whole world (I John 2:2). The death of Christ confirmed the unilateral covenant promise that God made to Adam after Adam and Eve were cast out of the Garden of Eden (Genesis 3:15), and it fulfilled the words of Jeremiah (Jeremiah 31:31-34) and many other old Testament prophets. That covenant was that a Messiah would be sent from God to permanently forgive sins and save the people. Justification and propitiation of sin for *all* people was settled on the cross. However, there was a conditional covenant made with all people that did not involve sin but faith. Forgiveness of sins was accomplished on the cross, but that only opened the path to salvation. Eternal life can never be obtained without *faith*....Faith that Jesus Christ is the only Son of God who came to forgive all sins and that He will one day return and resurrect all who would believe from death and the grave. Eternal life is a free Gift of God by grace but it can only be appropriated by *Faith*.

The Millennial Covenant

The *Millennial Covenant* is sometimes called the *Kingdom Covenant*. The Millennial covenant was spoken of and prophesied by prophets of God that arose throughout all of scripture. The Millennial Kingdom was repeatedly alluded to by Jesus Christ during His earthly ministry. The phrase Millennial Kingdom does not appear anywhere in scripture, but it corresponds to the 1,000-year dispensation that will immediately follow the Tribulation Period described in the Book of Revelation. We discuss the Millennial Kingdom promises in detail because of its significance in God's eternal plan for mankind. The most definitive revelation of the Millennial Kingdom to come is found in the book of Revelation.

[1] *And I saw an angel come down from heaven, having the key of the bottomless pit and a great chain in his hand.*
[2] *And he laid hold on the dragon, that old serpent, which is the Devil, and Satan, and bound him* **a thousand years,**
[3] *And cast him into the bottomless pit, and shut him up, and set a seal upon him, that he should deceive the nations no more, till* **the thousand years** *should be fulfilled: and after that he must be loosed a little season.*
[4] *And I saw thrones, and they sat upon them, and judgment was given unto them: and I saw the souls of them that were beheaded for the witness of Jesus, and for the word of God, and which had not worshipped the beast, neither his image, neither had received his mark upon their foreheads, or in their hands; and they lived and reigned with Christ a thousand years.*
[5] *But the rest of the dead lived not again until* **the thousand years** *were finished. This is the first resurrection.*
[6] *Blessed and holy is he that hath part in the first resurrection: on such the second death hath no power, but they shall be priests of God and of Christ, and shall reign with him* **a thousand years.**
[7] And when **the thousand years** are expired, Satan shall be loosed out of his prison,
[8] *And shall go out to deceive the nations which are in the four quarters of the earth, Gog and Magog, to gather them together to battle: the number of whom is as the sand of the sea.*
[9] *And they went up on the breadth of the earth, and compassed the camp of the saints about, and the beloved city: and fire came down from God out of heaven, and devoured them.*
[10] *And the devil that deceived them was cast into the lake of fire and brimstone, where the beast and the false prophet are, and shall be tormented day and night forever and ever.*
[11] *And I saw a great white throne, and him that sat on it, from whose face the earth and the heaven fled away; and there was found no place for them.*
[12] *And I saw the dead, small and great, stand before God; and the books were opened: and another book was opened, which is the book of life: and the dead were judged out of those*

things which were written in the books, according to their works.
[13] And the sea gave up the dead which were in it; and death and hell delivered up the dead which were in them: and they were judged every man according to their works.
[14] And death and hell were cast into the lake of fire. This is the second death.
[15] And whosoever was not found written in the book of life was cast into the lake of fire.
   Revelation 20: 1-15

It is the purpose of this book to not only explain the meaning of Revelation 20: 1-15, but present and explain the prophecies of Daniel, Ezekiel, Isaiah and Zachariah as they relate to the Millennial Kingdom. For additional study of how the Millennial Kingdom relates to the great tribulation, the reader is referred to Phillips, The Book of Revelation: *Mysteries Revealed*.

The Millennial Kingdom: Theological Views

There are four basic interpretations of the Millennial Kingdom that have surfaced over the past 200 years. These are the (1) Amillennial (2) Postmillennial (3) Premillennial and (4) Preterist views of the Millennial Kingdom.
   Amillennial   The term Amillennial literally means "no Millennial". Those who propose this theology spiritualize Revelation 20 and do not believe that there is any period of 1000 years that follow the end of the Church Age. They believe that Christ will rapture and resurrect all saints; fight the Battle of Armageddon; judge all believers at the Bema Seat Judgment and then judge all unbelievers at the Great White Throne Judgment. This will then be immediately followed by the creation of New Heavens and a New Earth.

   Postmillennial   The Postmillennial view seems to have originated centuries after the death of Christ, and popularized by *Darwin*. The belief called *Postmillennialism* is that Christ will not return a second time until after the Millennial Kingdom has run its course. Most Postmillennialists also believe that the 1000 years mentioned in Revelation 20 is not literal but figurative; it is a long period of time but not 1000 years. During a period of time which will follow the Great Tribulation, the church will finally evangelize all the world and a period of peace and tranquility will be ushered in. After the earth is evangelized, then Christ will return again and establish New Heavens and New Earth.

   Premillennial   The Premillennial view seems to have originated...or at least popularized... by *Ron Darby* in 1830 who was a pastor in Bristol, England. It was later adopted by C.I. Scofield in his Scofield reference bible. Premillennial theology was certainly not a belief of early Christians or the early Roman Catholic Church. The basic belief is that Revelation 20 should be taken literally, and that Christ will return a second time before the 1000 years begins. The basic premise is that God has preordained specific rewards and duties for both his chosen people (Israel) and for the Church or the Body of Christ (Ecclesia). The Premillennial view embraces the following beliefs (Extracted from: A Comparison of Three Millennial Views: Kenneth J. Morgan).

Preterist Finally, it should be mentioned that there are "Christians" who are called *preterists*. A preterist believes that all end-time prophecies....including the Book of Revelation and the Millennial Kingdom have already occurred. Everything described in the Book of Revelation has already happened, and Christ has already returned. In other words, those who are preterists do not believe that the Book of Revelation is the true, inerrant word of God.

Comment by the Author: A real, 1000 year Millennial Kingdom is believed by many biblical commentators and scholars to be a biblical principle which cannot be supported by scripture. Both Amillennial and Postmillennial expositors spiritualize Revelation 20 and deny that the Millennium will actually last 1000 years. Amillennialists maintain that it simply does not exist, and Postmillennialists teach that 1000 years should be interpreted as a "long time". Many also deny the clear biblical prophecies of the Old Testament in which God promises Israel that they will live in the land which was promised to the 12 tribes of Israel and confirmed by a blood oath. It is the basic assumption and belief of this author that all scripture is inerrant in its principles and precepts and that *all scripture is God inspired*. In particular, if there is not a dispensation called the *Millennial Kingdom* which is to last 1000 years, then the inspired words and visions given to the apostle John in Revelation 20 are a deception at best and a lie at worst. Revelation 20: 1-8 refers to a literal, 1000 year future kingdom *six* times. If God had not meant this to be revelation truth, He would not have referred to a future 1000 year period of time in 6 different places. It also follows that if Revelation 6: 1-8 is not true, then the entire Book of Revelation may not be true. If the Book of Revelation is not true, then the entire Holy Bible may not be true: This is heresy of the highest degree. I personally categorically reject any view which contradicts scripture. Specifically regarding Revelation 20, we can only quote the very words of Jesus Christ concerning the Book of Revelation.

[**18**] *For I testify unto every man that hear the words of the prophecy of this book, If any man shall add unto these things, God shall add unto him the plagues that are written in this book:*
[**19**] *And if any man shall take away from the words of the book of this prophecy, God shall take away his part out of the book of life, and out of the holy city, and from the things which are written in this book.*
[**20**] *He which testifieth these things saith, Surely I come quickly. Amen. Even so, come, Lord Jesus* Revelation 22: 18-20

The correct understanding of both Dispensations and Covenants as the history of man unfolds is important to understanding how God's purpose and plan is being revealed throughout the ages. However, it is crucial to understand how the literal fulfillment of the Millennial Kingdom is necessary to completely fulfill the covenant promises that God made with Abraham, Moses and King David concerning Israel and their inheritance of the promised land.

God's Plan for the Ages

1.0   The Old Testament, after Abraham to the Book of Acts, deals with God's prophetic program for Israel. The New Testament after the Book of Acts deals with God's prophetic program for the Ecclesia or the saints.

2.0   Christ came to redeem all mankind from sin (including the Old Testament believers who died in faith). He established a New Covenant based upon faith and grace by which both Jews and Gentiles are offered salvation and eternal life.

3.0   When the Jews corporately rejected their promised Messiah and crucified Him on the Cross of Calvary, they were "blinded in part" until "the fullness of the Gentiles" comes to pass, which would terminate the *Church Age* or the *Dispensation of Grace*. When the New Covenant began, the Old Covenant was finished and the Nation of Israel temporarily set aside. The New Covenant which offered salvation to Jews and Gentiles alike was a *mystery* not revealed to the Old Testament prophets.

4.0   The *Ecclesia* or the Body of Christ has a *heavenly calling* and the Jews have an *earthly calling.* The New Covenant saints will rule and reign with Jesus Christ during the 1000 year Millennial Kingdom, during which time the Jews will live upon this earth in the land that was promised to them by God to Abraham, Moses and King David. The Jewish inheritance and occupation of the promised land is central to the purpose of the Millennial Kingdom. It was prophesied by the Old Testament men of God and ratified in a unilateral covenant between God and Abraham.

Israel's Promise of the Land

One of the most important and far-reaching events in the history of Israel was the covenant that God made with Abram. Abram was living in Ur of the Chaldees when God called him forth to father the Nation of Israel. He promised (Covenanted) with Abram that:

[2] *I will make of thee a great nation, and I will bless thee, and make thy name great; and thou shalt be a blessing:*
[3] *And I will bless them that bless thee, and curse him that curseth thee: and in thee shall all families of the earth be blessed.*
[4] *So Abram departed, as the LORD had spoken unto him; and Lot went with him: and Abram was seventy and five years old when he departed out of Haran.*
[5] *And Abram took Sarai his wife, and Lot his brother's son, and all their substance that they had gathered, and the souls that they had gotten in Haran; and they went forth to go into the* **land of Canaan***; and into the land of Canaan they came.*
[6] *And Abram passed through the land unto the place of Sichem, unto the plain of Moreh. And the Canaanite was then in the land.*

[7] *And the LORD appeared unto Abram, and said,* **Unto thy seed will I give this land**
Genesis 12: 2-7

God at that time gave Abram and his seed all of the land that he could see.

[14] *And the LORD said unto Abram, after that Lot was separated from him, Lift up now thine eyes, and look from the place where thou art northward, and southward, and eastward, and westward:*
[15] *For all the land which thou sees, to thee will I give it, and to thy seed* **forever**
Genesis 13: 14-15

The extent of this land promise was later clarified and defined in Genesis 15 and in Deuteronomy 30.

In the same day the LORD made a covenant with Abram, saying, Unto thy seed have I given this land, from the river of Egypt unto the great river, the river Euphrates Genesis 15:18

[3] *That then the LORD thy God will turn thy captivity, and have compassion upon thee, and will return and gather thee from all the nations, whither the LORD thy God hath scattered thee.*
[4] *If any of thine be driven out unto the outmost parts of heaven, from thence will the LORD thy God gather thee, and from thence will he fetch thee* Deuteronomy 30: 3-4

God also promised the people of Israel that *He* would gather the dispersed people of Israel back into the land. This was not the return of Israel from 70 years of Babylonian Captivity and this is not the steady migration of the Jews back to Israel since Israel became a nation again on May 14, 1948. This is a prophecy concerning the return of all the 12 tribes of Israel to inherit and live in the land that God promised to them. Many television evangelists and well meaning Christians have boldly declared that because the Jews are returning to Israel today that the tribulation period is about to begin. This cannot not be true because the tribulation period of time described by John in the Book of Revelation *must* be completed before the Millennial Kingdom can begin, God recovers a remnant of Jews back to Israel and the land divided among 12 tribes of Israel. The return of many Jews to Israel since May 8, 1948 is *not* a fulfillment of Deuteronomy 30: 3-4.

The Lord *himself* will regather His chosen people into Israel *after* the Church Age has finished and not before. The regathering of Israel is mentioned in a multitude of bible prophecies. The Jews have been conquered by the Assyrians, the Babylonians and the Romans; and they experienced horrible and senseless genocide under the Germans in WW II. This is all because they failed to uphold the conditional Mosaic Covenant. In spite of their domination by the Gentiles they have never lost their identity and have clung to the Old Testament economy of salvation by works. What is taking place today is **not** the calling of Israel back to their promised land. Every Christian today who has been saved by grace and has had their sins forgiven by Jesus Christ on the Cross of Calvary should pray every day that The Jews will have the scales removed from their eyes that have temporarily blinded them in part. Then and only then will they accept Jesus Christ as their Lord and Savior.

[**25**] *For I would not, brethren, that ye should be ignorant of this mystery, lest ye should be wise in your own conceits; that blindness in part is happened to Israel, until the fullness of the Gentiles be come in.*
[**26**] *And so all Israel shall be saved: as it is written, There shall come out of Zion the Deliverer, and shall turn away ungodliness from Jacob:*
[**27**] *For this is my **covenant** unto them, when I shall take away their sins*   Romans 11:25-27

And so it will come to pass that: All of Israel will be saved. Consider the following Old Testament prophecies.

[**10**] *And **in that day** there shall be **a root of Jesse**, which shall stand for an ensign of the people; to it shall the Gentiles seek: and his rest shall be glorious.*
[**11**] *And it shall come to pass **in that day**, that the Lord shall set his hand again the **second time to recover the remnant of his people**, which shall be left, from Assyria, and from Egypt, and from Pathros, and from Cush, and from Elam, and from Shinar, and from Hamath, and from the islands of the sea.*
[**12**] *And he shall set up an **ensign for the nations,** and shall assemble the outcasts of Israel, and **gather together the dispersed of Judah from the four corners of the earth***   Isaiah 11: 10-12

The *Day of the Lord* of which Isaiah prophesied was identified previously in Isaiah 2 and the *Root of Jessie* is Jesus Christ. A *remnant* will be regathered to the promised Land from the *four corners of the earth*. *And it shall come to pass in that day, that the Lord shall set his hand again the **second** time to recover the remnant of his people* (Isaiah 11:11). The 1st time was after the 70 year Babylonian captivity.

[**21**] *And say unto them, Thus saith the Lord GOD; Behold, I will take the children of Israel from among the heathen, where they be gone, and will gather them on every side, and **bring them***

into their own land:

[**22**] *And I will make them **one nation** in the land upon the mountains of Israel; and **one king** shall be king to them all: and they shall be no more two nations, neither shall they be divided into two kingdoms any more at all:*

[**23**] *Neither shall they defile themselves any more with their idols, nor with their detestable things, nor with any of their transgressions: but I will save them out of all their dwelling places, wherein they have sinned, and will **cleanse them**: so shall they be my people, and I will be their God.*

[**24**] *And **David my servant shall be king over them**; and they all shall have one shepherd: they shall also walk in my judgments, and observe my statutes, and do them.*

[**25**] ***And they shall dwell in the land that I have given unto Jacob** my servant, wherein your fathers have dwelt; and they shall dwell therein, even they, and their children, and their children's children for ever: and my servant David shall be their prince **forever***

Ezekiel 37: 21-25

Christ himself will supernaturally gather those Jews that are alive and remain to inhabit the 1000 year millennial Kingdom after the Tribulation Period has ended at the Battle of Armageddon. This cannot be referring to either the gathering of the people to Moses at the Exodus because Isaiah promised that a *remnant* would be regathered the second time: *For though thy people Israel be as the sand of the sea, yet a **remnant** of them shall return* (Isaiah 10:22) from each of 12 tribes of Israel. Ezekiel 37: 21-25 cannot refer to either the return from Babylonian exile or the exodus from Egypt. When the Jews were regathered to Israel and Jerusalem after the 70 years of Babylonian captivity, only 2 1/2 tribes from the Southern Kingdom returned. At the exodus from Egypt *all of the people* left Egypt with Moses at that time. In addition, when Israel is regathered by God to populate the Millennial Kingdom Jerusalem and the surrounding area will be leveled by a great earthquake....the area which now holds the temple mount will be raised up to a large plateau.... and the Throne of Jesus Christ will be built from which He will rule and reign over all nations. King David will be resurrected and reign beside Christ over all Israel. This was prophesied by the prophet Ezekial.

[**21**] *And say unto them, Thus saith the Lord GOD; Behold, I will take the children of Israel from among the heathen, where they be gone, and will gather them on every side, and bring them into their own land:*

[**22**] *And I will make them one nation in the land upon the mountains of Israel; and one king shall be king to them all: and they shall be no more two nations, neither shall they be divided*

into two kingdoms any more at all:

[23] Neither shall they defile themselves any more with their idols, nor with their detestable things, nor with any of their transgressions: but I will save them out of all their dwelling places, wherein they have sinned, and will cleanse them: so shall they be my people, and I will be their God.

[24] And David my servant shall be king over them; and they all shall have one shepherd: they shall also walk in my judgments, and observe my statutes, and do them.

[25] And they shall dwell in the land that I have given unto Jacob my servant, wherein your fathers have dwelt; and they shall dwell therein, even they, and their children, and their children's children for ever: and my servant David shall be their prince forever

Ezekiel 37:24

The Lord will rule over the whole world from a plateau that will be raised above the land surrounding Jerusalem (See Chapter 5).

*[2] And it shall come to pass in the last days, **that** the mountain of the LORD's house shall be established in the top of the mountains, and shall be exalted above the hills; and all nations shall flow unto it.*

*[11] The lofty looks of man shall be humbled, and the haughtiness of men shall be bowed down, and the LORD alone shall be exalted in **that** day.*

*[12] For the day of the LORD of hosts shall be upon every one **that** is proud and lofty, and upon every one **that** is lifted up; and he shall be brought low:*

*[17] And the loftiness of man shall be bowed down, and the haughtiness of men shall be made low: and the LORD alone shall be exalted in **that** day.*

[20] In that day a man shall cast his idols of silver, and his idols of gold, which they made each one for himself to worship, to the moles and to the bats   Isaiah 2: 2, 11-12, 17, 20

The *Mountain of the Lord's House* is where Jesus Christ will rule and reign during the Millennial Kingdom. *ALL* nations will worship there. The god of the Muslims and gods of the Hindus will no longer be worshipped...only Jesus Christ here on earth, and Jehovah God in His heavenly home. This can only happen when Christ rules in the Millennial Kingdom. There are many other places in the Old Testament that testify Israel is destined to inherit **all** of the land that was promised to them by the Abramic and Davidic covenants; God will regather all of His chosen people that remain alive from the four corners of the world; and Jesus Christ with King David will rule and reign *on this earth* during the 1000 year Millennial Kingdom.

We are now ready to describe all of the wonders and glory of the Kingdom.

Chapter 2

The Millennial Kingdom

This chapter will provide a short overview of what to expect in the Millennial Kingdom. Most of the topics which will be mentioned will be explored in greater detail in subsequent chapters. The 1000 Year Millennial Kingdom will not start until the *Age of Grace* and the period of *Great Tribulation* has been completed. As the Great Tribulation comes to an end, several important events must happen before the Millennial Kingdom can begin

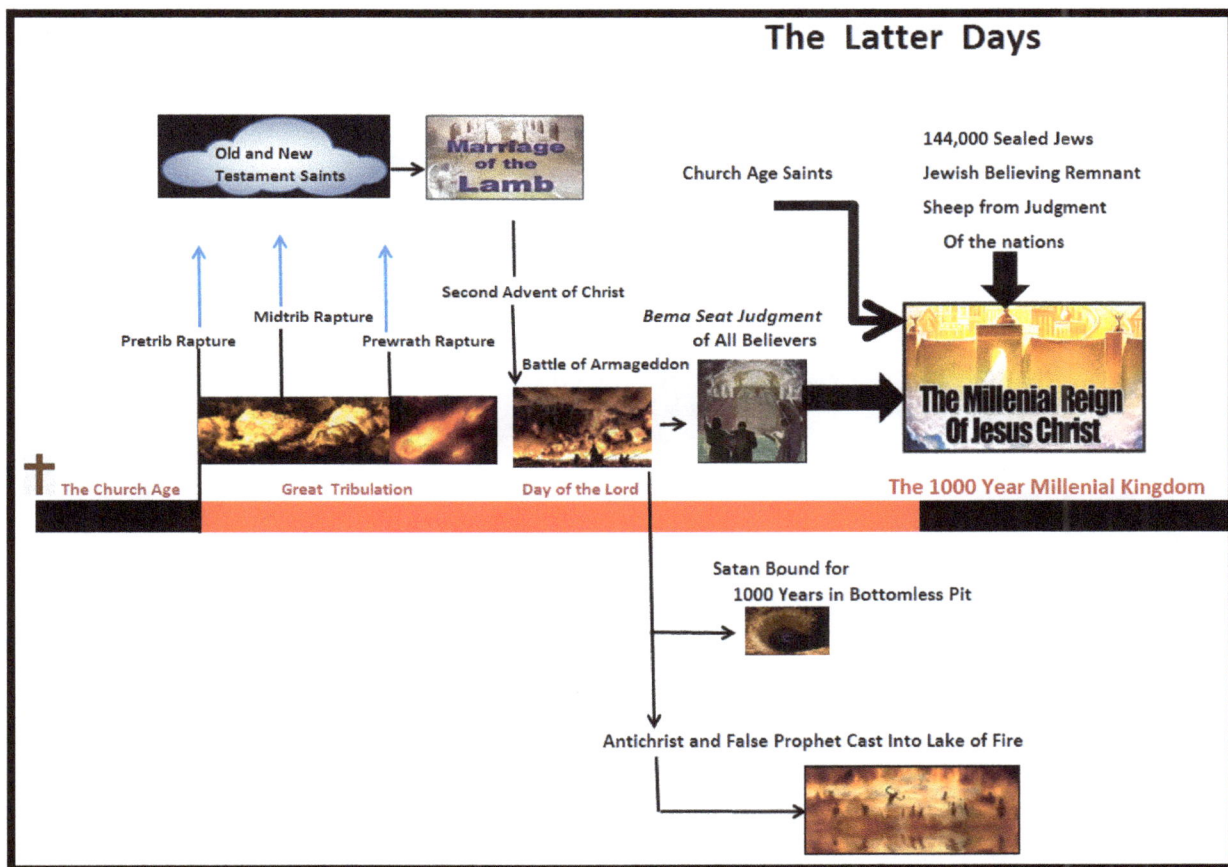

The Latter Days

The *Church Age* has been going on now for almost 2000 years, and soon God will tell His Son that it is time for Him to return a 2nd time. The 1st advent of Christ terminated on the Cross of Calvary and began the current *Age of Grace*. By the sacrifice of Jesus Christ on the Cross of Calvary as the perfect Passover Lamb, the price for all sin was paid and a New Covenant established which would offer salvation and eternal life to Jews and Gentiles alike. When Christ returns a 2nd time it will be in two stages.

First, Christ will appear in the air above the earth to gather to Him all of those who have died in faith and accepted Him as Lord and Savior. This gathering of the saints is known as the *rapture* (I Corinthians 15: 51-52). At the call of a great trumpet, Christ will resurrect all of those who have died in faith...both Jew and Gentile. Then He will gather to Him all of those who remain alive and have believed in faith that they would be redeemed from sin. There are 4 main theological lines of thought regarding when this might occur: (1) Pretribulation rapture.....The rapture will take place before the tribulation begins (2) Midtribulation rapture......The rapture will take place half-way between when the tribulation begins and when it ends (3) Pre-wrath Rapture..... The rapture will take place before the Wrath of God falls upon the earth (4) Post tribulation rapture.....The rapture will not occur until the entire tribulation period of time is over. It is not the intention of this book to debate the merits and beliefs underlying each rapture position. For those that are interested see Phillips: The Book of Revelation: *Mysteries Revealed.* It is sufficient to note that there will be a rapture of the saints and that it will take place before the Church age can come to a close. When Christ returns to rapture or resurrect all who believed upon Him in faith, He will not set foot upon this earth but the saints will rise to meet Him in the air. Those who are alive at that time will be raptured out to escape the *Wrath of God* (Romans 1:18, Romans 5:9, Ephesians 5:6, Colossians 3:6, I Thessalonians 5:9, Revelation 14:19, Revelation 15:7, Revelation 16:1). As the Wrath of God is being poured out upon the earth the *Wedding of the Lamb* will take place in heaven (Revelation 19: 6-7). Those who have accepted Christ as their Lord and savior and are still alive will be spared from the Wrath of God (Revelation 15:1, 7, Revelation 16:1)

Let us be glad and rejoice, and give honor to him: for the Marriage of the Lamb is come, and his wife hath made herself ready   Revelation 19:7

Much more then, being now justified by his blood, we shall be saved from wrath through him   Romans 5:9

Let no man deceive you with vain words: for because of these things cometh the wrath of God upon the children of disobedience   Ephesians 5:6

For God hath not appointed us to wrath, but to obtain salvation by our Lord Jesus Christ   I Thessalonians 5:9

And one of the four beasts gave unto the seven angels seven golden vials (bowls) full of the wrath of God, who lives forever and ever   Revelation 15:7 (Revelation 16:1)

After the *Wedding of the Lamb* takes place in Heaven, Christ will return to fight the *Battle of Armageddon* outside of Jerusalem (Revelation 19: 1-21).

Second, when Christ returns to gather all believers to Him in what we call the *rapture* he will meet all believers (living and dead) *in the air*. When Jesus Christ returns to the earth in His *second advent*, He will descend to the Mount of Olives from where He will go to meet Satan and his army of unbelievers in the *Valley of Megiddo* (Zachariah 12: 1-9) for the *Battle of Armageddon*. The battle will not last long (Revelation 20:9). Christ will completely destroy Satan and his army of unbelievers in a short and decisive battle (Revelation 19: 11-18). After the battle is over, the *Antichrist* and the *False Prophet* will be cast into the *Lake of Fire* and *Brimstone* (Revelation 19:20). Satan will then be bound and placed into the *Bottomless Pit* where he will remain for the next 1000 years until the Millennial Kingdom has run its course (Revelation 20: 1-2). Those who followed Satan to Armageddon and were slain will be sent to a *Place of Torments* where they will remain for 1000 years awaiting the final judgment of all unbelievers at the *Great White Throne Judgment* (revelation 20:11). For those who wish to study these events in more detail, see Phillips, Revelation: *Mysteries Revealed*.

Characteristics of The Kingdom

As previously discussed in Chapter 1, there here are three theological positions concerning the fulfillment of the Millennial Kingdom: (1) Amillennial (2) Postmillennial and (3) Premillennial.

Premillennialists believe that the Book of Revelation provides an accurate description of end-time events, and that immediately following the tribulation a 1000 year Millennial Kingdom will begin. This view also holds that the church age will exist between the 1st and 2nd coming of Jesus Christ. The *Premillennial* theology believes in the inerrancy of scripture, and that the 1000 year kingdom described in Revelation 20 is a real, future Kingdom. Although there are several variations of how the end-time events will unfold and the actual sequence of end-time events will occur, everything described in the Book of Revelation will come to pass. Jesus will return to earth at the Battle of Armageddon and He will rule and reign for a literal 1000 years. After this period of time, all evil and sin will be purged from the earth, the earth will be renovated with fire, and eternity will begin.

The reader of this book should pause and understand that this author believes without question or doubt that the Holy Bible is truth and that it was inspired by God.

All scripture is given by inspiration of God, and is profitable for doctrine, for reproof, for correction, for instruction in righteousness   II Timothy 3:16

[20] *Knowing this first, that no prophecy of the scripture is of any private interpretation.*
[21] *For the prophecy came not in old time by the will of man: but holy men of God spoke as they were moved by the Holy Ghost*   I Peter 1: 20-21

If one believes that the word of God is inerrant and true, there is no basis for any Millennial Kingdom theology but Premillennialism.

The Millennial Kingdom will not be like anything that has existed since Adam and Eve were cast out of the Garden of Eden. During the 1000 year Millennial Kingdom will there will be a dramatic change in the world structure and how it operates. The earth will undergo radical and unprecedented changes, and Jesus Christ will rule in a theocracy from His palace and throne north of Jerusalem. Living conditions in the Millennial kingdom will be unlike any that previously existed upon the earth. The following is a short summary of what the Millennial Kingdom will be like for 1000 years.

- The purpose of the Millennial Kingdom is twofold: (1) The land covenant with Abraham and King David will finally be fulfilled. The 12 tribes of Israel will inherit and dwell in the promised land....Jeremiah 16: 14-15 (2) Jesus Christ came the 1st time as a suffering servant who died on the Cross for all sinners. During the 1000 year Millennial Kingdom He will rule and reign as King of Kings and Lord of Lords.

- There will be significant and dramatic changes in the Land of Israel during the Millennial Kingdom. When Jesus returns to fight the Battle of Armageddon, He will descend to the Mount of Olives. His feet will touch the ground and the Mount of Olives will split into two parts creating a valley which will run North and South. After He fights the Battle of Armageddon there will be a great disturbance in the land of Israel. Jerusalem will be supernaturally destroyed and in its place a great plateau will rise where the *Throne of Jesus* will be built where He will rule and reign for 1000 years. All of the land surrounding the Jerusalem site will be leveled and transformed into a great plain. The land will be fertile and in it all manners of crops and fruits will be grown. (Zachariah 14: 4-5, Ezekiel 47: 1-7, Isaiah 32:15, 51:3)

  For the seed shall be prosperous; the vine shall give her fruit, and the ground shall give her increase, and the heavens shall give their dew; and I will cause the remnant of this people to possess all these things. Zachariah 8:12

- Jesus Christ will fulfill all prophecy which predicted that He will someday rule as the King of Kings and the Lord of Lords. He will rule over the entire world in righteousness and power with a *Rod of Iron* sitting upon the His Throne with King David assisting Him in Jerusalem. Jesus Christ will rule on political, social, economical and religious issues that will arise in the Kingdom. The palace and throne from which Christ will

reign will be built over the site where Herod's temple once stood (Ezekiel 43:7, Isaiah 9: 6-7).

- The world government will be a theocracy and Jesus Christ will be the King (Isaiah 11: 1-5). He will rule and reign with King David by His side (Ezekiel 37:24)

- His throne will be lifted up high above the old temple mount on a new plateau (Ezekiel 40-48)

- The Jews who have accepted Christ as their prophesied Messiah will live in the land which was promised to them long ago. The land will be divided among 12 tribes of Israel and they will prosper and live in peace (Ezekiel 48, Isaiah 11:11)

- Peace will reign in the animal kingdom, and the Lion will lay down with the Lamb (Isaiah 11:6-9)

- A baby will be able to hold and play with a poisonous snake without being bitten (Isaiah 11:8)

- Animals and predators in the animal kingdom will become vegetarians, just as they were in the Garden of Eden (Isaiah 11: 6-7, Isaiah 65:25).

- Jesus Christ will know the needs of all men, and He will answer prayers before they are even spoken or finished (Isaiah 65:24)

- The lifespan of man will be greatly increased and death will not reign. If a person dies before he/she is 100 years old, they will be considered a child (Isaiah 65: 19-20)

- The Lord Jesus Christ will celebrate His reign with great banquets in His Holy Palace for all people who want to celebrate and attend (Isaiah 25:6)

- All who dwell upon the earth will be required to come to Jesus at least once a year and worship Jesus Christ on the Feast of Tabernacles (Zachariah 14:1, 16). Those who refuse to attend will be punished (Zachariah 14: 16-19)

- Sin will still be present and unbelievers will still be upon the earth (Revelation 20:1-9)

- Deserts will be fertile, contain water and produce crops (Isaiah 35:1)

- The saints (ecclesia) will rule and reign under Christ throughout the land (Revelation 5:10)

- The animal kingdom will return to their peaceful state which existed in the Garden of Eden. The Lion will lay down with the Lamb. Children will be able to hold and play with a poisonous snake without being bitten. Man will once again live in peace and harmony with nature. There will be a great river which will emerge from the site of Christ's throne room. It will run north to south and then split into two pieces; one to the Dead Sea and one to the Mediterranean Sea. There will be an abundance of fish in each body of water (Isaiah 11: 6-9).

- The world will live in peace and there will be no more wars (Jeremiah 23: 5-6)

- Israel will be the Center of the World, and nations will be ruled by a dictatorship (theocracy) in which Jesus Christ will have sovereign rule. The Kingdom will be ruled by Jesus Christ, but He will be joined by (1) Martyrs from all Ages (2) New Covenant saints (3) The 12 disciples and (4) King David

- *Israel* will inhabit the kingdom. More specifically, all inhabitants will be redeemed Jews. Those who were converted either before or during the Great Tribulation; those gathered from the nations after the Battle of Armageddon; those chosen from among the nations at the *Sheep and Goats Judgment* and possibly the 144,000 Jews who were sealed from the Wrath of God in Revelation 7: 1-8

- Satan will not be on the earth but will be bound in the *Bottomless Pit* for 1000 years

- The inhabitants of the Millennial Kingdom will live in peace and prosperity (Micah 4:4, Isaiah 32: 17-18), but contrary to popular belief sin will still exist in this near perfect Kingdom. This is because real people with earthly bodies will live on the earth during this period of time, and each will have inherited the sin nature from Adam (Revelation 20: 7-9).

- People living in the Millennial Kingdom will experience long lifetimes. A person of 100 years of age will be considered to be a young child (Isaiah 65: 20-25)

- People living in the promised land will plant gardens, raise cattle and sheep and build houses just as in other ages (Amos 9: 13-14).

- Jews and people from the Judgment of the Nations (Sheep and Goats) will initially be the only inhabitants of earth, but they will eventually migrate to other nations of the world. Even though they are outside of Israel, it appears they will also lead normal (long) lives, live in harmony with the animal kingdom and will multiply. Jesus Christ will reign as King over all the nations of the world.

- All people will be required to honor Jesus Christ and make a pilgrimage to Jerusalem every year on the Feast of Tabernacles (Zachariah 14: 16-19). Failure to do so will result in severe punishment.

- People from all over the earth will regularly visit the Throne of Jesus in Jerusalem to seek wisdom, settle any disputes which might arise and worship Him as King of Kings (Zachariah 8: 20-23, Isaiah 62:2, Revelation 16:16)

All of these wonderful things will be enjoyed by those who have accepted our Lord Jesus Christ as their personal Savior. But those who *do not* accept Christ as their long awaited Messiah (Old Testament believers) or as their Savior before the Kingdom begins (New Covenant saints) will not see this wonderful Kingdom ....They will be cast into the Lake of Burning Fire for all eternity

The millennium will be the period of the full manifestation of the glory of the Lord Jesus Christ. There will be the manifestation of glory associated with the humanity of Christ. There will be the glory of a glorious dominion, in which Christ, by virtue of his obedience unto death, is given universal dominion to replace that dominion which Adam lost. There will be the glory of a glorious government, in which Christ, as David's son is given absolute power to govern. There will be the glory of a glorious inheritance, in which the land and the seed promised to Abraham are realized through Christ

Dr. J. Dwight Pentecost

Who Will Populate the Millennial Kingdom ?

The Millennial Kingdom will be populated by several groups of people. Group 1 and Group 2 will populate and inhabit the Millennial Kingdom. Groups 3-6 will rule and reign for 1000 years with Jesus Christ.

1.0 144,000 Jewish converts to Christianity

2.0 Inhabitants of the earth from all nations that have survived the Great Tribulation. These are the sheep in the *Sheep and Goat Judgment* at the end of the Church

Age. The *Jewish Remnant* who will be saved and *Gentiles who* have helped and given food, clothing and a place to sleep are the sheep.

3.0   Martyrs from all ages and those that were executed during the *Wrath of Satan*

4.0   The 12 Apostles of Christ

5.0   The *Ecclesia* or those who died in faith from all ages

6.0   King David

The 144,000 Jewish converts and the sheep from the judgment of the sheep and goats will both be the initial inhabitants of the Millennial Kingdom. Although not specifically stated in the scriptures, it is proposed that anyone who will enter into the 1000 year kingdom will be saved by faith, believe that Jesus Christ died for their sins and accepts Him as not only their Savior but Lord of Lords and King of Kings. Both groups will be discussed in some detail in Chapter 4: Kingdom Inhabitants. The martyrs, the 12 apostles of Christ, the ecclesia and King David will all rule and Reign in some capacity during the 1000 tears Millennial Kingdom. These will be discussed in Chapter 3: Rule and Reign in the Kingdom.

There is one other group of initial Kingdom Inhabitants that is a distinct possibility. This group is almost never recognized and discussed. We will call this group of people the *Bozrah Remnant*.

The Bozrah Remnant

An event which is usually overlooked is that one of the first things that will happen after Satan is cast down to the earth (Revelation 12: 7-8) and his reign of terror begins (Revelation 12:17). In his rage he will assemble his forces and together they will seek to destroy Jerusalem (Daniel 8: 9-12) and desecrate the rebuilt holy temple (Daniel 8:11, II Thessalonians 2: 3-4)

[3] *Let no man deceive you by any means: for that day shall not come, except there come a falling away first, and that man of sin be revealed, the son of perdition;.*
[4] *Who opposes and exalts himself above all that is called God, or that is worshipped; so that he as God sits in the temple of God, showing himself that he is God*   II Thessalonians 2: 3-4

And the king shall do according to his will; and he shall exalt himself, and magnify himself above every god, and shall speak marvelous things against the God of gods, and shall prosper till the indignation be accomplished: for that that is determined shall be done   Daniel 11:26

This invasion of Jerusalem is what we will call the *Jerusalem Campaign* (See Chapter 6: The Three Invasions of Israel). Satan will attack Jerusalem and during the ensuing battle, 1/2 of all inhabitants will either be captured or killed and only 1/2 will survive (Zachariah 14:1-2). Those who survive will flee to the south through a valley which will be formed when Jesus Christ sets His feet upon the Mount of Olives (Zachariah 14: 3-5). Satan will pursue them to destroy them all, but as he begins to overtake them God will intervene. A great earthquake will occur which will *swallow up* many who pursue (Revelation 12: 12-16). Satan will turn back and it is conjectured that this Jewish remnant will continue to flee south and west to the ancient fortress of Petra in Edom where they will be divinely protected. After the Battle of Armageddon, this remnant will be recovered by Christ Himself from somewhere in Edom. This is revealed by applying the following prophecy in Isaiah.

[1] *Who is this that cometh from Edom, with dyed garments from Bozrah? this that is glorious in his apparel, travelling in the greatness of his strength? I that speak in righteousness, mighty to save.*
[2] *Wherefore art thou red in thine apparel, and thy garments like him that treadeth in the winefat?*
[3] *I have trodden the winepress alone; and of the people there was none with me: for I will tread them in mine anger, and trample them in my fury; and their blood shall be sprinkled upon my garments, and I will stain all my raiment.*
[4] *For the **day of vengeance** is in mine heart, and the **year of my redeemed is come***
Isaiah 63: 1-4

This is a prophecy concerning Jesus Christ: (1) He is coming from Bozrah which is in Edom, south of Jerusalem (2) He is glorious but His garments are stained *red* with blood (3) He has trampled His enemies and tread over them in anger...at the bloody Battle of Armageddon (4) He Has tread the *winepress* alone. This last prophecy can only fit the following passage in Revelation 15.

[19] *And the angel thrust in his sickle into the earth, and gathered the vine of the earth, and cast it into the great winepress of the wrath of God.*
[20] *And the winepress was trodden without the city, and blood came out of the winepress, even unto the horse bridles, by the space of a thousand and six hundred furlongs*
Revelation 14: 19-20

Revelation 14: 19-20 is clearly describing the *Battle of Armageddon* described in Revelation 19: 1-21 where Christ is pictured as trampling Satan and all of his followers in the great *winepress* of His wrath outside of Jerusalem. This is after the rapture and will likely take place on the *Feast of Yom Kippur* on the last day of the Church Age. We assume that the Jews who have fled Jerusalem in the *Jerusalem Campaign* been also been divinely protected to enter into the Millennial Kingdom. We again conjecture that they have fled to Edom....possibly Petra. Christ will evidently leave following the Battle of Armageddon and retrieve those who have been hiding there. His garments are stained with blood from the Battle of Armageddon. Once again, this is conjecture derived from biblical clues: It is not stated definitively in scripture. In any case, it is strongly believed that those Jews from Jerusalem have been protected so that they can enter into the land promised to the 12 tribes of Israel by God.

Jews and Gentiles in the Kingdom

It must be understood that the main purpose of the 1000 year Millennial Kingdom is for the Jews to live upon this earth in their promised land. We will have more to say about this later. The New Covenant saints will participate in the Millennial Kingdom by serving Jesus Christ as a royal priesthood. The 12 Tribes of Israel which will live in the land are people with corruptible bodies and flesh and blood. The New Covenant saints have been redeemed from the earth at the rapture and have received their incorruptible bodies, crowns of glory and robes of white. They will not live in the land promised to Israel; their calling is *heavenly*. We are not told exactly where all of those who are believers will reside in the Millennial Kingdom, but there is no doubt that they will rule and reign (See Chapter 3).

[5] *And from Jesus Christ, who is the faithful witness, and the first begotten of the dead, and the prince of the kings of the earth. Unto him that loved us, and washed us from our sins in his own blood,*
[6] *And hath made us kings and priests unto God and his Father; to him be glory and dominion forever and ever. Amen*   Revelation 1 :5-6

*And hast made us unto our God kings and **priests**: and we shall reign on the earth*
Revelation 5:10

The other purpose of the Millennial Kingdom is to establish Christ as King in Jerusalem, sitting on the throne of David (Luke 1: 32-33), and to fulfill all prophecy concerning the promises God has made to Israel. The Jews will be a blessing to all other nations, fulfilling the Abrahamic covenant (Genesis 12: 1-3). They will live in portions of land given to them by Jesus Christ as the Millennial Kingdom begins. At that time they will experience forgiveness and a renewed relationship with God, fulfilling the Davidic covenant (II Samuel 7: 10-13).

Authors Note: It is believed that from examining and comparing scripture to scripture that the 144,000 Jews in Revelation 7: 1-8 are sealed (they are all born-again Jews) and will be protected from the *Wrath of God* so that 12,000 Jews from each of the 12 tribes of Israel can enter and live in the land during the Millennial Kingdom. It is also believed that the remnant of Jews who flee from Jerusalem when the Antichrist invades the city of Jerusalem (*The Jerusalem Campaign*) will be protected in Bozra during the tribulation period. Even if both groups are divinely protected by God so that they can populate the Millennial Kingdom, this does not exempt them from judgment. The *Great White Throne Judgment* at the end of the 1000 year

Millennial Kingdom seems to be the most logical choice but this is not specifically stated in scripture and remains a mystery. We only know that *every person* will stand before the Judgment of God

And as it is appointed unto men once to die, but after this the judgment   Hebrews 9:27

It is interesting and instructive to see what the prophet Ezekiel wrote long ago.

[21] *And say unto them (Israel), Thus saith the Lord GOD; Behold, I will take the children of Israel from among the heathen, where they have gone, and will gather them on every side, and bring them into their own land:*
[22] *And I will make them one nation in the land upon the mountains of Israel; and one king shall be king to them all: and they shall be no more two nations, neither shall they be divided into two kingdoms any more at all:*
[23] *Neither shall they defile themselves any more with their idols, nor with their detestable things, nor with any of their transgressions: but I will save them out of all their dwelling places, wherein they have sinned, and will cleanse them: so shall they be my people, and I will be their God.*
[24] *And David my servant shall be king over them; and they all shall have one shepherd: they shall also walk in my judgments, and observe my statutes, and do them.*
[25] *And they shall dwell in the land that I have given unto Jacob my servant, wherein your fathers have dwelt; and they shall dwell therein, even they, and their children, and their children's children for ever: and my servant David shall be their prince forever* Ezekiel 37: 21-25

People from the 12 tribes of Israel will live and prosper in the Promised Land: Jesus Christ and King David will reign over them from Jerusalem, but this is *not* the eternal Kingdom of God. The reason is clear. God will eventually return to earth to join His son (after the Millennial Kingdom) but not until after the earth has been cleansed and purged by fire. In Genesis 1:17 God told Adam and Eve after they had been expunged from the Garden of Eden: ...*cursed is the ground for thy sake.*

[18] *Thorns also and thistles shall it bring forth to thee; and thou shalt eat the herb of the field;*
[19] *In the sweat of thy face shalt thou eat bread, till thou return unto the ground; for out of it wast thou taken: for dust thou art, and unto dust shalt thou return* Genesis 1: 18-19

The earth had a curse placed upon it, and that curse must be lifted before God can set His foot upon its soil. This will not take place until *after* the 1000 year Millennial Kingdom has run its course.

[1] *And I saw a new heaven and a new earth: for the first heaven and the first earth were passed away; and there was no more sea.*
[2] *And I John saw the holy city, new Jerusalem, coming down from God out of heaven, prepared as a bride adorned for her husband.*

*[3] And I heard a great voice out of heaven saying, Behold, **the tabernacle of God is with men, and he will dwell with them**, and they shall be his people, and God himself shall be with them, and be their God.*
[4] And God shall wipe away all tears from their eyes; and there shall be no more death, neither sorrow, nor crying, neither shall there be any more pain: for the former things are passed away
Revelation 21 :1-4

The End of the Millennial Kingdom

John now gazes even farther into the future......many years.....as if it were tomorrow. John does not know when Christ will return to physically rule upon this earth, but He is certain that one day He will. The *Rapture and resurrection* of all true believers has taken place; The *Wrath of God* (7 Bowl Judgments) has fallen upon all unbelievers (Revelation 15:1, 16:1); the *Battle of Armageddon* has been fought; the *Beast* (Antichrist), the *False Prophet* have been defeated and cast into the *Lake of Fire and Brimstone* where they will be tortured forever (Revelation 19:20). Satan has been bound by a mighty angel and cast into the *Bottomless Pit* where he will be confined for 1000 years until the *Millennial Kingdom* has run its course (Revelation 20: 1-2). At that time, Satan will be loosed for just a *little while* (Revelation 20:3) to gather to Him all of the unbelievers which are alive on earth after this 1000 year period of time. They will be assembled by Satan and march on Jerusalem one more time (the 3rd assault on Jerusalem will be called *Satan's last Stand* (See Chapter 6). Satan will once again try and destroy the Holy City (Revelation 20: 7-9a), but this time **God Himself** will totally defeat Satan and his army of unbelievers (Revelation 20: 9b). This time the victory will be complete. Satan will be thrown into the Lake of Burning Fire where the Antichrist and the False Prophet were cast 1000 years earlier (Revelation 19:20, Revelation 20:10).

The time has now come for the *Great White Throne Judgment*. Almost without exception, biblical teachers and commentators equate the Great White Throne with a final judgment of all *unbelievers* who have died without accepting Christ as their Lord and Savior. This is true, but it is only partially true. All unbelievers from all ages will be judged, but there are three other groups which must also be judged at this time. (1) Those who have entered the Millennial Kingdom alive and then died (2) Those who have been born in the Millennial Kingdom and then died (3) Those who have been born into the Millennial Kingdom and are still alive. Each of these three groups will be composed of both believers and unbelievers and all must now be judged (Chapter 7). Those who have died in faith will be rewarded good works manifested in the Kingdom and will join those who were judged at the *Bema Seat Judgment* for unknown assignments and duties throughout eternity. Many will be saved if their names are found written in the *Book of Life*, and many who did not accept Jesus Christ as their Lord and Savior will be cast into the Lake of Burning Fire (Revelation 20: 12-15}. This will all take place at the

White Throne Judgment (See Chapter 7). Only one question might be asked by God: *What did you do with my Son?*

[**13**] *And the sea gave up the dead which were in it; and death and hell delivered up the dead which were in them: and they were judged every man according to their works.*
[**14**] *And death and hell were cast into the lake of fire.* **This is the second death.**
[**15**] *And whosoever was not found written in the* **book of life** *was cast into the lake of fire*
Revelation 20: 13-15

Finally, it should be clearly understood that the Millennial Kingdom will *not* be a restored Garden of Eden. Many pastors and biblical scholars teach that the Millennial Kingdom will be utopia and sin free...but this is not scriptural. Even though Satan has been bound and chained for 1000 years, the Adamic sin nature is still in all men from Adam. Incredibly, men will reject the rule of Jesus Christ, turn away from Him and love sinful acts more than righteousness. This is hard to believe, but recall that during the exodus from Egypt the children of Israel turned away from God within days after they miraculously passed through the Red Sea by the mighty hand of God! The presence of sin and rebellious, sinful people is the precise reason why Satan will be released from the *Bottomless Pit* after 1000 years for a *little season* (Revelation 20:3). Satan will gather all unbelievers to him and march on Jerusalem (Revelation 20: 7-9). He will once again be defeated along with all of the sinful people of the world, who will be as numerous as the *sand in the sea* (Revelation 20:8). *All unbelievers from all ages*....dead or alive (Revelation 20: 13-15, Matthew 25:46)....will then be gathered to the Great White Throne Judgment where they will be condemned to everlasting punishment. They will all be cast into the Lake of Burning Fire to join the Antichrist, the False prophet and Satan (Revelation 19:20, Revelation 20:10). After the earth is purged of all evil, the earth will be cleansed and renovated with fire (Revelation 21:1, II Peter 3: 10-12.

[**7**] *And when the thousand years are expired, Satan shall be loosed out of his prison,*
[**8**] *And shall go out to deceive the nations which are in the four quarters of the earth, Gog and Magog, to gather them together to battle: the number of whom is as the sand of the sea.*
[**9**] *And they went up on the breadth of the earth, and compassed the camp of the saints about, and the beloved city: and fire came down from God out of heaven, and devoured them.*
[**10**] *And the devil that deceived them was cast into the lake of fire and brimstone, where the beast and the false prophet are, and shall be tormented day and night forever and ever*
Revelation 20: 7-10

What will take place after the final judgment at the Great White Throne ? We will see that God will join Christ in His Millennial Palace and sit with him on His Millennial Throne. Yes...God will descend from heaven once the earth has been cleansed of all sin and live upon this earth for eternity. We are not given any more details than this, but: *Eye hath not seen, nor ear heard, neither have entered into the heart of man, the things which God hath prepared for them that love him* (I Corinthians 2:9). We will now describe the wonders of the Millennial Kingdom.

Chapter 3

Rule and Reign In the Millennial Kingdom

The Millennial Kingdom is not a kingdom which is in heaven but it is a literal, physical kingdom which will exist here on this earth for 1000 years. The government in the Millennial Kingdom is a *theocracy*, ruled by Jesus Christ. A possible hierarchy of rule and reign based upon scriptural clues is shown below.

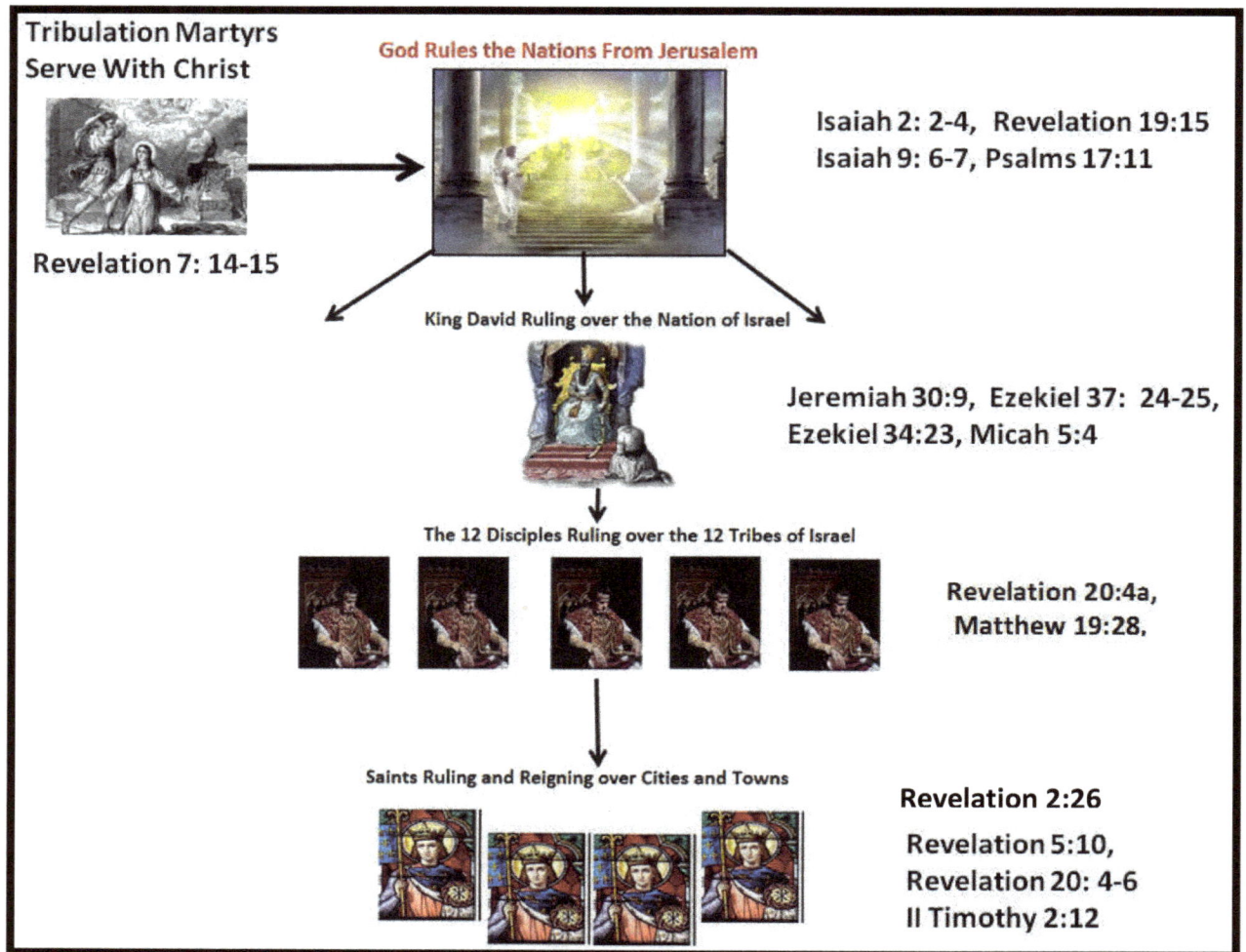

God Rules the Nations From Jerusalem

Paul wrote that all of Israel will not be saved before the *fullness of the Gentiles be come in* (Romans 11:25). This prophecy is also explained by Luke who wrote that:

*And they shall fall by the edge of the sword, and shall be led away captive into all nations: and Jerusalem shall be trodden down of the Gentiles, **until the times of the Gentiles be fulfilled*** Luke 21:24

Luke clearly says that the *Jerusalem shall be trodden down of the Gentiles, until the times of the Gentiles be fulfilled*. From the scriptures, we know that Jerusalem will be trodden down until Christ comes in His 2nd advent to fight the Battle of Armageddon. When the 7th angel pours out the 7th bowl (vial) of wrath upon the earth, there will be a great earthquake (Revelation 16:18). which will split the City of Jerusalem into *three parts* (Revelation 16:19). The temple Mount where the Muslim controlled Dome of the Rock now stands will be completely leveled and the old temple completely destroyed (Revelation 16:20). This earthquake will also raise up the old geographical area surrounding the temple mount.   *After* those things take place Christ will set up His *throne* on the old site of the temple mount, and He and King David will rule over those who inhabit the land during the 1000 years to follow. Jerusalem will no longer exist as it does today. There will be a great earthquake after Christ fights the battle of Armageddon that will elevate Mt. Zion, and all of the surrounding hills will be leveled (Zachariah 14: 4, 10). Christ will rule and reign from atop this new mountain and a throne will be built from which Christ and King David will rule and reign for 1000 years (Isaiah 2:2-4)

[**16**] *After this I will return, and will build again the tabernacle of David, which is fallen down; and I will build again the ruins thereof, and I will set it up:*
[**17**] *That the residue of men might seek after the Lord, and all the Gentiles, upon whom my name is called, saith the Lord, who doeth all these things*   Acts 15: 16-17

[**2**] *And it shall come to pass in the last days, that **the mountain of the LORD's house shall be established in the top of the mountains**, and shall be exalted above the hills; and all nations shall flow unto it.*
[**3**] *And many people shall go and say, Come ye, and let us go up to the mountain of the LORD, to the house of the God of Jacob; and he will teach us of his ways, and we will walk in his paths: for **out of Zion shall go forth the law, and the word of the LORD from Jerus**alem*   Isaiah 2: 1-2

After Ezekiel describes how Israel will be gathered to their own land as promised, he describes the new throne of Jesus Christ in great detail in Ezekiel 40-48. The prophet Isaiah spoke of this judgment long ago in Isaiah 11.

[**11**] *And it shall come to pass in that day, that the Lord shall set his hand again **the second time** to recover the remnant of his people, which shall be left, from Assyria, and from Egypt, and from Pathros, and from Cush, and from Elam, and from Shinar, and from Hamath, and from the islands of the sea.*
[**12**] *And he shall set up an **ensign** for the nations, and shall assemble the outcasts of Israel, and **gather together the dispersed of Judah from the four corners of the earth**.* Isaiah 11: 11-12

Most commentators identify the *first time* that Christ gathered his people together as referring to the Exodus from Egypt. However, this cannot be the case since at the Exodus all the people were gathered only out of Egypt. This regathering of the people will be from the *four corners of the earth*. The *first regathering* is referring to when God regathered His people out of Babylon and returned them to Israel after 70 years captivity. The lost 10 tribes of the Northern Kingdom who were exiled to Assyria were never recovered, but the 12 tribes will once again be united to inherit the Millennial Kingdom. Ezekiel prophesied of this reunion long ago.

[16] *Moreover, thou son of man, take thee one stick, and write upon it, For Judah, and for the children of Israel his companions: then take another stick, and write upon it, For Joseph, the stick of Ephraim, and for all the house of Israel his companions:*

[17] *And join them one to another into one stick; and they shall become one in thine hand*
Ezekiel 37: 16-17

There will be only one supreme ruler over all mankind, and that will be Jesus Christ. There will be no Catholic Church, no Baptist Church , no Muslims, Etc. but there will be a single world-wide religious system that only worships our Lord Jesus Christ. Jerusalem will be the religious and political center of the world:

And the LORD shall be king over all the earth: in that day shall there be one LORD, and his name one   Zachariah 14:9

[3] *Thus saith the LORD; I am returned unto Zion, and will dwell in the midst of Jerusalem: and Jerusalem shall be called a city of truth; and the mountain of the LORD of hosts the holy mountain.*

[4] *Thus saith the LORD of hosts; There shall yet old men and old women dwell in the streets of Jerusalem, and every man with his staff in his hand for very age.*

[5] *And the streets of the city shall be full of boys and girls playing in the streets thereof.*

[6] *Thus saith the LORD of hosts; If it be marvelous in the eyes of the remnant of this people in these days, should it also be marvelous in mine eyes? saith the LORD of hosts.*

[7] **Thus saith the LORD of hosts; Behold, I will save my people** *from the east country, and from the west country;*

[8] *And **I will bring them**, and they shall dwell in the midst of Jerusalem: and they shall be my people, and I will be their God, in truth and in righteousness.*

[9] *Thus saith the LORD of hosts; Let your hands be strong, ye that hear in these days these words by the mouth of the prophets, which were in the day that the foundation of the house of the LORD of hosts was laid, that the temple might be built.*

On May 14, 1948, in Tel Aviv, Jewish Agency Chairman David Ben-Gurion proclaimed the State of Israel and established the first Jewish state in almost 2,000 years. As soon as Israel was restored to a sovereign state once again, Jews from all over the world began to re-gather in the Land of Israel. Tele-evangelists and many prophecy teachers loudly decreed: *The end is near....prophecies concerning Israel regathering to the land are coming true before your eyes....this continues today.* Do not be deceived and just believe what the Holy Bible prophesies. Yes, there will be a regathering of Jews to the land but it will not be because a new State of Israel now exists. Prophecy concerning the return of Israel to the land of Israel is speaking of the end times when Jesus Christ will divide the land into 13 sections... one for Himself, His administration, His throne room, His royal palace, and the City of Jerusalem... and one for each of the 12 tribes of Israel to inherit and live upon. A regathering of the Jews will be by the mighty hand of Jesus Christ and *will not* occur until after the tribulation period and the Church age has come to an end.

*For, lo, the days come, saith the LORD, that **I will bring again** the captivity of my people Israel and Judah, saith the LORD: and I will cause them to return to the land that I gave to their fathers, and they shall possess it*   Jeremiah 30:3

*Afterward shall the children of Israel return, and seek the LORD their God, and David their king; and shall fear the LORD and his goodness **in the latter day**s*   Hosea 3:5

The Throne of Jesus Christ

Jesus Christ will rule and reign from just north of where the City of Jerusalem now stands (Isaiah 2:4; 11:3-4). It will be a "New Jerusalem" because the old Jerusalem will be completely destroyed and replaced by a new city also called Jerusalem. This is not the *New Jerusalem* described in Revelation 21: 1-27. The hill on which the city and the current temple mount now sits will become a large, elevated plateau and the surrounding land will become a level plain. This transformation will begin when Christ descends from heaven to meet Satan and his army outside of Jerusalem on the Plains of Megiddo.

*[**2**] And it shall come to pass in the last days, that the mountain of the LORD's house shall be established in the top of the mountains, and shall be exalted above the hills; and all nations shall flow unto it.*

*[**3**] And many people shall go and say, Come ye, and let us go up to the mountain of the LORD, to the house of the God of Jacob; and he will teach us of his ways, and we will walk in his paths: for out of Zion shall go forth the law, and the word of the LORD from Jerusalem.*

*[**4**] And he shall judge among the nations, and shall rebuke many people: and they shall beat their swords into plowshares, and their spears into pruning hooks: nation shall not lift up sword against nation, neither shall they learn war any more*
Isaiah 2: 2-4

When Jesus Christ returns to earth a 2nd time there will be a transformation of the land which surrounds Jerusalem when He descends from heaven to the Mount of Olives, from which He ascended after His resurrection.

[4] *And **his feet shall stand in that day upon the mount of Olives**, which is before Jerusalem on the east, and the **Mount of Olives shall** cleave in the midst thereof toward the east and toward the west, and there shall be a very great valley; and half of the mountain shall remove toward the north, and half of it toward the south*   Zachariah 14:4

Zachariah 4:1 seems to settle a long debated argument. The *Day of the Lord* is often presented as the entire period of time that Satan will war against the saints as the 6 seals are opened and the 7 trumpets sound. Many call the duration of the 6 seals, 7 trumpet judgments and the 7 bowl/vial judgments to be the Day of the Lord (Joel 1:15, Isaiah 13:9, Jeremiah 46:10, Joel 3:14). The Day of the Lord is exactly what it says... a single glorious day when Jesus Christ arrives back on earth to fight the Battle of Armageddon.

*The lofty looks of man shall be humbled, and the haughtiness of men shall be bowed down, and the LORD alone shall be exalted **in that day***   Isaiah 2:11

*Behold, **the day of the LORD** cometh, cruel both with wrath and fierce anger, to lay the land desolate: and he shall destroy the sinners thereof out of it*   Isaiah 13:9

*In that **day**, saith the LORD, I will smite every horse with astonishment, and his rider with madness: and I will open mine eyes upon the house of Judah, and will smite every horse of the people with blindness*   Zachariah 12:4

Before Christ returns a 2nd time, Satan and his forces will have gathered in the Valley of Jehosephat (Joel 3: 1-2). They will then begin to attack Jerusalem. Satan and his forces will overrun the City of Jerusalem and slaughter its inhabitants. People will flee from this carnage but about 50 % of the people will be captured or killed (Zachariah 14: 2-3). This is the 2nd attack on Jerusalem during the Tribulation period (The Jerusalem Campaign as the Wrath of Satan begins was the first). Christ will suddenly descend from heaven....probably to the exact location on the Mount of Olives from which He ascended to heaven 40 days after his resurrection (Acts 1: 1-12). It is also likely that Jesus will descend from the east (Matthew 24:27). When Christ touches the earth, His feet will split the Mt. of Olives into two pieces, one to the east and one to the west (Zachariah 14:4). As the 600 foot hill splits in half, it will flatten and spread creating a valley running north and south. Those who are fleeing Jerusalem will run through that valley (Zachariah 14:5) towards a small village east of Jerusalem called Azel (Zachariah 14:5). Satan will evidently see Christ, and it appears that he will move to encounter Him. As Satan moves against Christ, He will destroy them all (Revelation 19). There is yet another cataclysmic event which changes the land surrounding Jerusalem which will take place after the Battle of Armageddon is completed.

*All the land shall be turned as **a plain** from Geba to Rimmon south of Jerusalem: and it shall be lifted up, and inhabited in her place, from Benjamin's gate unto the place of the first gate, unto the corner gate, and from the tower of Hananeel unto the king's winepresses*
Zachariah 14:10

All of the hills and ridges near Jerusalem will be turned into level plains. *Geba* is a small town near the northern border of Judah about 5 miles from Jerusalem, and Rimmon is a town near the southern border of Judah. The Mount of Olives and all of the *mountains around Jerusalem* (Psalms 125:2) will be leveled, but the site where Jerusalem now stands will be raised up and will be higher than the surrounding plains. This elevated portion of the land is where the temple of God and the throne of Jesus Christ will be built (See Chapter 5).

*But **in the last days** it shall come. to pass, that the **mountain of the house of the LORD** shall be established in the top of the mountains, and it shall be exalted above the hills*   Micah 4:1

The purpose of Israel being elevated is to lift the Lord Jesus Christ high above the land of Israel and to display the place where Christ will rule and reign to anyone that might approach from any direction.

*Thus saith the Lord; **I am returned unto Zion, and will dwell in the midst of Jerusalem**: and Jerusalem shall be called a city of truth; and the mountain of the Lord of hosts the holy mountain.*   Zechariah 8:3

[2] *And it shall come to pass **in the last days**, that the mountain of the LORD's house shall be established in the top of the mountains, and **shall be exalted** above the hills; and all nations shall flow unto it*
[3] *And many people shall go and say, Come ye, and let us go up to the mountain of the LORD, to the house of the God of Jacob; and he will teach us of his ways, and we will walk in his paths: for **out of Zion shall go forth the law, and the word of the LORD from Jerusalem**.*
[4] *And he shall judge among the nations, and shall rebuke many people: and they shall beat their swords into plowshares, and their spears into pruning hooks: nation shall not lift up sword against nation, neither shall they learn war any more.*   Isaiah 2: 2-4

Isaiah prophesied that during the earthly reign of Jesus Christ He will judge *among the nations* and would *rebuke many people* (Isaiah 2:4). Evidently he will rule as a fair and just monarch, but will not tolerate rebellion against the laws of God. Although any transgression will result in immediate righteous judgment, the general condition among all of the nations will be one of peace. Following the Battle of Armageddon, the implements and weapons of war will be burned for *7 years* (Ezekiel 39:8). There will be so many weapons and implements of war that contain wood the people of Israel will not cut down any trees for warmth or cooking for *7 years* (Ezekiel 39:10). The dead that are laying in the fields will take *7 months* to bury (Ezekiel 39:12).

[8] *Behold, it is come, and it is done, saith the Lord GOD;* **this is the day** *whereof I have spoken.*
[9] *And they that dwell in the cities of Israel shall go forth, and shall set on fire and burn the weapons, both the shields and the bucklers, the bows and the arrows, and the hand staves, and the spears, and* **they shall burn them with fire seven years**:
[10] *So that they shall take no wood out of the field, neither cut down any out of the forests; for they shall burn the weapons with fire: and they shall spoil those that spoiled them, and rob those that robbed them, saith the Lord GOD.*
[11] *And it shall come to pass in that day, that I will give unto Gog a place there of graves in Israel, the valley of the passengers on the east of the sea: and it shall stop the noses of the passengers: and* **there shall they bury Gog and all his multitude**: *and they shall call it The valley of Hamon-gog.*
[12] *And* **seven months shall the house of Israel be burying of them**, *that they may cleanse the land.*
[13] *Yea, all the people of the land shall bury them; and it shall be to them a renown the* **day that I shall be glorified**, *saith the Lord GOD*　　　　　Ezekiel 39: 8-13

War as a solution to national problems will no longer be practiced.

[5] *Behold, the days come, saith the LORD, that I will raise unto David a righteous Branch, and a King shall reign and prosper, and shall execute judgment and justice in the earth.*
[6] *In his days Judah shall be saved, and* **Israel shall dwell safely**: *and this is his name whereby he shall be called, THE LORD OUR RIGHTEOUSNESS*　　　　　Jeremiah 23: 5-6

And he shall judge among the nations, and shall rebuke many people: and they shall beat their swords into plowshares, and their spears into pruning hooks: nation shall not lift up sword against nation, neither shall they learn war any more.　　　　　Isaiah 2:4

As I live, saith the Lord GOD, surely with a mighty hand, and with a stretched out arm, and with fury poured out, will I **rule** *over you*　　　　　Ezekiel 20:33

The Ruling Hierarchy

Jesus Christ will rule and reign over all of the nations from his elevated throne room for 1000 years. Initially, there would only be a few people living in the promised land. There will be at least 12,000 people in each section of land allocated to the 12 tribes of Israel (Revelation 7: 1-8). However, this relatively small population would grow to a very large number over a 1000 year period of time.

It is not clear as to whether the *sheep* in the judgment of the Nations (Matthew 25: 31-46) will return to their own land or whether they will join the 12 tribes of Israel in the promised land.

Since there is no clue in scripture that gentiles would share the promised land with the Jews, it is speculated that they would enter into the Millennial Kingdom by returning to their own land...but this is only conjectured. It any case, as the 1000 years unfolds, there will be many who will choose to leave the promised land for other parts of the world. This conjecture becomes near certainty when it is realized that after Satan is released from his chains in the bottomless pit, He will return to earth and gather all unbelievers from the *four corners of the earth* (Revelation 20:8). Although Christ will rule and reign over the entire world, he will not be omnipresent and omniscient as God the Father, but He will be advised and aided by those who will rule and reign with Him. Christ will be ruling and reigning as an absolute monarch, but He will be joined by several groups of saints who have accepted Him as Lord and Savior by faith: (1) Martyrs from all ages (2) The 12 apostles who spread the gospel message about the known world (3) King David (4) Old Testament men of faith who died with the faith of Abraham and (5) Many New Covenant saints. It is not absolutely positive how each of these people will rule and reign throughout the Kingdom. The following discussion and the introductory graphic of this chapter are presented based upon available clues and prophecies found in the Holy Scriptures.

Jesus Christ: *Sovereign Ruler*

Jesus the Christ will rule and reign over all of the nations of the world from a high plateau that will be raised at the current site of the Dome of the Rock in Jerusalem (Isaiah 2:2). The elevation of the throne of Jesus above all of the land surrounding Jerusalem is symbolic of the exalted and risen Christ. He will destroy and renovate the desecration of the Temple site by the Muslim Dome of the Rock and destroy all of the filth and sin that the modern Jerusalem represents. The center of this high plateau will be the Temple of Jesus Christ. This graphic was constructed from biblical descriptions in Zachariah and Ezekiel by Henry Sully, who was an architect in England (1845-1940).

Martyrs

Those who have been martyred for Christ rather than deny Him will hold a special place in the Millennial Kingdom. It appears that those who have been martyred between the resurrection of Christ and the Great Tribulation have been waiting for Jesus Christ to return a 2nd time in Heaven beneath the Throne of God.

[9] *And when he had opened the fifth seal, I saw under the altar the souls of them that were slain for the word of God,*

and for the testimony which they held:

[10] And they cried with a loud voice, saying, How long, O Lord, holy and true, dost thou not judge and avenge our blood on them that dwell on the earth?

[11] And white robes were given unto every one of them; and it was said unto them, that they should rest yet for a little season, until their fellowservants also and their brethren, that should be killed as they were, should be fulfilled Revelation 6: 9-11

These martyred saints will be joined by their *brethren* who would be *killed as they were* (Revelation 6: 9-11). The first New covenant martyred saint is believed to be *Stephen*. He was stoned to death as he preached the gospel to Jews in Jerusalem. He did not compromise the gospel message in any way, and when he had finished the Jews were so infuriated that they turned on him and stoned him to death. As he was being martyred, Stephen looked up and saw Christ standing by His Father (Acts 7-8). Earlier, Christ had prophesied that His disciples would see Him sitting next to His Father in heaven on the throne of glory (Matthew 26:64). When Stephen was martyred, he saw Jesus *standing*. We can imagine that Christ was so grieved at the death of His *friend* that He suddenly stood wanting to go to his aid. But Christ knew that this could not be so. All of His 12 apostles except for John were also martyred, and there would be many more before the Church Age would come to an end. When Stephen died we can imagine that Christ might have stood to welcome His faithful servant into His loving arms and then to place Stephen beneath His throne where he would wait for those who must suffer the same fate.

[22].....The Son of man must suffer many things, and be rejected of the elders and chief priests and scribes, and be slain, and be raised the third day.

[23] And he said to them all, If any man will come after me, let him deny himself, and take up his cross daily, and follow me.

[24] For whosoever will save his life shall lose it: but whosoever will lose his life for my sake, the same shall save it Luke 9: 22-24

What role will these martyrs play in the Millennial Kingdom? The scriptures are silent on this issue but it is certain that they will hold a special place in the administration of Jesus Christ. It is conjectured that these martyred saints will be special emissaries for Christ as he rules and reigns. It is possible that they might assume earthly roles similar to Michael and Gabriel who will remain in heaven with God the Father. Angels will not have an active role in the Millennial Kingdom except to worship and praise God in heaven as Jesus reigns on earth as Lord of Lords and King of Kings.

King David Ruling over the Nation of Israel

The United Kingdom of David was inherited by his son Solomon. At the death of King Solomon it was split into two different kingdoms: One ruled by Solomon's son Rehoboam (Judah) and the other by Jeroboam (Israel). Eventually both were conquered by a foreign country because of disbelief, apostasy and idol worship: Judah by Babylon and Israel by Assyria. The Northern

Kingdom disappeared into history (the 10 lost tribes) and the Southern Kingdom of Judah spent 70 years in Babylonian captivity. Judah was later reconstituted in the land...eventually giving rise to Jesus Christ. The 12 tribes of Israel will be united once again in the Millennial kingdom. (Ezekiel 37: 16-19).

[21] *And say unto them, Thus saith the Lord GOD; Behold,* **I will take the children of Israel from among the heathen,** *where they be gone, and will gather them on every side, and* **bring them into their own land:**
[22] *And I will make them one nation in the land upon the mountains of Israel; and one king shall be king to them all: and they shall be no more two nations, neither shall they be divided into two kingdoms any more at all:*
[23] *Neither shall they defile themselves any more with their idols, nor with their detestable things, nor with any of their transgressions: but I will save them out of all their dwelling places, wherein they have sinned, and will cleanse them:* **so shall they be my people, and I will be their God** Ezekiel 37: 21-23

This is an amazing prophecy! (1) The children of Israel will gathered from among the Gentiles (heathen) (2) They will become one nation with only one King (Jesus Christ) (3) They will no longer defile themselves (4) God will cleanse them and (5) They will be His people and He will be their God. Of course, it was not known in the Old Testament that Jesus Christ would rule over them during the 1000 year Millennial Kingdom. Paul revealed to us that: *He hath put all things under his feet. But when he saith, all things are put under him, it is manifest that he* (God) *is excepted, which did put all things under him* (I Corinthians 15:27).

[25] *Thus saith the Lord GOD; When I shall have gathered the house of Israel from the people among whom they are scattered, and shall be sanctified in them in the sight of the heathen, then shall* **they dwell in their land** *that I have given to my servant Jacob.*
[26] *And* **they shall dwell safely** *therein, and shall build houses, and plant vineyards; yea, they shall dwell with confidence, when I have executed judgments upon all those that despise them round about them; and* **they shall know that I am the LORD their God** Ezekiel 28: 25-26

[24] *And* **David my servant shall be king over them**; *and they all shall have one shepherd: they shall also walk in my judgments, and observe my statutes, and do them* Ezekiel 37:24

Ezekiel 28: 25-26 and Ezekiel 37:24 are loaded with prophecy and must be carefully interpreted. (1) David is His *servant*. He serves *under* God by and beside His Son (2) David will be their (Israel) *shepherd* (3) God will gather all of the House of Israel from the nations and *then* they (all of the 12 tribes) will *safely dwell in the land* (4) They (the 12 tribes) will build houses....plant vineyards.....dwell confidently (securely). None of this has ever come to pass....but it will.

Jesus Christ will be their exalted King, but they will have only *one shepherd* (one God, one king, one shepherd). These verses in Ezekiel make it quite clear that King David will rule over the 12 tribes of Israel during the 1000 year Millennial Kingdom, but he will serve under the monarchy of Jesus Christ. There are many other verses that confirm this conclusion. For example:

[4] *For the children of Israel shall abide* **many days** *without a king, and without a prince, and without a sacrifice, and without an image, and without an ephod, and without teraphim:*
[5] *Afterward shall the children of* **Israel return**, *and seek the LORD their God, and David their king; and shall fear the LORD and his goodness in the latter* days   Hosea 3: 4-5

But they shall serve the LORD their God, and David their king, whom I will raise up *unto them*
Jeremiah 30:9

A Teraphim (Hosea 3:4) is an image made of gold or silver...an idol. A careful examination of Jeremiah, Hosea and Ezekiel will confirm that during the 1000 year Millennial Kingdom Jesus will rule and reign from His throne just north of the City of Jerusalem, probably at the site of the ancient city of Shiloh (Jeremiah 7:12). In a type of the Millennial Kingdom, Joshua divided the land among the 12 tribes of Israel after they had *subdued the land*. The tabernacle remained there from the days of Joshua until the days of Samuel (Joshua 19:1). In the Millennial Kingdom, David will be the King over all 12 tribes of Israel and is called a *Prince* (Ezekiel 37:25).

Old Testament Believers

There is no doubt that King David will be resurrected and that He will rule and reign with Christ. Considering prophecy as a whole, it is believed that the Old Testament saints who died in faith will be resurrected and taken up to Christ at the *rapture*. It is not clear what role they will play in the Millennial Kingdom, but it is logical that they might assist King David in ruling over the 12 tribes of Israel. Another possibility is based upon the fact that when the Jews became the *Bride of God* (Jeremiah 31: 31-33), He called them as His chosen people and they became the apple of His eye. This is parallel to the New Covenant *ecclesia* being the Bride of Jesus Christ. In this case, the Old Testament saints who believed in faith might remain with God in heaven and return with Him after the 1000 years are over. However, it is also likely that the dry bones prophecy of Ezekiel has a broader and far reaching meaning. After Satan kills or takes into captivity 50% of the Jews living in Jerusalem just after Christ descends in His 2nd advent to the Mount of Olives, Christ will rescue the other 50% as previously discussed. At that time, the Jews will finally realize that they have been wrong for over 2000 years, and that their only hope is in Jesus Christ. At that time *all of Israel will be saved* (Romans 11:26). Ezekiel spoke of this about 2500 years ago.

Thus saith the Lord GOD; Behold, O my people, I will open your graves, and cause you to come up out of your graves, and bring you into the land of Israel   Ezekiel 37:12

This is a difficult passage to understand, but it is proposed that it is *not* referring to a resurrection at all, but is a *metaphor* referring to how Israel will one day be reconciled to God and inherit the land promised to them. A metaphor is not a simile. A *simile* uses words such as *like* or *as* to compare: *Life is like a bowl of cherries.* A metaphor directly states a comparison: *God is love.* Israel must be restored to the land to honor the Abramic Covenant made between God and Jacob (Israel). Since the Jews rejected Christ and demanded that He be crucified, God has *set aside* the Jews and *blinded them in part* (Romans 11:25) until the Church Age is over and the *fullness of the Gentiles* has come in (Romans 11:25). The Jews (corporately) even today refuse to believe that Jesus Christ was their long awaited redeemer and Messiah. They are *spiritually dead.* To be spiritually dead is to be separated from God. The opposite of death is *life*, and life can only be obtained in Jesus Christ: *I am the way, the truth and the life.* Israel today is *dead in her sins*, nothing remains but *lifeless bones*. God said that one day those bones would rise (be restored to a covenant relationship through Jesus Christ); God would bring life into those bones (the Holy Spirit); and Israel will be restored to her land in blessing under the leadership of *David, My servant.*

[25] *And they shall dwell in the land that I have given unto Jacob my servant, wherein your fathers have dwelt; and they shall dwell therein, even they, and their children, and their children's children for ever: and my servant David shall be their prince forever.*
Ezekiel 37:25

What a glorious moment that will be! The dead, dry bones which represent Israel in disbelief and *dead in their own sins* will turn to Jesus Christ. Christ will then bring them into the Land of Israel....the promised land.

For if by one man's offence death reigned by one; much more they which receive abundance of grace and of the gift of righteousness shall reign in life by one, Jesus Christ   Romans 5:17

I will appoint a place for my people Israel, and will plant them, that they may dwell in a place of their own, and move no more; neither shall the children of wickedness afflict them any more, as beforetime   II Samuel 11:10

The 12 Apostles

The 12 apostles (original 11 plus Matthias) will also hold a special place in the Kingdom (Matthew 19:28). They were not only responsible for spreading the gospel message around the known world, but all suffered a horrible death(martyred) except for the apostle John. Jesus loved each of His apostles and He personally promised them that they would join Him in His Kingdom and rule (judge) over the 12 tribes of Israel.

[27] *Then answered Peter and said unto him, Behold, we have forsaken all, and followed thee; what shall we have therefore?*
[28] *And Jesus said unto them, Verily I say unto you, That ye which have followed me,* ***in the***

regeneration when the Son of man shall sit in the throne of his glory, ye also shall sit upon twelve thrones, judging the twelve tribes of Israel   Matthew 19: 27-28

The word *regeneration* only appears one other time in the New Testament and it is in the context of experiencing a new birth into Jesus Christ by the Holy Spirit (Titus 3:5). This cannot be the case here, but undoubtedly refers to a new beginning in the Millennial Kingdom. All of the final 12 apostles were Jews. They participated in every Jewish Feast and worshipped in the synagogs. It is certain that Matthias who replaced Judas was a Jew (Acts 1:26) and so was Saul of Tarsus (Paul). Timothy was not one of the 12 apostles but he was selected by Paul to accompany him on several missionary journeys. Paul called him a brother (II Corinthians 1:1). Timothy certainly thought that he would reign with Christ in some capacity.

If we suffer, we shall also reign with him: if we deny him, he also will deny us   II Timothy 2:12

And (He) *hast made us unto our God kings and priests: and we shall reign on the earth* Revelation 5:10

The New Covenant Saints

The new Covenant Saints have been promised that they would rule and reign with Christ. In Revelation 5:10 Christ makes a promise to the saints (Revelation 5:8) that they will rule and reign with Christ. Revelation 20:4 confirms that those saints who do not have the mark of the beast will rule and reign. During the 1000 year millennial Kingdom, many people will be born and many cities will be built all over the world. It is conjectured that the New Covenant saints will have some role in rule and reign over these municipalities. This is logical since between 30 AD and 70 AD, they were all responsible for preaching the gospel message throughout the known world.

The scriptures indicate that people who will live upon the earth during the Millennium will initially all believe that Jesus Christ is the Son of God and the Holy Spirit will dwell within them, but this is not clearly stated in the Holy Word of God. Some biblical scholars have taught that there is no need for the Holy Spirit to dwell in man as a promise of the resurrection to come since it has already taken place. This is false doctrine. Christ clearly said: And *I will pray the Father, and he shall give you another Comforter, that he may abide with you* **forever** (John 14:16). Many also teach and believe that the 1000 year Millennial Kingdom will be free from sin since Satan has been bound in chains and is being confined in the bottomless pit. However, this is also

Saints Ruling and Reigning over Cities and Towns

false doctrine. At the end of the 1000 years Satan will be released for a *short season* and allowed to again roam over the earth (Revelation 20: 1-3). *What does this mean*? Satan constantly lies to man and deceives him every day. However, man in and of himself does not need to Satan to sin. All mankind is born with a sin nature inherited from Adam. Matthew warned us that *the spirit is willing but the flesh is weak* (Matthew 26:41). The apostle Paul...perhaps the greatest evangelist that ever lived... revealed that even though he had died to Christ that his body still was alive to sin.

[14] *For we know that the law is spiritual: but I am carnal, sold under sin.*
[15] *For that which I do I allow not: for what I would, that do I not; but what I hate, that do I.*
[16] *If then I do that which I would not, I consent unto the law that it is good.*
[17] *Now then it is no more I that do it, but sin that dwelleth in me.*
[18] *For I know that in me (that is, in my flesh,) dwelleth no good thing: for to will is present with me; but how to perform that which is good I find not.*
[19] *For the good that I would I do not: but the evil which I would not, that I do.*
[20] *Now if I do that I would not, it is no more I that do it, but sin that dwelleth in me*
Romans 7: 14-20

The very earth that the Jews will live on in the Millennial Kingdom was placed under a curse ever since Adam and Eve were evicted from the Garden of Eden (Genesis 3:17). Incredibly, those who are living upon the earth during this magnificent Kingdom will rebel against God and abandon His precepts and laws. Satan will be released from his prison at the end of the 1000 years and he will go to the four corners of the earth to round up all unbelievers for one last battle (See Chapter 6, Revelation 20). At this last great battle....which we call *Satan's Last Stand*...Satan and all of those who will follow him will be destroyed by *God* (Revelation 20:9). The *Great White Throne Judgment* will immediately follow, and when this takes place *all* unbelievers will be *judged* and found guilty of not accepting Jesus Christ as their Lord and Savior. all unbelievers....those whose names are not written in the Book of Life (Revelation 20:15) will be cast into the Lake of Burning Fire with Satan where the Antichrist and the False Prophet have been for 1000 years (Revelation 20: 11-15). At this point, the earth will have finally been purged of *all* unbelievers. The earth will then be cleansed by *fire* (II Peter 3: 7, 12) and return to the pure and sinless state it was in when Adam and Eve lived in the Garden of Eden.

It is generally not realized by the average Christian, but eternity will not be spent in the 3rd heaven where God now rules and reigns (II Corinthians 12:2). Christians will not sit on clouds and play a harp all day for eternity! After the 1000 year Millennial Kingdom is over and the earth is purged of all sin, God will descend from where He now resides in the 3rd heaven and live here on this earth. The resurrected and regenerated saints will then live forever in a city called the *New Jerusalem*, which will descend from heaven and sit on this earth in the Nation of Israel (Revelation 22: 2-3). *What will happen next?* The scriptures are silent as to what will happen through all eternity, but we are told that God will be worshipped and praised by all of those who enter into His eternal Kingdom.

[1] *Praise ye the LORD. Praise, O ye servants of the LORD, praise the name of the LORD.*
[2] *Blessed be the name of the LORD from this time forth and for evermore.*
[3] *From the rising of the sun unto the going down of the same the LORD's name is to be praised*
Psalms 113: 1-3

But we will bless the LORD from this time forth and for evermore. Praise the LORD
Psalms 115:18

Where will all the saints live during the Millennial Kingdom? The scriptures do not specifically say, but it will be proposed that they will all receive an eternal home that Christ has built for us as a reward when the Millennial Kingdom begins. That home is called the *New Jerusalem*. During the Millennial Kingdom, the New Jerusalem will be it the 3rd heaven and if the New Covenant saints will live there they will need to go back and forth between the earth and the 3rd heaven (See Chapter 8).

[2] *In my Father's house are many mansions: if it were not so, I would have told you. I go to prepare a place for you.*
[3] *And if I go and prepare a place for you, I will come again, and receive you unto myself; that where I am, there ye may be also*   John 14: 2-3

A New Heaven and a New Earth

[1] *And I saw a new heaven and a new earth: for the first heaven and the first earth were passed away; and there was no more sea.*
[2] *And I John saw the holy city,* **New Jerusalem**, *coming down from God out of heaven, prepared as a bride adorned for her husband.*
[3] *And I heard a great voice out of heaven saying, Behold,* **the tabernacle of God is with men**, *and he will dwell with them, and they shall be his people, and God himself shall be with them, and be their God.*
[4] *And God shall wipe away all tears from their eyes; and there shall be no more death, neither sorrow, nor crying, neither shall there be any more pain: for the former things are passed away*
Revelation 21: 1-4

Recall that the *ecclesia* or the *ones called out....*true believers from all of the ages past ....will be raised at the Rapture and will be rewarded at the Bema seat Judgment. The holiness of all the saints would be honored by having them live in the New Jerusalem throughout eternity, but the New Jerusalem will not descend to the earth until after the Kingdom is completed (Chapter 8). This is such an interesting prophecy that an entire chapter will be devoted to who will live in the Kingdom, and why the New Jerusalem cannot be here on earth until the Millennial Kingdom is over (Chapter 8).

The Spirit of the Lord GOD is upon me; because the LORD hath anointed me to preach good tidings unto the meek; he hath sent me to bind up the brokenhearted, to proclaim liberty to the captives, and the opening of the prison to them that are bound;

The New Jerusalem

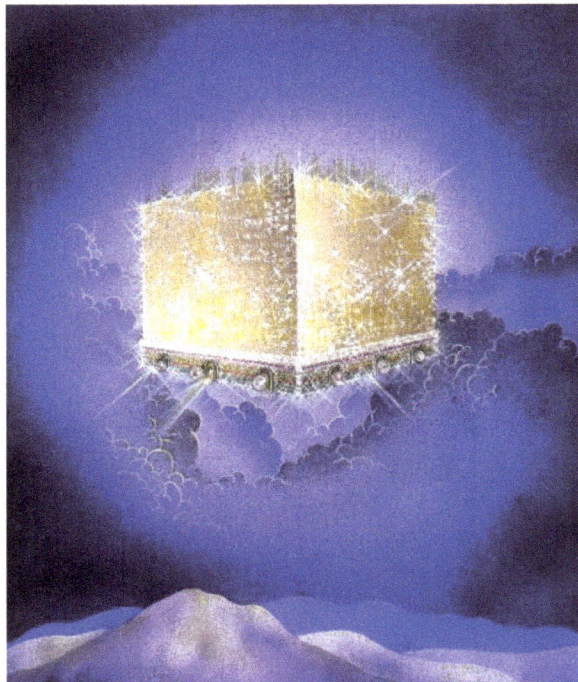

Chapter 4

Kingdom Inhabitants

The Millennial Kingdom will be inhabited by both *spiritual* people and *ordinary people.* The people who will be in spiritual bodies will be involved in the administration (Chapter 3) of the Kingdom. The people in natural bodies will live in the land during the Millennial Kingdom. (1) Jesus Christ will sit on His earthly throne in Jerusalem and be the supreme ruler over all of the earth (2) Martyrs will serve with Christ (3) King David will be restored to his throne and rule over all the 12 tribes of Israel (4) The 12 disciples will rule over the individual 12 tribes of Israel (5) New Covenant saints will rule and reign over cities and towns all over the world. The actual position, role and authority of those who will rule and reign with Christ for 1000 years will be determined by the magnitude of their rewards at the Bema Seat Judgment (Chapter 7).

The Promised Land will be inhabited by real people in ordinary human bodies. The life span of those who live on the earth will be greatly increased, but many will die natural deaths. The citizens of the Promised land and the Kingdom will be composed of: (1) The 144,000 Jews that were sealed from Wrath (2) A Jewish remnant who have survived the Great Tribulation and (3) The *sheep* from the Judgment of the Nations (Sheep and Goats Judgment). Of course, as time goes on there will be children born in every country and in every city.

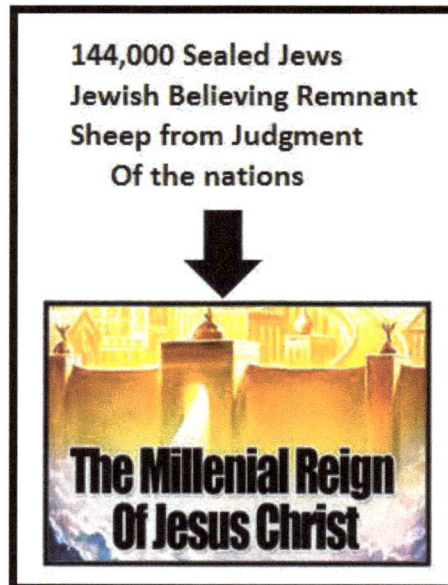

144,000 Sealed Jews
Jewish Believing Remnant
Sheep from Judgment
Of the nations

The Millenial Reign Of Jesus Christ

The Millennial 1000 year Kingdom will not be in some far-away heavenly place with God and Jesus Christ. This Kingdom will be here on earth. Jesus Christ will rule supreme and reign in a *theocracy* over the whole world for 1000 years, and He will be on this earth in His temple in Jerusalem.

And the LORD shall be king over all the earth: in that day shall there be one LORD, and his name one   Zachary 14:9

The current City of Jerusalem and the Muslim Temple Site will be destroyed and the surrounding land changed by supernatural forces of nature (Chapter 2). The Palace and throne of Jesus Christ will be built just north of the temple over the place where the ancient City of Shiloh once stood (Larkin).

On the *Day of the Lord* Christ will descend from heaven to this earth and His feet will stand upon the Mount of Olives. The Mount will split into two pieces forming a valley. He will rescue 1/2 of the people in Jerusalem from Satan and the *Jerusalem Campaign* (Chapter 6), and then He will leave to fight the Battle of Armageddon.

[1] *Behold, the day of the LORD cometh, and thy spoil shall be divided in the midst of thee.*
[2] *For I will gather all nations against Jerusalem to battle; and the city shall be taken, and the houses rifled, and the women ravished; and half of the city shall go forth into captivity, and the residue of the people shall not be cut off from the city.*
[3] *Then shall the LORD go forth, and fight against those nations, as when he fought in the day of battle.*
[4] *And his feet shall stand in that day upon the mount of Olives, which is before Jerusalem on the east, and the mount of Olives shall cleave in the midst thereof toward the east and toward the west, and there shall be a very great valley; and half of the mountain shall remove toward the north, and half of it toward the south*   Zachariah 14: 1-4

[16] *And he gathered them together into a place called in the Hebrew tongue Armageddon.*
[17] *And the seventh angel poured out his vial into the air; and there came a great voice out of the temple of heaven, from the throne, saying,* **It is done**.
[18] *And there were voices, and thunders, and lightnings; and there was a great earthquake, such as was not since men were upon the earth, so mighty an earthquake, and so great.*
[20] *And every island fled away, and the mountains were not found.*
[21] *And there fell upon men a great hail out of heaven, every stone about the weight of a* **talent** *(uncertain....60-80 pounds): and men blasphemed God because of the plague of the hail; for the plague thereof was exceeding great*   Revelation 16: 16-21

[10] *All the land shall be turned as a plain from Geba to Rimmon south of Jerusalem: and it shall be lifted up, and inhabited in her place, from Benjamin's gate unto the place of the first gate,*

unto the corner gate, and from the tower of Hananeel unto the king's winepresses.
[11] *And men shall dwell in it, and there shall be no more utter destruction; but Jerusalem shall be safely inhabited*   Zachariah 14: 10-11

[1] *Great is the LORD, and greatly to be praised in the city of our God, in the mountain of his holiness.*
[2] *Beautiful for situation, the joy of the whole earth, is mount Zion, on the sides of the north, the city of the great King.*   Psalms 48: 1-2

The Land of Israel will be supernaturally transformed when Christ returns to earth at His *Second Advent*

- As the 7th bowl in the Wrath of God is poured out upon Satan and unbelievers *every island fled away, and the mountains were not found* (Revelation 16: 16-20)

- All of the land surrounding the Throne of Jesus and His Palace (Chapter 5) will become a fertile *plain* (Zachariah 14:10).

- The place where Jesus will rule and reign will be lifted up above the surrounding land: The Sanctuary (Temple) and the throne of Jesus Christ will be built on a flat plateau (Zachariah 14:10)

After Jesus Christ returns to this earth He will rescue the inhabitants of Jerusalem from Satan (the Armageddon Assault, Chapter 6), and then He will engage Satan and his army of unbelievers at the *Battle of Armageddon* (Revelation 16:16, Revelation 19). Most of the unbelievers on earth will be slain by Jesus Christ (Revelation 19:20) at the Battle of Armageddon. We say *most* because there are others who have survived the Great Tribulation that are scattered throughout the world: Both *believers* and *unbelievers* (Revelation 6: 15:17). The *Wrath of Satan* (Seven Trumpet Judgments) and the *Wrath of God* (Seven Bowl or Vial Judgments) will have taken place in Israel and across the European Theatre. There is no reason to doubt that tribulation and devastation will also be worldwide (Revelation 6: 1-8). During the last 3.5 years of the Tribulation, the Antichrist will persecute and seek to kill all Jews and Christians, but the center of all tribulation activities will be in Israel. *The Church Age will end at Armageddon so how will Christ deal with those who have survived and are still alive?* Those who have hidden from the Antichrist and the Wrath of Satan in other countries will be *gathered* to Him for what Jesus Christ called the *Judgment of the Sheep and Goats* or what might be called the *Judgment of the Nations* (Matthew 25: 31-46). Christ will sit upon a throne of judgment after the Battle of Armageddon, and He will decide who will be saved and enter into the Millennial Kingdom and who will be cast away forever into the Lake of Burning Fire (Revelation 19:20). This is a unique judgment which is different from the Bema Seat Judgment of all believers, and the Great White Throne Judgment of all unbelievers. Because it is seldom studied or completely understood by many Christians, it will be described in some detail.

The Sheep and Goats Judgment

[**31**] *When the Son of man shall come in his glory, and all the holy angels with him, then shall he sit upon the throne of his glory:*

[**32**] *And before him shall be gathered all nations: and he shall separate them one from another, as a shepherd divides his sheep from the goats:*

[**33**] *And he shall set the sheep on his right hand, but the goats on the left.*

[**34**] *Then shall the King say unto them on his right hand, Come, ye blessed of my Father, inherit the kingdom prepared for you from the foundation of the world:*

[**35**] *For I was hungry, and ye gave me meat: I was thirsty, and ye gave me drink: I was a stranger, and ye took me in:*

[**36**] *Naked, and ye clothed me: I was sick, and ye visited me: I was in prison, and ye came unto me.*

[**37**] *Then shall the righteous answer him, saying, Lord, when saw we thee hungry, and fed thee? or thirsty, and gave thee drink?*

[**38**] *When saw we thee a stranger, and took thee in? or naked, and clothed thee?*

[**39**] *Or when saw we thee sick, or in prison, and came unto thee?*

[**40**] *And the King shall answer and say unto them, Verily I say unto you, Inasmuch as ye have done it unto one of the least of these my brethren, ye have done it unto me.*

[**41**] *Then shall he say also unto them on the left hand, Depart from me, ye cursed, into everlasting fire, prepared for the devil and his angels:*

[**42**] *For I was hungry, and ye gave me no meat: I was thirsty, and ye gave me no drink:*

[**43**] *I was a stranger, and ye took me not in: naked, and ye clothed me not: sick, and in prison, and ye visited me not.*

[**44**] *Then shall they also answer him, saying, Lord, when saw we thee hungry, or thirsty, or a stranger, or naked, or sick, or in prison, and did not minister unto thee?*

[**45**] *Then shall he answer them, saying, Verily I say unto you, Inasmuch as ye did it not to one of the least of these, ye did it not to me.*

[**46**] *And these shall go away into everlasting punishment: but the righteous into life eternal*
Matthew 25: 31-46

Matthew 25: 31-46 makes it clear that: (1) Jesus Christ Himself will judge all nations accompanied by His Holy angels (2) He will gather all of those who are still alive and remain upon earth to Him as He sits upon His throne in Jerusalem (3) He will divide all nations into two groups; *sheep* and *goats* (4) They will be *judged* on how each treated *His brethren* (5) One group will inherit life eternal (sheep) and one group will go into everlasting punishment (goats). *How can this strange judgment be explained and what is its purpose?*

The setting for this prophecy is in the fields of Israel where the sheppard would tend his sheep. Sheep tend to be docile, peaceful creatures. They will follow a sheppard and they hear and recognize his voice. Goats are sometimes disruptive... mischievous.... and often stray off. When evening comes, the good sheppard would sometimes herd them all together, and guiding them through a narrow gate into an area where they would be protected, he would separate the goats from the sheep with a *rod* which would direct the sheep to a place on his right and the goats to a place on his left.

Some have called this teaching by Christ a parable, but it is not. This is a real event which will take place *after* Christ returns (Matthew 25:31a). In the previous description of the Battle of Armageddon, it might have been suggested that Christ will gather *all* unbelievers including those which have taken the *Mark of the Beast* to a battle outside of Jerusalem near the *Valley of Jehoshaphat* on the *Plains of Megiddo*, but this cannot be true when one examines Matthew 25: 31-46. It is clear that *after* the Battle of Armageddon Jesus Christ will judge the *nations of the world* with *all of His Holy angels* (Matthew 25: 31b-31a).

Nations are physical geographical regions and political boundaries, and that cannot be what is in view here. Christ will judge *people* which still remain alive in the nations of the world after Satan has been defeated at the Battle of Armageddon. The English word *nations* has been translated from the Greek word *ethnos*. Ethnos means *race, nations, people or heathens*. The word *ethnos* was commonly used by Jews to describe *Gentiles,* who they considered to be heathens. We can infer from the Jewish use of *ethnos* that there will be Gentiles from all over the world who will be assembled in Jerusalem before Jesus Christ. Some will have turned to Jesus and accepted Him as their Lord and Savior...and some have not. It is not clear if a Jewish remnant will also be called from the nations at this time. If so, then they who are Jews (Messianic Jews or pure Jews) will be judged as to how they treated the *ethnos*...Jews or Gentiles.

After the Battle of Armageddon, Christ will establish His throne in Jerusalem where He will hold both the *Bema Seat Judgment* and the *Sheep and Goat judgment*. The Bema Seat Judgment is only for *rewards of the saints* and not a judgment of condemnation (II Corinthians 5:10). It is to prepare and anoint the saints for service in the Millennial Kingdom (Revelation 2:26). It should be understood that the Bema Seat Judgment is for all true believers who have previously been raptured out (I Corinthians 15: 51-57) to escape the Wrath of God (Revelation 16:1) which will fall upon Satan and all unbelievers (Revelation 14: 9-10). Those being judged have already been transformed into spiritual bodies and they will live forever serving Jesus Christ. They have already received their incorruptible and eternal bodies and been given robes of white

(Revelation 3:5, Revelation 19:8). The sheep and Goats judgment is to decide who will enter the Millennial Kingdom as real persons (Matthew 25:34).

The Sheep and Goats will be composed of: (1) A Jewish remnant of believers (2) A Jewish remnant of non-believers and (3) Gentiles who are scattered all over the earth and have turned to Christ as their Savior and (4) Gentiles who are still alive but have not accepted Christ.

The Jewish Believing Remnant

Scripture reveals that *all of Israel* (will) *be saved* (Romans 11:26). *How can every Jew who remains alive on earth accept Jesus Christ as their Savior?* This is not what Paul meant when He wrote this prophecy. When Paul said that " all Israel will be saved" he did not mean that every individual Jew that ever lived and every resident of Israel would be saved. There will be a believing *remnant* of Jews that will be called *sheep*, and a non-believing remnant that have not accepted Christ called *goats* (Chapter 7). At that time *all* who have called upon the name of Jesus Christ will be saved.

> In every age there has always been a remnant of Jews (Hebrews 11) that were saved. There was a remnant in Elijah's day; there was a remnant in David's day; there was a remnant in Paul's day; there has been a remnant saved over the last 2000 years and there will be a remnant saved during the Great Tribulation Period.   J. Vernon Mc Gee

Regardless of Israel's current state of unbelief, a future remnant will in fact repent and fulfill their calling to gain salvation by faith and grace (Romans 10: 1–8; Romans 11:5). This conversion will coincide with the fulfillment of God's covenant with Abraham which promised that Israel would someday inherit the land.

[26] *And it shall come to pass, that in the place where it was said unto them, Ye are not my people; there shall they be called the children of the living God.*
[27] *Esaias (Elijah) also cried concerning Israel, Though the number of the children of Israel be as the sand of the sea, **a remnant shall be saved***   Romans 9: 27

The prophet Ezekiel prophesied of the eventual redemption of Israel in the Old Testament. He prophesied when Israel was in Babylonian captivity and he was concerned about the eventual fate of his people. Hearing the prayers of Ezekiel, the Lord spoke to Him about how He would one day gather His chosen people back into the land.

[27] *When I have brought them again from the people, and gathered them out of their enemies' lands, and am sanctified in them in the sight of many nations;*
[28] *Then shall they know that I am the LORD their God, which cause them to be led into*

captivity among the heathen: but I have gathered them unto their own land, and have left none of them anymore there   Ezekiel 39: 27-28

This prophecy by Ezekiel was partially fulfilled by those Jews who were restored to the land of Israel after the 70 year Babylonian exile, but will ultimately be fulfilled after the Jews have been restored to the land during the Millennial Kingdom. After the Babylonian exile only 2 1/2 tribes were brought back into the land. This prophecy of Ezekiel 39:28 clearly states that when He re-gathers His people that He will leave *none of them anywhere.*

The redeemer (Jesus Christ) will come to Zion (Earthly Mt. Zion) and judge those tribulation survivors who are scattered among all the nations. They will be judged for *how they treated the brethren* (Matthew 25:40, 45). *Who are His brethren?*

The English word brethren is translated from the Greek word *adelphon* which can mean: (Strong's Concordance)

- brothers by blood
- all men
- apostles
- Christians, as those who are exalted to the same heavenly place

Jesus was born a Jew from the tribe of Judah, and it is almost universally agreed that His *brethren* were Jews. The entire tribulation period is concerned with bringing Jews to the point where they will finally turn to Him and accept Him as their redeemer, Lord and Savior. The Jews will be continually persecuted and hated between the 1st and 2nd coming of Jesus Christ. However, the brethren of Jesus are much broader than just the Jews. In the New Testament the word "brethren" is used over 230 times. In the Authorized King James Version *adelphon* is translated as *brethren* 226 times and brother(s) 120 times. It is sometimes used to describe His brothers, sometimes His disciples and sometimes Christians in general. Hence, Jesus is using the term *brethren* as referring to *all* of those who have accepted Him as Lord and Savior and suffered through the tribulation period. Note that those called to the Judgment of the nations are all alive somewhere and did not accept Christ as their Lord and Savior until after the church was raptured out....Otherwise they would not be in the world. A legitimate question is: *Have all of these survivors turned to Jesus Christ between the rapture and the end of the church age?* The scriptures are silent on this issue, but it is suggested that all who will be called sheep may not have accepted Christ as their Lord and Savior. Christ will supernaturally...probably with His holy angels....gather every person from the *4 corners of the world*; the people will all be set before Him....and the judgment will begin.

And he shall set the sheep on his right hand, but the goats on the left   Matthew 25:33

Note that in Matthew 25: 31-46 there is absolutely no mention of faith or of eternal salvation. The criteria is unique and it astounded those who were being judged. They will be judged on how they treated the *brethren* of Christ (Matthew 25: 31-46). Matthew 25:33 clearly states that the purpose of this judgment is to determine who from *the nations* will enter into a *Kingdom*...that kingdom is the *Millennial Kingdom*. Note that all of the sheep and goats are people that have survived both the Wrath of Satan (7 trumpet judgments) and the Wrath of God (7 Bowl judgments). They are scattered among the nations all over the world and they are all *alive* and not dead. Those who did not help God's chosen people and give them shelter, clothes or food are called the *goats*. They will be cast into *everlasting punishment*, but those who have given *His brethren* protection, help and provided those things necessary to sustain life during the tribulation. The Judgment of the sheep and goats are unique to every other judgment. In considering the full council of scripture, it may not be as unusual as it appears. Paul wrote to the church at Corinth:

[**11**] When I was a child, I spoke as a child, I understood as a child, I thought as a child: but when I became a man, I put away childish things.
[**12**] *For now we see through a glass, darkly; but then face to face: now I know in part; but then shall I know even as also I am known.*
[**13**] *And now abides faith, hope, charity, these three; but the greatest of these is charity*
I Corinthians 13: 11-13

There are three characteristics of a mature, blood-bought Christian: Love, hope and charity. All things may fade away but these 3 will never end. *God is love.* He loved the world so much that He gave His only son for the sins of the world. Love is the cornerstone of the three: Faith and hope may perish but love is forever. The Love of Jesus Christ and the father is what sustains and comforts us. Our hope is that some day we will be present with the Lord forever...a hope that is rooted in faith. But charity is the result of love and hope. Charity is an individual choice...it is the manifestation of love... and more that almost anything else characterizes a true Christian. Therefore, it should be no real surprise that when Christ gathered to him all of those that had survived the Great Tribulation he chose those to enter into the Millennial Kingdom based upon how they had treated his beloved brethren.

The *Sheep* will be those who will physically enter into the Millennial Kingdom. *Where will they live?* It is conjectured that they will not *all* live in the land that was promised to the Children of Israel by God. Some may, but it is proposed that many will be returned to their own nation. In any case, Jesus Christ will rule and reign over the entire world from Jerusalem. These are real people (gentiles and Jews) who are very much alive and in their human bodies, just as those who were chosen and sealed from 12 tribes of Israel. During the *tribulation period* of the last

3.5 years, all who profess Christ will need specific protection and refuge from the Wrath of Satan. When Satan is defeated by Michael and his angels and cast down to earth, there will be a remnant of believers from Jerusalem who will be protected and nourished for 1260 days. After Satan is cast out of the heavenlies, he will gather his forces of evil and attack Jerusalem (the First Jerusalem Campaign). After that, 2/3 of all the Jews in Israel will be killed over the next 3.5 years (Zachariah 13: 8-9). They will have no food, no extra clothes and no money. Those *brethren* of Christ will need both divine protection and the necessities of life from the *sheep*. The brethren of Christ will be all over the world during the great Tribulation. It should be noted that a basic assumption is that the Wrath of Satan will precede the Wrath of God, and that the persecution of all those who *do not* follow Satan will not be a part of the Wrath of God. They will be raptured out before the Wrath of God is unleashed from heaven.

The 144,000

In Revelation 7: 1-8 a mysterious and interesting interlude is revealed concerning 144,000 Jews; 12,000 from each of 12 tribes of Israel.

[1] *And after these things I saw four angels standing on the four corners of the earth, holding the four winds of the earth, that the wind should not blow on the earth, nor on the sea, nor on any tree.*
[2] *And I saw another angel ascending from the east, having the **seal of the living God:** and he cried with a loud voice to the four angels, to whom it was given to hurt the earth and the sea,*
[3] *Saying, Hurt not the earth, neither the sea, nor the trees, till we have sealed the servants of our God in their foreheads.*
[4] *And I heard the number of them which were sealed: and there were sealed an hundred and forty and four thousand of all the tribes of the children of Israel.*
[5] *Of the tribe of Judah were sealed twelve thousand. Of the tribe of Reuben were sealed twelve thousand. Of the tribe of Gad were sealed twelve thousand.*
[6] *Of the tribe of Asher were sealed twelve thousand. Of the tribe of Naphtali were sealed twelve thousand. Of the tribe of Manassas were sealed twelve thousand.*
[7] *Of the tribe of Simeon were sealed twelve thousand. Of the tribe of Levi were sealed twelve thousand. Of the tribe of Issachar were sealed twelve thousand.*
[8] *Of the tribe of Zebulon were sealed twelve thousand. Of the tribe of Joseph were sealed twelve thousand. Of the tribe of Benjamin were sealed twelve thousand*   Revelation 7: 1-8

It is proposed that this a group of 144,000 Jews who will enter the Millennial Kingdom after the great tribulation period of 3.5 years has ended. In order to justify this conclusion we need to address several Biblical principles. The most important one is the Principle of the *Firstfruits Harvest* (Leviticus 23)

The Principle of Firstfruits

In Leviticus 23 we are told that there are four stages in the Harvest Cycle: (1) *The ground is prepared* and the *seed is planted*. Throughout the Old Testament there were Holy Prophets who spoke of a Messiah who would be sent from God to redeem all from sin who would believe: *For the wages of sin is death; but the gift of God is eternal life through Jesus Christ our Lord* (Romans 6:23). Before Jesus Christ came to the Jews to fulfill all Old Testament prophecies, it was announced by John the Baptist who came preaching repentance from sins to prepare the way. Jesus Christ spent His entire 3.5 year ministry witnessing that salvation had now come to those Jews who believed upon His power and authority as the Son of God. He *planted the seed* that would give eternal life to all who believed in faith that He was the prophesied Messiah. The title of "Christ" comes from the Greek word *Christos* which means *anointed*. It is translated from the Hebrew word "Mashiach", or "Messiah". Both Christ and Messiah mean *the anointed one of God*. (2) The grain crop seed planted in Israel contained both *wheat* and *barley*. The barley would mature first and then the precious wheat (3) As the grain began to ripen, there would be a portion of the grain that would mature first....*The Firstfruits*. The barley always matured first and then precious wheat. One of the 7 Feasts of Israel was the *Feast of Firstfruits*. In the spring (March/April) the High Priest would offer up a *sheaf of barley* to the Lord. Nothing else could be harvested until the Barley Firstfruits had been accepted by the Lord. The wheat would mature later, and the Main Harvest of Wheat would begin 50 days later and celebrated on the *Feast of Pentecost*. (4) The farmer could not reap the wheat until it had fully ripened. The wheat is then separated from the chaff and the precious wheat is taken to the barn. The barley remains in the field. The barley and some wheat around the edge of the field would be left for the poor and strangers. These are called the *gleanings*. The gleanings are none other than the Jews who will be a part of the *sheep*. The basic principle of the Firstfruits is a model for the harvest of both barley and wheat which will take place during the great tribulation.

The Sun Clothed Woman and The Man Child

In Revelation 12 we are told about a magnificent sun-clothed woman who is travailing in birth.

[1] *And there appeared a great wonder in heaven; a woman clothed with the sun, and the moon under her feet, and upon her head a crown of twelve stars:*
[2] *And she being with child cried, travailing in birth, and pained to be delivered.*
[3] *And there appeared another wonder in heaven; and behold a great red dragon, having seven heads and ten horns, and seven crowns upon his heads.*
[4] *And his tail drew the third part of the stars of heaven, and did cast them to the earth: and the dragon stood before the woman which was ready to be delivered, for to devour her child as*

soon as it was born.

[5] And she brought forth a man child, who was to rule all nations with a rod of iron: and her child was caught up unto God, and to his throne.

[6] And the woman fled into the wilderness, where she hath a place prepared of God, that they should feed her there a thousand two hundred and threescore days   Revelation 12: 1-6

This wondrous event is a watershed for understanding the last 3.5 years of the church age. The Greek word translated as *wonder* in Revelation 12:1 is *semeion* or a *sign*. Whenever God gives a sign it is best to pay attention to what will follow. A glorious woman is seen *clothed with the sun, and the moon under her feet, and upon her head a crown of twelve stars.* She is said to be travailing in birth to bring forth a Man-Child, and she does: *And she brought forth a man child, who was to rule all nations with a rod of iron: and her child was caught up unto God, and to his throne.* She is being pursued by a *great red dragon* who seeks to kill the Man-child as soon as he is born (Revelation 12: 3, 5). This great red dragon is Satan (Revelation 12:9). She does give birth and the Man-child is caught up to God and His throne (Revelation 12:5). *Who is this magnificent woman and who is this Man-child* ? There are many theologians who teach that this woman is the *Mother Mary* and the child is *Jesus*. However, this has to be incorrect for the following reasons.

(1) Mary was not the glorious woman depicted here in spite of her deification by the Roman Catholic Church. She is shown with the moon under her feet, which is a position of control and authority.

(2) If the sun-clothed woman is Mary, then the dragon would be King Herod. But the dragon is specifically identified as Satan in Revelation (Revelation 12:9).

(3) When Mary conceived Jesus, she was a virgin and childless...but Revelation 12:17 clearly states that this woman already has other offspring.

(4) When Mary birthed Jesus, Herod sought to kill Him. Being warned by the Magi, Mary, Joseph and Jesus fled to *Egypt*. In Revelation 12:14 it is written that this woman *fled into the wilderness*.

(5) At this time, there is a great war in the heavenlies between Satan and 1/3 of all the angels which follow him and Michael and his angelic forces (Revelation 12: 4,7). There was no such war in the heavenlies when Jesus was born.

(6) The woman hides herself in the wilderness for a *time, times and half a time* or 1260 days or 3.5 years (Revelation 12:14). Jesus carried out his ministry all over Israel for 3.5 years.

64

(7) King Herod was not even aware that Christ had been born until the wise men told him so. The dragon is waiting for the Man-child to be born.

(8) If the Man -child is Jesus Christ and the woman is Mary, the events in Revelation 12: 1-17 would have happened almost 2000 years ago. If this was true, Revelation 12 would be revealing things which preceded the entire Book of Revelation. This cannot be because John was previously instructed by Jesus Christ to: *Write the things which thou hast seen, and the things which are, and the things which shall be hereafter* (Revelation 1:19). John did not witness the birth or death of Christ. The typology is all wrong. We must look elsewhere to identify the woman and the Man-child.

When this glorious woman appears in Revelation 12 she is: *clothed with the sun, and the moon under her feet, and upon her head a crown of twelve stars*. This woman is *clothed with the sun*.

*But unto you that fear my name shall the **Sun** of righteousness arise with healing in his wings; and ye shall go forth, and grow up as calves of the stall*   Malachi 4:2

The *woman* is the corporate Nation of Israel. The *sun* is Jesus Christ shining upon the woman. Jesus said: *I am the **light** of the world* (John 8:12). The woman has the *moon under her feet*. The moon does not *produce* light, it only *reflects* light. The moon represents the law which was only a shadow or reflection of the real thing that would be manifest when Christ came. Everything made manifest under the law was a shadow and type of what was to come when Jesus Christ established the New Covenant. The rituals and furniture in the tabernacle and later in the temple...The 7 Feasts of Israel....all only reflected Jesus Christ. The moon under her feet symbolizes that the law belongs to her...she is the one that gave it life. Israel was the one that was corporately given the law. All of the precepts and commands of the law were birthed by Israel. When the New Covenant was established, It came by Christ who was birthed by God into the House of Israel: He was born and died a Jew. The moon under her feet is symbolic that the law belonged to Israel.

[**20**] *Therefore by the deeds of the law there shall no flesh be justified in his sight: for by the law is the knowledge of sin.*
[**21**] *But now the righteousness of God without the law is manifested, being witnessed by the law and the prophets;*
[**22**] *Even the righteousness of God which is by faith of Jesus Christ unto all and upon all them that believe: for there is no difference:*
[**23**] *For all have sinned, and come short of the glory of God;*
[**24**] *Being justified freely by his grace through the redemption that is in Christ Jesus:*
[**25**] *Whom God hath set forth to be a propitiation through faith in his blood, to declare his*

righteousness for the remission of sins that are past, through the forbearance of God;

[26] To declare, I say, at this time his righteousness: that he might be just, and the justifier of him which believeth in Jesus.

[27] Where is boasting then? It is excluded. By what law? of works? Nay: but by the law of faith.

[28] Therefore we conclude that a man is justified by faith without the deeds of the law
Romans 3: 20-28

This sun-clothed woman has the *sun over her head* and the *moon under her feet*. This shows the intimate relationship between the woman, the Law and the New Covenant. She lived under the law which brought sin and death: She will be redeemed by faith and grace under the New Covenant. She also has upon her head a *crown of 12 stars*. These shows that the woman is not only related to the dispensation of the law but to the dispensation of grace. When Abraham gave birth to the Nation of Israel, he established 12 tribes out of his loins. He had 11 sons of his own and granted a birthright to two sons of Joseph. These were the 12 tribes of Israel who were blessed and spawned through Abraham by his *seed*. Abraham was not only the father of the nation of Israel, but the one who's seed would produce Jesus Christ through the tribe of Judah.

*[16] Now to Abraham and his **seed** were the promises made. He saith not, And to **seed**s, as of many; but as of one, And to thy **seed**, which is Christ.*

*[19] Wherefore then serveth the law? It was added because of transgressions, till the **seed** should come to whom the promise was made; and it was ordained by angels in the hand of a mediator.*

*[29] And if ye be Christ's, then are ye Abraham's **seed**, and heirs according to the promise*
Galatians 3: 16, 19, 21)

So who is this woman? The evidence is strong and the typology correct....This woman represents *Israel*, not only the unbelieving Jews, but also those that believe in the faith of Abraham. Paul said that:

[6] Not as though the word of God hath taken none effect. For they are not all Israel, which are of Israel:

[7] Neither, because they are the seed of Abraham, are they all children: but, In Isaac shall thy seed be called.

[8] That is, They which are the children of the flesh, these are not the children of God: but the children of the promise are counted for the seed   Romans 9: 6-8

The sun clothed woman is Israel. *Who is the Man-child?* The woman s travailing in birth pains to deliver a child....not in the singular but in the plural. Satan is well aware that the child is being birthed in the earth and he is seeking to destroy that child before it can be birthed. He attempted to destroy Jerusalem many times but the place where God has designated to be His home will never be completely destroyed. The child is produced by the woman (Israel) but before Satan can destroy this Man-child it is caught up to God and His throne. Here we see once again that this Man-child cannot be Jesus Christ who was born of the virgin Mary. Jesus experienced a full childhood and later taught all over Israel for 3.5 years. This child is berthed and then *immediately* caught up. The Man-child is a newly formed Child and yet is a fully matured man....a Man-child. The Greek work translated as *caught up* is *harpazo*, which means to be *snatched away* (Strong's Dictionary Red Letter edition). It is the same Greek word used by Paul when he was transported into Paradise which is in the 3rd heaven (II Corinthians 12: 2-4). In I Thessalonians 4, Paul reveals the mystery of the rapture and in I Thessalonians 4:17 he uses the exact same phrase: *snatched away*: to reveal the removal of people from earth to heaven. The inescapable conclusion is that the Man-child is *raptured* away to God and to His throne. Why has this been so difficult to believe among modern theologians? Note that this Man-child is *not* all of Israel...it comes *out of Israel*. Christ told Thomas who was a Jew: *Jesus saith unto him, I am the way, the truth, and the life: no man cometh unto the Father, but by me.* The conclusion is that this Man child is a group of Believing Jews who have come to Christ by faith. They are to *Rule all nations with a Rod of Iron* (Revelation 12:5). This is a promise to the overcomers who are identified with the church of Thyatira.

[26] *And he that overcometh, and keepeth my works unto the end, to him will I give power over the nations:*
[27] *And he shall* **rule them with a rod of iron**   Revelation 2: 26-27

To him that overcometh will I grant to **sit with me in my throne,** *even as I also overcame, and am set down with my Father in his throne*   Revelation 3:21

This was promised to the overcomers in the Church at Laodicea, and it is exactly what is promised to the Man-child in Revelation 12:5. The conclusion is that this group of Jews out of Israel has believed upon Jesus Christ and accepted Him as their long-awaited Messiah. They are the *overcomers* identified in Revelation 2 and 3. *Can this be substantiated anywhere else in scripture?* Yes it can. In Revelation 14 a group of 144,000 believers is seen standing on Mount Zion with Jesus Christ. This clearly shows us that these 144,000 are standing on the *heavenly* Mount Zion before the throne of God.

[1] *And I looked, and, lo, a Lamb stood on the Mount Zion, and with him an hundred forty and four thousand, having his Father's name written in their foreheads.*   Revelation 14:1

The name of the Father is written on their foreheads. This is again a promise made to overcomers in the Church of Sardis (Revelation 3:12). Of course, the promises made to an overcomer in any one church applies to the overcomers in all churches :

He that hath an ear, let him hear what the Spirit saith unto the **churches**   Revelation2:29

So just as the earthly Zion is the place of the throne of Jesus Christ during the Millennial Kingdom, God's throne will be in heaven as His Son rules and reigns on earth. The earthly Mount Zion is a type of the heavenly Mount Zion. Who *are these that are seen before the throne of God who are snatched out of Satan's wrath?*   (Revelation 12:5)

These were redeemed from among men, being the **firstfruits** *unto God and to the Lamb.* Revelation 14:4

The Man-child is 144,000 Jews who are the first to come to Christ. They are the *firstfruits* of Israel, and the firstfruit offering is always made directly to God. They are the guarantee of those that will come afterward before the Great Tribulation is finished.

There are 144,000 in this group of firstfruits. The astute Christian and those who are reading and studying this book might cry; *But wait!*.... is this group of redeemed Jews not the same as those 144,000 that were seen in Revelation 7: 1-8 ? No they are not. The 144,000 seen in Revelation 14: 1-5 are **not** the same group seen in Revelation 7: 1-8.

      (1) The 144,000 seen by John in Revelation 7: 1-8 are Jews.....12,000 from each of the 12 tribes of Israel. The 144,000 seen in Revelation 14: 1-5 have been *purchased from among men* (Revelation 14:4)

      (2) The 144,000 Jews in Revelation 7: 1-8 are *sealed* with a seal from the living God. This is Jewish, Old Testament symbology. New testament believers are sealed with the Holy Spirit (Ephesians 1:13). The 144,000 of Revelation 14: 1-5 are sealed in both the name of the Father and of the lamb. This is New Covenant symbology. Those people in Revelation 12: 1-5 must be part of those saved in Christ.

      (3) The 144,000 in Revelation 7: 1-8 must be sealed for protection as they walk the earth during the Great Tribulation. Otherwise, why would they be sealed against things that are taking place on the earth if they are in heaven? (Revelation 7: 1-2). The 144,000 in Revelation 14: 1-5 are seen after the 3.5 years of tribulation and wrath are almost over (Revelation 14:7).

      (4) The group seen in Revelation 14: 1-5 are intimately associated with the lamb of God. Those in Revelation 7: 1-8 are not.

(5) The 144,000 *sealed* in Revelation 14: 1-5 *are singing a new* song in heaven before the throne of God. The group in Revelation 7: 1-8 have no song.

Note that Revelation 14: 2-3 reveals that John looked and saw Jesus Christ standing on Mount Zion (Revelation 14:1), and then he heard a voice *from heaven* (Revelation 14:2). It does not say that John was in heaven, but that he heard a voice and song *from* heaven. This is strange terminology if all of this is taking place in heaven. The entire setting of Revelation 14: 1-20 is prolyptic and provides a glimpse of what will be seen after the Church Age comes to a conclusion. The 144,000 in Revelation 14:1-5 are seen standing with the lamb (Jesus) on Mount Zion which is Jerusalem. Christ will rule and reign there for 1000 years. The 144,000 sealed Jews will serve Christ and follow Him where ever He goes (Revelation 14:5). We could provide other contrasts, but those just given should be sufficient to conclude that the group in Revelation 7: 1-8 are *not the same* as those in Revelation 14: 1-5.

The 144,000 seen in Revelation 14: 1-5 are identical to the Man-child in Revelation 12. The Man-child is composed of the group of *overcomers* who were typed by those found in each of the 7 churches in Asia that Paul established. These churches are all a type of Christian Churches found today throughout the world. They are the firstfruits of all Jews who will be saved before the Great Tribulation ends. They will join the rest of the Jewish and Gentile believers after the rapture. If this line of reasoning is correct...and evidence points to its correctness....then what is the purpose of the 144,000 Jews sealed in Revelation 14: 1-5 ? We will now show that this group of 144,000 Jews will enter the 1,000 year Millennial kingdom and inherit the land to fulfill God's promises to Abraham, Moses and King David.

The 144,000 Sealed Jews of Revelation 7

In Revelation 7: 1-8 the apostle John sees 4 angels who are *standing on the earth* to withhold the wind from blowing upon the earth. The wind will be prevented from blowing upon *the earth, nor on the sea, nor on any tree* (Revelation 7:1). *What does this mean?* The position of this event is of great importance. It is before any of the *7 trumpets* are blown that unleash the *Wrath of Satan* and also before the *7 bowls* are poured out which unleash the *Wrath of God*. This places the subsequent sealing of the 144,000 either just before or just after the great heavenly conflict in Revelation 12. The symbology of the four winds is rooted in many Old Testament passages which represent God's destructive action against something or someone upon the earth (Cf.. Jeremiah 49: 36-38, Daniel 7:2 and Hosea 13:15). Those 144,000 Jews that are sealed in Revelation 7:1 are exemption from wrath that will fall upon all *4 corners of the earth* (Revelation 7:1). The *4 winds* are symbolic of the agents of wrath and destruction. The realization of these *winds of wrath* seem to come with the blowing of trumpets 1-4 in Revelation 8.

The interlude sustained by the four angels which precede the Wrath of Satan (7 trumpets) is commanded by the action of a 5th angel.

[2] *And I saw another angel ascending from the east, having the seal of the living God: and he cried with a loud voice to the four angels, to whom it was given to hurt the earth and the sea,*
[3] *Saying, Hurt not the earth, neither the sea, nor the trees, till we have sealed the servants of our God in their foreheads*   Revelation 7: 2-3

This angel is carrying a seal from God which he (the angel) is about to place on the forehead of 144,000 Jews from 12 tribes of Israel.

And I heard the number of them which were sealed: and there were sealed an hundred and forty and four thousand of all the tribes of the children of Israel
Revelation 7:4 (Revelation 7: 5-8)

This type of seal of protection is not unique to these 144,000 Jews. In Ezekiel 9 the iniquity of Judah and the Jewish population of Israel were so great that God brought destruction upon the City of Jerusalem. However, there was a *remnant* who were *saved and spared* by God. He called a man *clothed in linen* (almost certainly an angel...maybe the same angel) to *place a seal of protection* on the forehead of a remnant of righteous men (Ezekiel 9: 1-11). It is interesting that after these 144,000 are sealed, the great heavenly conflict between good and evil will result in Satan being cast out of the heavenly realm down to earth. Satan will then launch an attack upon Jerusalem which will devastate the city and kill 1/2 of the inhabitants (The Jerusalem Campaign).

What is the purpose of this seal? The seal is placed upon the forehead of each man... not to exempt them from tribulation.... but to protect them from the Wrath of God (7 Bowls) and physical death. Those who are sealed are real people who will be on this earth during the last 3.5 years of the tribulation period. The other saints along with these 144,000 Jews must endure the Wrath of Satan and witness to those Jewish brethren who can still accept Christ as their Lord and Savior. The *Ecclesia* will all be spared from the Wrath of God by the rapture of all true believers living or dead, but These 144,000 sealed Jews must go through the Wrath of God and then enter into the Millennial Kingdom. They are kept alive for one prophetic reason: They will be the Jews from 12 tribes of Israel that will enter into the promised land and live there during the 1000 year Millennial Kingdom. *Where else would they come from in such guaranteed and balanced numbers?* These are also a part of the chosen people of God that will need protection and nourishment to survive. This must a large part of those that are protected by the *sheep* in the *Judgment of the Sheep and Goats.* These 144,000 are not the firstfruits of Jewish Israel to turn to Jesus Christ as their Redeemer and Savior. This group of Firstfruit Jews have already been shown to be those 144,000 in Revelation 14: 1-5 who are the Man-child of Revelation 12.

The seed (plural) of Abraham are destined for two distinct groups. One is like the stars in heaven; they have a *heavenly calling*: And one is like the sands of the sea; they have an *earthly calling*. The seed (singular) is Jesus Christ who is the promised Messiah for both groups.

[14] *And the LORD said unto Abram, after that Lot was separated from him, Lift up now thine eyes, and look from the place where thou art northward, and southward, and eastward, and westward:*
[15] *For all the land which thou see, to thee will I give it, and to thy seed for ever.*
[16] *And I will make thy seed as the dust of the earth: so that if a man can number the dust of the earth, then shall thy seed also be numbered.*   Genesis 13: 14-16

Those of Abraham's seed that have a heavenly calling are seen in Revelation 14: 1-5. This group started with the *little flock* of Luke 12:32. they are being formed today by many Jews worldwide called *Messianic Jews*.). Those that have an earthly calling are those in Revelation 14: 1-7 who will populate the Millennial Kingdom and will be completed after the *Judgment of the Sheep and Goats*. The church is not all spiritual Israel, but spiritual Israel...those seen in Revelation 14: 1-5 and those of Revelation 7: 1-8 who have or will come to Christ....... are a part of the body of Christ.

Summary

To summarize, scripture *clearly teaches* that eternal life can only be attained by *faith* in Jesus Christ and by grace ... not by works. One cannot be just "good" and work their way into heaven. This would violate too many New Testament scriptures. Those who are *sheep* in the Judgment of the Nations will have come to Christ as all of those before them....*by faith.* The sheep are not saved by their good works, but their good works are a consequence of having a servant's heart and how they treated the *brethren* of Christ during the Great Tribulation. These *good works* must have been done both before and during the tribulation period, but the *sheep* did not accept Christ as their savior *before* the rapture of the saints, but *after*..... otherwise they would have been taken up to Christ at the Rapture of the saints. Hence, *all* of these individuals (sheep and goats) missed the rapture, but *some* like the repentant thief who was crucified with Christ would have turned to Jesus Christ at the last minute and attained both the privilege of entering the Millennial Kingdom and eternal life. All over the world there will be both unbelievers and new believers who have survived both the Wrath of Satan and the Wrath of God but did not accept Christ until after the rapture. This Judgment of the Nations is a very difficult event to fully explain...it is a real *Mystery*. Those who *will not* accept Christ during the

Millennial Kingdom and those that *will* come to Christ will all be judged at the *Great White Throne Judgment*. All unbelievers...all whose names are not written in the Book of Life.... will be doomed to the Lake of Burning Fire (Revelation 20: 11-15).

The Man-child of Revelation 12: 5 is a Firstfruit harvest of Jewish believers. They will be "snatched up" to heaven and will later join those taken up to heaven in the rapture of all true believers. The firstfruits *always precede* the main harvest and are waved before God the Father as a guarantee of the main harvest to come. They will serve Jesus Christ throughout the 1000 year Millennial Kingdom.

The 144,000 Jews....12,000 from 12 tribes of Israel...are sealed by god to protect and preserve then through the Wrath of Satan and the Wrath of God. They will live in the land that was promised to the seed of Abraham through the line of King David.

144,000 Sealed Jews
Jewish Believing Remnant
Sheep from Judgment
Of the nations

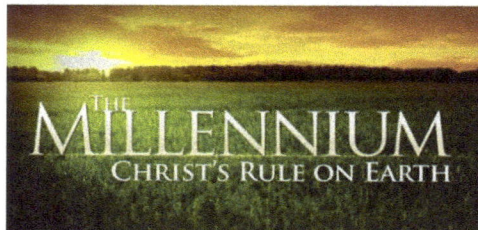

Chapter 5

The Land of Israel

The Millennial Kingdom will be a worldwide Kingdom which is ruled and reigned by Jesus Christ. Although people will live in different countries across the earth, the center of the world will be *Jerusalem*. The Nation of Israel will be restored to a place of prominence and inherit the land which was promised to them long ago. When *Abram* (Abraham) was called by God to birth the Nation of Israel, God made an *unconditional covenant* (Genesis 12-22) with Abraham which involved three promises: (1) Land (2) Seed and (3) Blessing. The nature, content and character of the Abrahamic Covenant will span time from when Israel was birthed as a new nation until the world as we know it will end after the 1000 year *Millennial Kingdom.*

Land (Genesis 13: 14-15)

[14] *And the LORD said unto Abram, after that Lot was separated from him, Lift up now thine eyes, and look from the place where thou art northward, and southward, and eastward, and westward:*
[15] *For all the land which thou see, to thee will I give it, and to thy seed for ever*
 Genesis 13: 14-15

In the same day the LORD made a covenant with Abram, saying, Unto thy seed have I given this land, from the river of Egypt unto the great river, the river Euphrates Genesis 15:18

Seed (Genesis 13:16, Genesis 17: 7-8, Genesis 22:18, Galatians 3:16)

And *the LORD appeared unto Abram, and said, Unto thy seed will I give this land*
Genesis 12:17a

And I will make thy seed as the dust of the earth: so that if a man can number the dust of the earth, then shall thy seed also be numbered Genesis 13:16

[7] *And I will establish my covenant between me and thee and thy seed after thee in their generations for an everlasting covenant, to be a God unto thee, and to thy seed after thee.*
[8] *And I will give unto thee, and to thy seed after thee, the land wherein thou art a stranger, all the land of Canaan, for an everlasting possession; and I will be their God* Genesis 17: 7-8

And in thy seed shall all the nations of the earth be blessed; because thou hast obeyed my voice Genesis 22:18

Now to Abraham and his seed were the promises made. He saith not, And to seeds, as of many; but as of one, And to thy seed, which is Christ Galatians 3:16

Blessing (Genesis 22: 17-18, Genesis 12: 2-3)

[**17**] *That in blessing I will bless thee, and in multiplying I will multiply thy seed as the stars of the heaven, and as the sand which is upon the sea shore; and thy seed shall possess the gate of his enemies;*
[**18**] *And in thy seed shall all the nations of the earth be blessed; because thou hast obeyed my voice* Genesis 22: 17-18

[**2**] *And I will make of thee a great nation, and I will bless thee, and make thy name great; and thou shalt be a blessing:*
[**3**] *And I will bless them that bless thee, and curse him that curse thee: and in thee shall all families of the earth be blessed* Genesis 12: 2-3

The Lord made a covenant with Abraham that he would have many sons and daughters. The Lord gave the land of Canaan as a blessing to Abraham and his seed. God promised Abraham that he would give the seed of Abraham *land*, where God would live with him and his offspring forever. His *seed* would be as many as the *stars in heaven*, and as the *sand on a sea shore* (Genesis 2:17). The *starry seed* is a great host of Jews that will accept Christ as their Messiah during the Church age and before the rapture of all believers, Jews and Gentiles. The *earthly seed* is the Jews who will fulfill the Abramic Covenant at the end of the tribulation period, inherit the land and populate the Millennial Kingdom. God has always wanted to live with man. When Adam and Eve were forced out of the Garden of Eden because they sinned, God made a plan to restore humanity in the land of promise through Abraham. God promised that He would give all the land of Canaan to Abraham and his descendants. He made a covenant with Abraham:

the LORD made a covenant with Abram, saying, Unto thy seed have I given this land, from the river of Egypt unto the great river, the river Euphrates Genesis 15:18

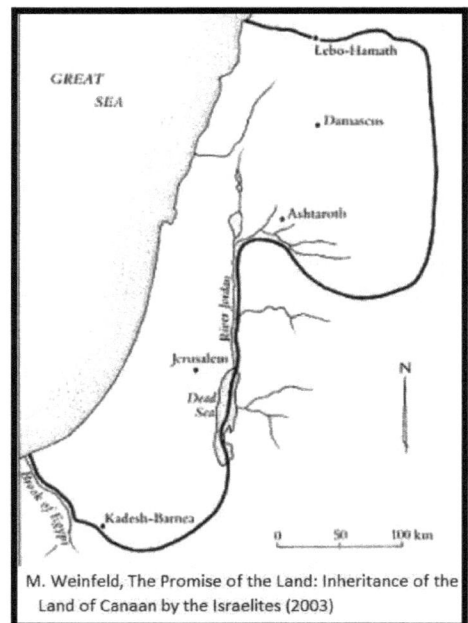

M. Weinfeld, The Promise of the Land: Inheritance of the Land of Canaan by the Israelites (2003)

According to Genesis 15:18 and Joshua 1:4, the land that God gave to Israel included everything from the *River of Egypt* in the south to the *River Euphrates* in the north; and everything from the Mediterranean Sea to a boundary defined from the *Gulf of Suez* north to t*he Sea of Galilee.* Then about 100 miles to the south and west of Capernaum and on north to part of Syria and Damascus. The River of Egypt is disputed among modern scholars. Some say that it is the Nile River, but most say that it is what is now called the *Wady el-'Arish* which runs east to west through the Sinai Peninsula. The present boundary between Egypt and Palestine is about midway between this Wady and Gaza. The land that God had promised to Abraham includes all of the land which constitutes modern Israel: all of the land of the Palestinians (the West Bank and Gaza); some of Egypt and Syria; all of Jordan; and some of Saudi Arabia and Iraq. Israel currently possesses only a fraction of the land God has promised. In any case, Israel has never had possession of all the land that was promised to the seed of Abraham. God made an unconditional covenant with Abram that He would one day recall the seed of Abraham from all over the world to inherit the land that He had promised.

[4] *Since thou wast precious in my sight, thou hast been honorable, and I have loved thee: therefore will I give men for thee, and people for thy life.*
[5] *Fear not: for I am with thee: I will bring thy seed from the east, and gather thee from the west;*
[6] *I will say to the north, Give up; and to the south, Keep not back: bring my sons from far, and my daughters from the ends of the earth*   Isaiah 43: 4-6

And I will set thy bounds from the Red sea even unto the sea of the Philistines, and from the desert unto the river   Exodus 23:31

This gathering will take place as the Millennial kingdom begins. Since Israel was reconstituted as a formal nation in 1948, there have been Jews from other countries who have returned to the land. However, this is only a partial fulfillment of prophecy. It is not exactly clear from Old Testament prophets when and where this will take place, but we now know that it will likely be after the Battle of Armageddon. If there is to be a regathering of the Jews to Israel, there most certainly would have been a dispersement. When Israel was ready to cross over the river Jordan after 40 years of wandering in the wilderness, Moses warned them what would happen if they did not obey the Lord and keep His commandments.

[27] *And the **LORD shall scatter you among the nations**, and ye shall be left few in number among the heathen, whither the LORD shall lead you.*
[28] *And there ye shall serve gods, the work of men's hands, wood and stone, which neither see, nor hear, nor eat, nor smell.*
[29] *But if from thence thou shalt seek the LORD thy God, thou shalt find him, if thou seek him with all thy heart and with all thy soul.*
[30] ***When thou art in tribulation**, and all these things are come upon thee, **even in the latter days**, if thou turn to the LORD thy God, and shalt be obedient unto his voice*

[31] *(For the LORD thy God is a merciful God;) he will not forsake thee, neither destroy thee, nor forget the covenant of thy fathers which he swore unto them*   Deuteronomy 4: 27-30

But every tribe of Israel did forsake the Lord: They went their own way and set up idols of silver and gold to worship. God was true to His word: The united kingdom of King David was split into two parts after the death of His son Solomon. The *Northern Kingdom* called *Israel* was conquered by the Assyrians and taken into captivity and most were never heard from again; These are the 10 lost tribes of Israel. Later, the *Southern Kingdom* of *Judah* was taken into captivity by the Babylonian Empire. After seventy years of captivity, God allowed the Southern Kingdom to return to Jerusalem. A remnant of the Jews returned to the land of Israel and the city was rebuilt. About 650 years later in 70 AD, Titus and his Roman soldiers attacked Jerusalem and Herod's Temple. The city and the Temple were both destroyed and all except the old and weak were again taken from the land. It was not until 1948 that the Nation of Israel was reconstituted when Israel declared its independence on May 14, 1948. Many Jews returned to their homeland, and this prompted many prophecy teachers to declare that the end was near. That was over 70 years ago and Christ has not returned yet.

A regathering of Israel *in the end times* will most certainly take place, and exactly how and when is known from prophecy. All Old Testament prophecies concerning the Jews being restored to their promised land will not happen until the end of the Tribulation period and not before. From Biblical Clues the following scenarios seem likely. Only those who are alive and remain after the tribulation will enter into the land.

      (1) 144,000 Jews....12,000 from each of 12 tribes of Israel.... are sealed in Revelation 7: 1-8 by 4 angels who are about to *hurt the earth* (Revelation 7: 1-2). This is assumed to be the four angels who will initiate the 1st four trumpet judgments which are a part of the *Wrath of Satan* (the 7 trumpet judgments are all initiated by God and His angels) upon all of the earth's inhabitants. By positioning and context, this protection will also allow these 144,000 Jews to survive the *Wrath of God* (the 7 Bowl judgments). The purpose of these Jews being sealed is not so that they can be exempt from tribulation and the Wrath of Satan, but that they would survive and enter alive into the promised land after the Church Age is over (Chapter 4).

      (2) When Jesus Judges all of the nations (Sheep and Goats Judgment) after the Battle of Armageddon, many Jews will be saved from eternal damnation by accepting Christ as their long awaited Messiah between the rapture and the Battle of Armageddon. Those who are classified as *sheep* will be able to enter into the Millennial Kingdom.

Christ will reign as a monarch over the entire earth, but King David will be resurrected and will exercise special kingship over Israel and the 12 tribes of Israel. Under this dual kingship, it is proposed that the *twelve apostles* will help King David rule and reign over the twelve tribes of Israel (Matthew 19:28). Isaiah tells us that there will be *judges* and *counselors* in Israel (Isaiah 1: 26-27). Zerubbabel, who returned from Babylonian exile to re-establish a Jewish remnant in Jerusalem, will also be placed in some unnamed position in Israel (Haggai 2:23). The Gentile nations and cities of the world will be ruled by Gentile kings.....probably the overcomers who were promised that they would rule and reign in some capacity (Revelation 5:10). The tribulation martyrs will also rule as well (Revelation 20: 4-6). How these different groups will be organized is unknown, but it is certain that they will all serve under the theocracy of Jesus Christ who will rule from His Millennial throne.

[1] *But in the last days it shall come to pass, that the mountain of the house of the LORD shall be established in the top of the mountains, and it shall be exalted above the hills; and people shall flow unto it.*
[2] *And many nations shall come, and say, Come, and let us go up to the mountain of the LORD, and to the house of the God of Jacob; and he will teach us of his ways, and we will walk in his paths: for the law shall go forth of Zion, and the word of the LORD from Jerusalem*
Micah 4: 1-2

Civil laws will be implemented in the Kingdom (Micah 4:1-2) and temple worship will be reinstated (Chapter 3). God has revealed how the land will be divided among the 12 tribes of Israel in the Millennial Kingdom.

The 1st Division of the Land

There are two places in the Holy Scriptures where division of the land is detailed. The 1st is when Joshua led Israel across the Jordan River 40 years after they left Egypt. We can prove that Joshua took 7 years to subdue the Gentiles which were living in the land (Joshua 9-12). However, It can be verified by reading the Biblical Records that there were potions of the promised land that were never occupied. In particular, the *Canaanites* were never fully conquered (Joshua 13: 1-7). Israel did not capture every Canaanite city or slay every Canaanite as God commanded. Another problem arose when Joshua first began to conquer the land. The tribes of Reuben and Dan, and half the tribe of Manasseh chose to stay east of the Jordan River while the other 9 1/2 tribes crossed the Jordan River. Seven years later Joshua divided the land (Joshua 13-19) west of the Jordan River to 9 1/2 tribes while the other 2 1/2 tribes stayed east of the Jordan River. Although Joshua found favor with the Lord and was blessed his entire life, the division of the land and was not as originally intended by God. The 2nd division of the land of Israel will take place before the Millennial Kingdom begins. It is described in Numbers 34 and Ezekiel 37.

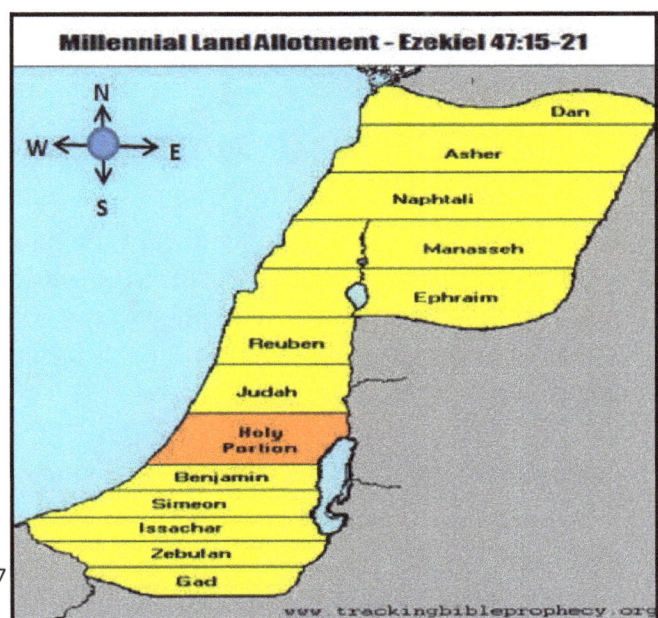

Millennial Land Allotment – Ezekiel 47:15-21

The 2nd Division of the Land

The 1st division of the land was determined by lot to all of the 9 1/2 tribes who were with Joshua (2 1/2 tribes remained east of the Jordan River). When Jesus Christ divides the Millennial Kingdom among 12 tribes, Jews will be supernaturally gathered from the four corners of the world (Leviticus 26: 40-45). The

77

land that God had promised to Abraham, Moses and King David will be divided into **13** different sections of land. A section of land will be given to each of 12 tribes of Israel. The 13th section of land will be called the *Holy Portion* (Ezekiel 45), and it will serve 4 purposes: (1) It will be where Jesus Christ will establish His throne and His palace from which He will rule and reign over the Nation of Israel and the whole world (2) It will be where the Levites will serve and live and (3) It will be where the City of Jerusalem will be rebuilt and (4) Sacrifices and three of the 7 Feasts of Israel will be celebrated in the temple complex . The exact dimensions of the Holy Portion are not revealed in scripture, but it is about 48 miles from the Dead Sea to the Mediterranean Sea. The Holy Portion is positioned between 7 tribes to the North (Dan, Asher, Naphtali, Manasseh, Ephraim, Reuben and Judah) and 5 tribes to the South (Benjamin, Simeon, Issachar, Zebulan and Gad). The 12 tribes of Israel are prominent in both the Old and New Testament scriptures. It is interesting to compare the 12 tribes of Israel that are mentioned at different times and in different dispensations in the Holy Bible. The original 12 tribes of Israel were all direct descendents of Abraham and were born from the direct descendents of *Jacob*, who was born of Isaac and Rebecca. Jacob had six sons by his wife Leah; two sons by Leah's servant Zilpah; two sons by his other wife Rachel and two sons by Rachel's servant Bilhah. Reuben was the oldest and Benjamin was the youngest.

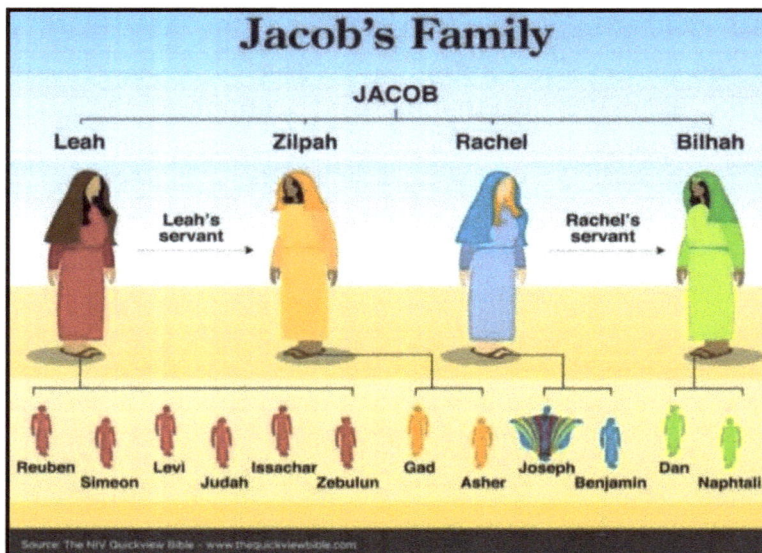

Birth Order	Name	Bible Reference
1	Reuben	Genesis 29:32
2	Simeon	Genesis 29:33
3	Levi	Genesis 29:34
4	Judah	Genesis 29:35
5	Dan	Genesis 30:5-6
6	Napthali	Genesis 30:7-8
7	Gad	Genesis 30:10-11
8	Asher	Genesis 30:12-13
9	Issachar	Genesis 30:17-18
10	Zebulun	Genesis 30:19-20
11	Joseph	Genesis 30:23-24
12	Benjamin	Genesis 35:16-18

Leah and Rachel were sisters and were the daughters of Laban (Genesis 29:16). These were the *original* 12 tribes of Israel. The next time we see the 12 tribes referenced as a group was after the exodus from Egypt. Moses spoke to the Lord on Mount Sinai, and the Lord commanded Moses to build a Tabernacle where He would come and be with the people, and talk with Moses outside of the camp.

And let them make me a sanctuary; that I may dwell among them   Exodus 25:8

The tabernacle stood for almost 650 years before it disappeared into history. Moses called the Levites to serve in the tabernacle and appointed Aaron as the High Priest. The High Priest had a breast plate which contained 12 precious gems...one for each of the original 12 tribes of Israel (Bible study.org).

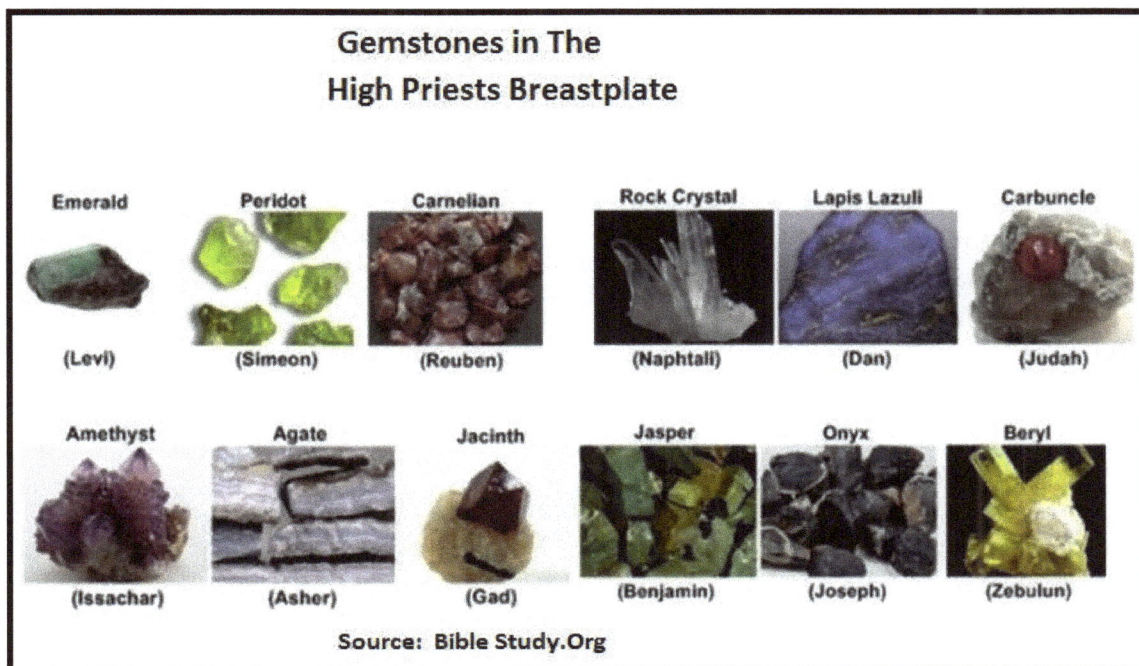

Gemstones in The High Priests Breastplate

Emerald	Peridot	Carnelian	Rock Crystal	Lapis Lazuli	Carbuncle
(Levi)	(Simeon)	(Reuben)	(Naphtali)	(Dan)	(Judah)

Amethyst	Agate	Jacinth	Jasper	Onyx	Beryl
(Issachar)	(Asher)	(Gad)	(Benjamin)	(Joseph)	(Zebulun)

Source: Bible Study.Org

When Moses established the Levites as a royal priesthood, he set them apart from the other tribes. At this point in time, the composition of the original 12 tribes changed . It was not arbitrary, but a result of a decision that Jacob had made over 200 years earlier. The story is long and complicated but it began when Jacob held Joseph to be his favorite child. This made the other brothers jealous, and so they told Jacob that Joseph had been killed by a wild animal. To conceal their plan they sold Joseph to a traveling caravan who later sold Joseph into Egyptian slavery. But the Lord protected Joseph, and after he interpreted a dream for the Pharaoh that no one else could interpret he rose to a place of prominence in Egypt and was placed in charge of all the grain. During this period of time, a great famine fell upon the Land of Canaan and Jacob decided to move his family to Egypt. When he got there, Joseph saved them all by divine appointment but Joseph and all of Israel were placed into slavery by the Pharaoh. After 215 years, the Lord heard their cry and called Moses to lead them out of Egypt. After the Lord through Moses brought 10 plagues against the Egyptians, the Pharaoh finally agreed to *let them go*. They fled Egypt, but in an act of rage the Pharaoh and his army pursued them to the Red Sea. The God of all creation saved them by allowing them to cross dry through the seabed: He then drowned all of the pursuing Egyptian army in the Sea. Moses and God's people continued on to Mount Sinai where they received the 10 commandments, built the Ark of the Covenant and the Tabernacle and then left for the promised land. Before leaving, Moses arranged all of the people into 12 tribes. This is when they were formed a second time. The 12 tribes that marched in the exodus were not the same as the original 12 tribes! This can be briefly explained as follows

Joseph was the favorite son of Jacob, and after he rose to prominence in Egypt he had two sons: *Manasseh* and *Ephraim*. When Jacob found that Joseph was not dead but alive, he blessed Joseph and declared that Manasseh and Ephraim would be *adopted* as *his own sons*. This would result in *14 tribes* after Manasseh and Ephraim were called his own sons. This was resolved as follows: The tribe of Levi was set apart which resulted in 13 possible tribes. Jacob had been one of the original 12, but he passed his position on to the two sons of Joseph.....Bingo!   When Moses left Mount Sinai he marched tribe-by-tribe through the wilderness in the following order.

The 12 tribes would surface three more times in the New Testament: (1) 12 tribes of Israel will be sealed by God for protection during the tribulation period of time ....Revelation 7: 1-8 (2) Before the Millennial Kingdom begins, Jesus Christ will call a remnant of Israel to Him which are alive and remain

The Order of March

and allocate a section 0f land to each tribe. (3) When the New Jerusalem descends to earth after the 1000 year Millennial Kingdom is over, it will have 12 gates of entry....named after the 12 tribes of Israel (Revelation 21: -12). We are not told the tribe of Israel which will be assigned each gate. The following table is a comparison of the 12 tribes listed in each case.....They are not identical!

Reuben, Simeon, Judah, Issachar, Zebulun, Benjamin, Dan, Naphtali, Gad, Asher	Joseph, Levi	The Original 12 Tribes of Israel
Reuben, Simeon, Judah, Issachar, Zebulun, Benjamin, Dan, Naphtali, Gad, Asher	Manassah, Ephraim	The Second 12 tribes of Israel (Exodus)
Reuben, Simeon, Judah, Issachar, Zebulun, Benjamin, Naphtali, Gad, Asher	Manassah, Levi, Joseph	144,000 in The Book of Revelation
Reuben, Simeon, Judah, Issachar, Zebulun, Benjamin, Dan, Naphtali, Gad, Asher	Joseph, Levy	12 Stones/Tribes in Breastplate
Reuben, Simeon, Judah, Issachar, Zebulun, Benjamin, Dan, Naphtali, Gad, Asher	Manasseh and Ephraim	The 12 Tribes in the Millennial Kingdom
Not Given>>>	>>>>>>>>>>>>>>>>>>>>>>>>>>>>>>>>>	The 12 Gates in t1e new Jerusalem

As this applies to the Millennial Kingdom, note that the 12,000 sealed from each of the 12 tribes of Israel (144,000) in the Book of Revelation (Revelation 7: 1-8) are different from everything else. The tribes of Dan and Ephraim were not sealed and they were replaced by the tribes of Levy and Joseph. This can be explained as follows. When the united kingdom of King David was ripped apart upon the death of King Solomon, both the tribe of Dan and the tribe of

Ephraim joined the northern kingdom of Israel. Dan was the tribe that was responsible for establishing Baal worship in Israel. Ephraim was so mired in sin that God spoke one of the most terrible judgments upon them that was recorded in the Old Testament.

Ephraim is joined to idols: let him alone   Hosea 4:17

The Millennial Kingdom: Israel Inherits The Land

When the Millennial Kingdom begins, Christ will divide the land that He promised to Abraham and his seed into 13 sections of land. The 13th section of land will be allocated to Jesus Christ and it is called the **Holy Portion**.

The *Holy Portion* is situated between 7 tribes of Israel to the North (Dan, Asher, Naphtali, Manasseh, Ephraim, Reuben and Judah) and 5 tribes of Israel to the South (Benjamin, Simeon, Issachar, Zebulon and Gad): Notice again that the tribe of Levi will have no portion of land given to them, and that a portion of land will not be allocated to Joseph. Recall that Jacob adopted the two sons of Joseph (Manasseh and Ephraim) as his own, and Joseph passed his legitimate birthright on to his two sons. Manasseh and Ephraim replaced Joseph and Levi. The *Holy Portion* will be bounded by the section of land

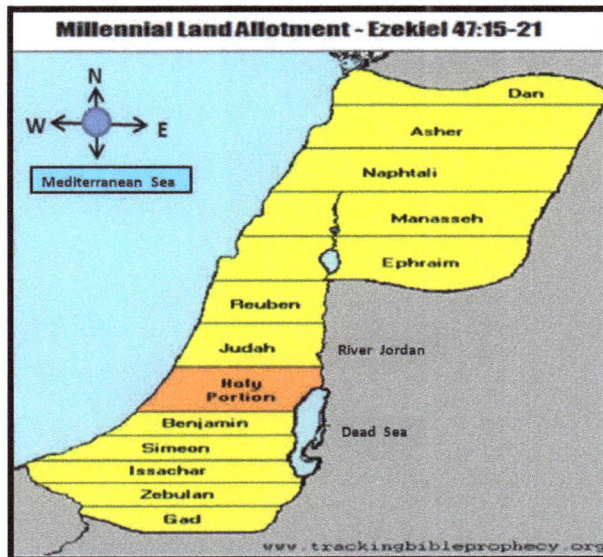

Millennial Land Allotment – Ezekiel 47:15-21

allocated to the Tribe of Dan on the north and the tribe of Benjamin to the south. In the middle of the Holy Portion is an area called the *Holy Oblation*.

The Holy Oblation

The *Holy Portion* all belongs to Jesus Christ. In the middle of the Holy Portion is a place called the *Holy Oblation*. The Holy Oblation is 25,000 reeds by 25,000 reeds or about 50 square miles. It is composed of three parts: (1) The *Holy District* or the *Levite's Portion*; which is 25,000 reeds by 10,000 reeds (about 20 square miles): (2) *The Lord's District* or the *Priests Portion* which is also 25,000 reeds by 10,000 reeds : and (3) The *City District* which is 25,000 reeds by 5,000 reeds (about 10 square miles) which is for the rebuilt City of Jerusalem. The *Lord's district* contains both the *sanctuary* and the *throne room* where Christ will rule and reign for 1000 years (Ezekiel 45: 1-6, 48:21)

Note: Ezekiel describes the Lord's District in great detail in Chapters 45-48. When he gives a measurement, the unit of measurement is usually not given. Ezekiel uses two units: a *reed* and a *cubit*. In carefully examining Chapters 45-48, it is believed that all basic measurements are in *cubits*. In the Original Greek text Ezekiel 45:1 uses cubits, but in the KJV Ezekiel 45:1 uses reeds.

The *cubit* was a unit of measurement which was used by the ancient Egyptians, Babylonians, and Jews. A cubit in this discussion will be assumed to be 18 inches in length, although it can vary from 18" to 37". All measurements will be in cubits unless reeds are specifically stated.

 [1] *Moreover, when ye shall divide by lot the land for inheritance, ye shall offer an oblation unto the LORD, an holy portion of the land: the length shall be the length of five and twenty thousand cubits, and the breadth shall be ten thousand. This shall be holy in all the borders thereof round about*
[2] *Of this there shall be for the sanctuary five hundred in length, with five hundred in breadth, square round about; and fifty cubits round about for the suburbs thereof*
Ezekiel 45: 1-2, 10

The 500 square enclosure is almost certainly in reeds; Ezekiel 42:16-20, KJV. The enclosure is surrounded by an open area which is 50 cubits wide.

And the five and twenty thousand of length, and the ten thousand of breadth, shall also **the Levites**, *the ministers of the house, have for themselves, for a possession for twenty chambers*
                    Ezekiel 45:5

And ye shall appoint the possession of **the city** *five thousand broad, and five and twenty thousand long, over against the oblation of the holy portion: it shall be for the whole house of Israel*   Ezekiel 45:6

And the five thousand, that are left in the breadth over against the five and twenty thousand, shall be a profane place for the city, for dwelling, and for suburbs: and the city shall be in the midst thereof   Ezekiel 48:15

[2] *And it shall come to pass in the last days, that the mountain of the LORD's house shall be established in the top of the mountains, and shall be exalted above the hills; and all nations shall flow unto it.*
[3] *And many people shall go and say, Come ye, and let us go up to the mountain of the LORD, to the house of the God of Jacob; and he will teach us of his ways, and we will walk in his paths: for out of Zion shall go forth the law, and the word of the LORD from Jerusalem.*
Isaiah 2: 2-3, (Micah 4: 1-2)

There are other Old Testament prophets who have also had a vision (s) of the temple complex, but Ezekiel provides more detail than all of the others put together.

> Joel 3: 15-21
> Isaiah 2: 2-3
> Isaiah 60: 13-14
> Haggai 2: 6-9

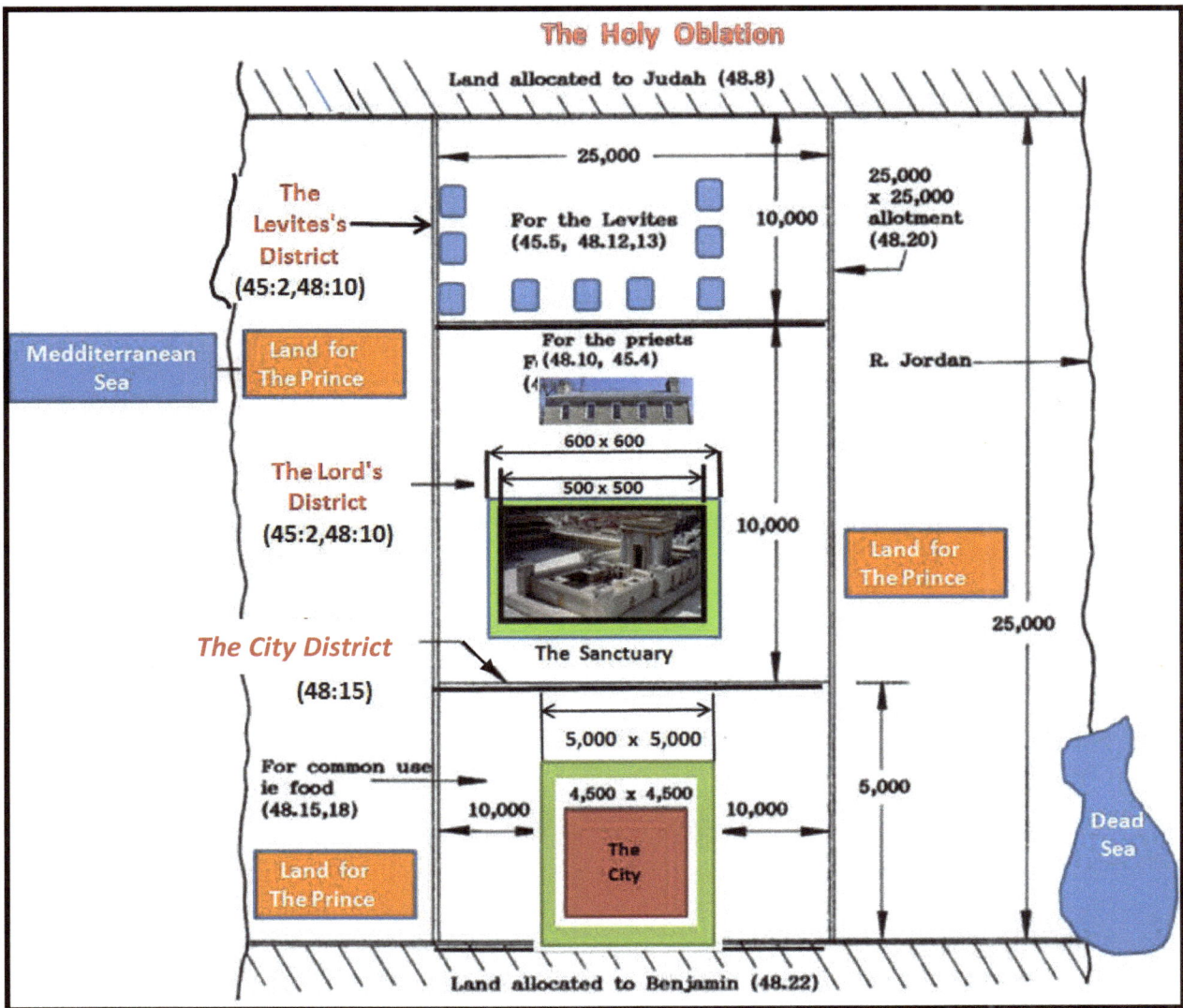

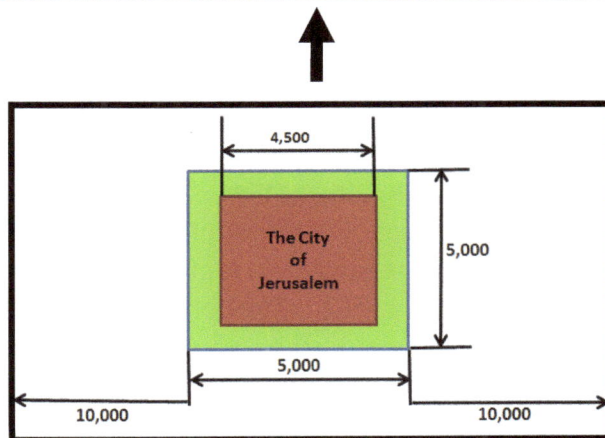

The Lord's District

In the middle of the Holy Oblation is *The Lords District*.
It is 25,000 cubits by 10,000 cubits (20.2 square miles).
The *Lord's Sanctuary* will be built exactly in the center of
the Lord's District. The sanctuary is a vast complex
which will be 500 x 500 *reeds* square (1 mile square). A
Biblical *Reed* is 10.5 feet. The Temple and Throne of
Jesus Christ will be in the Lords Sanctuary. The *Lord's
Throne Room* will be built on one end of the Sanctuary.

There are no dimensions given for the throne of Jesus, however we can be sure it will be a
glorious Temple which will surpass the beauty and majesty of Herod's Temple which was

destroyed in 70 AD. The Temple complex is surrounded by an open
area which is 50 cubits by 50 cubits. This is a Holy Area to separate
the Temple from the land. That area is surrounded by a *Common
Area* which is 10,000 cubits by 5,000 cubits. This is for farming and
raising sheep or cows.

The Temple and the Throne of Jesus Christ will be elevated above
the surrounding land (Zachariah 14:10) , and it will be built on the site where the ancient City of
Shiloh once stood (C. Larkin). It was in Shiloh that Joshua gathered the people to him to
distribute the land of promise, and it was here that the Tabernacle of Moses rested after the
death of Eli.

Our Lord Jesus Christ will be served and attended to by the *Sons of Zadok* (Ezekiel 48:11). *Who
are these sons*? Zadok was a Levite priest in the days of King David. *Absalom*, who was a son of
King David. conspired against David and usurped the throne. David was forced to flee into
hiding. While in hiding, Zadok overheard a plan to kill King David and sent word to him. Shortly
thereafter, a man called Joab killed Absalom. When David heard that his son was dead he went
back to Jerusalem and returned to his throne. When David was much older, he chose Solomon
to replace him over another son called Adonijah. Another plot was hatched by David's son
Adonijah to kill Solomon before He could take the throne. Nathan, who was a prophet, along
with Zadok and Bathsheba all convinced David to have Solomon taken to the *City of Gihon*,
where he would be officially announced and chosen as the next King of Israel. David agreed,
and directed Zadok take Solomon to the City of Gihon. Solomon was anointed and was divinely
accepted as the next king by the people. For his faithful and devoted service to King David,
Zadok was chosen as the 1st High Priest to serve under King Solomon and his sons were chosen

to serve in the Holy Temple (Ezekiel 44: 9-16). The Sons of Zadok
will live in a Holy Portion of land adjacent to the temple. This
holy portion of the land shall be for the Sons of Zadok who
administer to Jesus Christ in the sanctuary They will live in houses
overlooking the Sanctuary.

The City District

Just south of the Lord's District is the third section of the Holy Oblation: *The City District*. The City District is 25,000 cubits long and 10,000 cubits wide. It is divided into two separate parts: (1) The City of Jerusalem and (2) The surrounding land. The *City of Jerusalem* will be located in the exact center of the *City District*. It will be 4500 cubits by 4500 cubits. The City of Jerusalem will be rebuilt and beautified. The City area is surrounded by a "green belt" which is 50 cubits wide (75 feet). This land will be used for farmland (Ezekiel 48:18b). People from all of the 12 tribes of Israel will live in Jerusalem and they will cultivate the land (Ezekiel 48:19). It is often overlooked, but there will be land which is 5,000 cubits wide and 10,000 cubits long that will surround the city and its green belt. This land will belong to the whole house of Israel (Ezekiel 45:6) and will be used for houses and common usage. This will make the entire complex 25,000 cubits by 5,000 cubits or about 11 square miles.

The Holy District

The *Holy District* is just north of the Lord's District. It will house the tribe of Levy. The Holy District will be 25,000 cubits long and 10,000 cubits wide. Recall that the Tribe of Levy was not given a portion of land with the other 12 tribes either by Moses or by Christ in the Millennial Kingdom. The Levites will be banned from priestly duties in the Sanctuary and will be replaced by the Sons of Zadok. The Sons of Zadok were chosen to serve our Lord in the Sanctuary and offer sacrifices. The Levites are to perform other duties in the Holy Oblation and to serve the people (Ezekiel 44: 10-15), but they are not to touch or come near Holy things in the temple (Ezekiel 44:14). They will live in 20 large housing units 3 stories high. The entire sanctuary will be surrounded by a great will 50 cubits wide. The enclosed complex will have an outer court and an inner court. The outer court will be accessed by 4 gates on the north, south, east and west. Our Lord Jesus Christ will rule and reign in glory never previously seen upon the planet earth.

The River of Life

Perhaps the most interesting topological feature is that there will be a River which will flow from beneath the Temple (Sanctuary) south through the City District. Upon leaving the Holy Oblation, it will split into two pieces: One east and one west. The east branch will flow into the Dead Sea and the west branch will flow into the Mediterrannean Sea. The two branches of the river will be aquatic *living water* which will turn the Dead Sea into a body of water teeming with all manners of fish and aquatic creatures. The west branch will cause the Mediterrannean Sea to increase the fish and creatures which live there also. Peter is going to be overjoyed! No more will he fish all night without catching anything in his nets.

And it shall come to pass, that everything that lives, which moves, whithersoever the rivers shall

come, shall live: and there shall be a very great multitude of fish, because these waters all come thither: for they shall be healed; and everything shall live whither the river cometh
Ezekiel 47:9

Along the banks of this river will grow trees laden with fruit (Zachariah 14:8) which will nourish all who eat there (Zachariah 14:8).

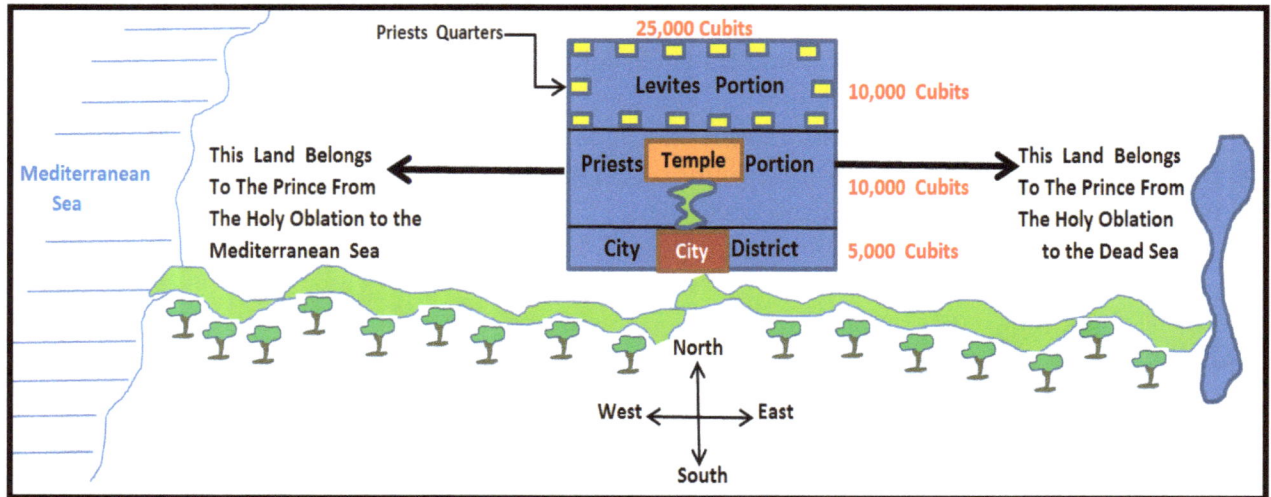

Sacrifices in the Millennial Kingdom

The Lord's District will contain the *Sanctuary of the Temple*. It is in the outer court of this sanctuary that temple that sacrifices will be made to the Lord during the year by the people on every weekly Sabbath day (Ezekiel 45:17), and on solemn or appointed times (Ezekiel 46: 9-11). These will include the Feast of Passover, the Feast of Unleavened Bread (Ezekiel 45:21, and the Feast of Tabernacles (Ezekiel 45:25, Zachariah 14: 16-19).

The word *Oblation* refers to not only a holy section of land but a holy offering to our Lord Jesus Christ (Numbers 18:9, Ezekiel 20:40). In Ezekiel 44:30 offerings are described which will be made to King Jesus during the Millennial Kingdom. Ezekiel 45: 13-17 gives details of annual sacrifices that will be offered by the people of the land to honor Jesus Christ, who will in turn offer Holy Oblations to His Father on behalf of the house of Israel when the yearly Feasts are observed. Christ is now our eternal High Priest. Ezekiel 45 identifies the festivals and special days that will be observed in the Millennium. The set days are: (1) The first day of the first month ....Ezekiel 45: 18,19 (2) The seventh day of the first month ...Ezekiel 45:20 (3) The fourteenth day of the first month Ezekiel 45: 21-24) and (4) The fifteenth day of the seventh month.... Ezekiel 45:25). Sacrifices will be made by the *prince* on each of these occasions for the house of Israel (Ezekiel 45:17). Sin offerings, meat offerings and burnt offerings will all be re-initiated.

[1] *Moreover, when ye shall divide by lot the land for inheritance, ye shall offer an oblation unto the LORD, a holy portion of the land*

 [2] *Of this there shall be for the sanctuary five hundred in length, with five hundred in breadth, square round about; and fifty cubits round about for the suburbs thereof.*

[3] *And of this measure shalt thou measure the length of five and twenty thousand, and the breadth of ten thousand: and in it shall be the sanctuary and the most holy place* Ezekiel 45: 1-3

Rituals and Offerings in The Temple

It may come as a surprise to many students of prophecy, but the sacrificial system under the Old Covenant will be partially reinstated in the Millennial Kingdom. There is no question about this fact if a real, physical Millennial Kingdom of 1000 years is to take place as described in the Book of Revelation. There are multiple Old Testament prophets who spoke of this happening.

> Isaiah 56: 6-7
> Isaiah 60: 7
> Jeremiah 33:18
> Zachariah 14: 16-21
> Ezekiel 45: 21-24

There are significant differences between the offerings that were conducted under the Law, as the following table indicates for the *Feast of Unleavened Bread*. These differences emphasize that the original Mosaic Law has been superseded by a "better covenant".

Offerings during the feast of unleavened bread		
	Numbers 28:18-25	**Ezekiel 45:21-24**
Burnt offering	2 bulls 1 ram 7 lambs	7 bullocks 7 rams
Meat offering	3 tenth deals per bullock 2 tenth deals per ram 1 tenth deal per lamb	1 ephah per bullock 1 ephah per ram 1 hin of oil for each ephah
Sin offering	1 kid of the goats	1 kid of the goats

During the millennial reign of Jesus Christ, the animal sacrifices will be to look *BACK* in remembrance of what Jesus has done for us, similar to the way that the Old Testament sacrifices looked *FORWARD* to what He would do. These sacrifices in no way take away our sins. Only faith in the finished work of the shed blood of Jesus can take away sin. Everything done in this temple points us to Jesus, because all things can be summed up in Jesus *"in whom dwells all the fullness of the Godhead bodily."* (Colossians 2:9)

[13] *This is the oblation that ye shall offer; the sixth part of an ephah of an homer of wheat, and ye shall give the sixth part of an ephah of an homer of barley:*
[14] *Concerning the ordinance of oil, the bath of oil, ye shall offer the tenth part of a bath out of the cor, which is an homer of ten baths; for ten baths are an homer:*
[15] *And one lamb out of the flock, out of two hundred, out of the fat pastures of Israel; for a meat offering, and for a burnt offering, and for peace offerings, to make reconciliation for them, saith the Lord GOD.*
[16] ***All the people of the land*** *shall give this oblation for the prince in Israel.*
[17] ***And it shall be the prince's part*** *to give burnt offerings, and meat offerings, and drink offerings, in the feasts, and in the new moons, and in the Sabbaths, in all solemnities of the house of Israel: he shall prepare the sin offering, and the meat offering, and the burnt offering, and the peace offerings, to make reconciliation for the house of Israel*   Ezekiel 45: 13-17

Jesus Christ is now our eternal High Priest, and He will act as such when these oblations are offered (Ezekiel 45:17). Some who do not believe that the Holy Scriptures are the inspired word of God have objected and even rejected the thought of a renewed sacrificial system, claiming (correctly) that the sacrifice on Calvary was sufficient for all eternity. In this they are correct, but these Holy Oblations are not for the atonement of sins as they were in the Old Testament economy. These new sacrifices are to honor Jesus Christ (Ezekiel 45:16) who permanently forgave sins on the Cross of Calvary and by Jesus Christ to honor His Father.

The Feasts of Israel During the Millennial Kingdom

The Seven Feasts of Israel were ordained by God at the Exodus from Egypt. A careful study of these Jewish Feasts will reveal that they are for *remembrance* of how Israel was liberated from Egyptian slavery and also as *Moeds* or *rehearsals* for what Jesus Christ would accomplish in both His 1st and 2nd comings (See Phillips; The Book of Revelation: *Mysteries Revealed*). During the Millennial Kingdom, there will still be three of these feasts which will be celebrated in Jerusalem: The Feasts of *Pentecost*, *Unleavened Bread* and *Tabernacles*. The purpose of these 3 feasts will be to conduct sacrifices of remembrance and praise. The Feast of Tabernacles appears to be more important than any other Feast during the Millennial Kingdom. Failure to attend this Feast will bring dire consequences.

[16] *And it shall come to pass, that every one that is left of all the nations which came against Jerusalem shall even go up from year to year to worship the King, the LORD of hosts, and to keep the feast of tabernacles.*
[17] *And it shall be, that whoso will not come up of all the families of the earth unto Jerusalem to worship the King, the LORD of hosts, even upon them shall be no rain.*
[18] *And if the family of Egypt go not up, and come not, that have no rain; there shall be the plague, wherewith the LORD will smite the heathen that come not up to keep the feast of tabernacles.*
[19] *This* shall be the punishment of Egypt, and the punishment of all nations that come not up to keep the feast of tabernacles*   Zachariah 14: 16-19

[1] *Moreover, when ye shall divide by lot the land for inheritance, ye shall offer an* **oblation** *unto the LORD,* **an holy portion** *of the land: the length shall be the length of five and twenty thousand reeds, and the breadth shall be ten thousand. This shall be holy in all the borders thereof round about*

[7] *And a portion shall be for the prince*

[8] **and the rest of the land shall they give to the house of Israel according to their tribes.**
Ezekiel 45:1,7, 8b

[20] *All the oblation shall be five and twenty thousand by five and twenty thousand: ye shall offer the holy oblation foursquare, with the possession of the city.*

[21] *And the residue shall be for the prince, on the one side and on the other of the holy oblation, and of the possession of the city, over against the five and twenty thousand of the oblation toward the east border, and westward over against the five and twenty thousand toward the west border, over against the portions for the prince: and it shall be the holy oblation; and the sanctuary of the house shall be in the midst thereof.*

[22] *Moreover from the possession of the Levites, and from the possession of the city, being in the midst of that which is the prince's, between the border of Judah and the border of Benjamin, shall be for the prince* Ezekiel 48: 20-22

[9] *The oblation that ye shall offer unto the LORD shall be of five and twenty thousand in length, and of ten thousand in breadth.*

[10] And *for them, even for the priests, shall be this holy oblation; toward the north five and twenty thousand in length, and toward the west ten thousand in breadth, and toward the east ten thousand in breadth, and toward the south five and twenty thousand in length: and the sanctuary of the LORD shall be in the midst thereof* Ezekiel 48: 9-10

[1] *But in the last days it shall come to pass, that the mountain of the house of the LORD shall be established in the top of the mountains, and it shall be exalted above the hills; and people shall flow unto it.*

[2] *And many nations shall come, and say, Come, and let us go up to the mountain of the LORD, and to the house of the God of Jacob; and he will teach us of his ways, and we will walk in his paths: for the law shall go forth of Zion, and the word of the LORD from Jerusalem.*
   Micah 4: 1-2 (Isaiah 2: 2-3)

Summary and Conclusions

The Millennial Kingdom will not be a *new heaven and a new earth*. It will be the same heavens and the same earth, but there will be marvelous and unprecedented things which will take place. The *seed of Abraham* (12 tribes of Israel) will be regathered by God from the *4 corners of the earth* to which they have been scattered. They will live in peace and prosperity upon the land which has been given to each tribe. Jesus Christ will finally establish *His Kingdom* which will last for 1000 years. His Kingdom will be here upon this earth, and He will rule and reign from a section of land called the *Holy Oblation* just North of where the City of Jerusalem now exists. The Millennial Kingdom will be a *theocracy* ruled by Christ with a *rod of iron* (Revelation 2:27). He will rule over the entire world (many nations) with King David at His side, who will reign once again over the 12 tribes of Israel. Both Jesus Christ and King David will be assisted by (1) The saints *...Ecclesia* (2) *Martyrs* from the tribulation and probably from all ages past and (3) The *12 disciples*. People from all over the world will worship Jesus on the Feasts of Passover, Unleavened Bread and Tabernacles each year. It will be a wonderful time which has been unprecedented since Adam and Eve were removed from the Garden of Eden.

A depiction of the Millennium by an unknown artist. Jerusalem is shown in the background, lifted up as the highest place on planet earth (Isaiah 2:2 and Zechariah 14:10). The glory of the Lord beams forth from Jerusalem (Isaiah 24:23), and people come from all over the world to worship the King of kings (Zechariah 14:16-18). Swords are hammered into plowshares (Isaiah 2:4), the wolf dwells peaceably with the lamb (Isaiah 11:6), and children play with cobras (Isaiah 11:8).

Chapter 6

The Three Invasions of Jerusalem

The center of God's universe has always been the holy city of Jerusalem. It was at this place that God told King David to build a temple where the people could come to worship Him. Jerusalem was the city where every male Jew was commanded to appear on the Feast of Passover, The Feast of Pentecost (Shavuot), the Feast of Unleavened Bread and the Feast of Tabernacles. Jesus Christ will rule and reign here on earth just north of Jerusalem during the Millennial Kingdom. The history of the Jews is intermingled with the history of Jerusalem. The first mention of Jerusalem was shortly after Abraham was called by God to begin the Nation of Israel. When Abraham rescued his brother Lot from being taken captive by a group of pagan kings (Genesis 14: 1-12), he returned with the spoils of war and was met by Melchisedec, who was the King of Salem (Genesis 14:18). Melchisedec was a type of Jesus Christ and it is believed that Salem was the same as Jerusalem. This seems to be verified by Psalms 76:2. About 3,000 years ago, King David conquered Jerusalem in a war against the Jebusites and established the capital of his kingdom on this site. The city continued as the capital of Israel for about another 400 years until its 1st destruction at the hands of the Babylonians in 586 BC. After the Babylonian captivity of 70 years, Zerubbabel (539 BC), Ezra (458 BC) and Nehemiah (444 BC) rebuilt the city, the city walls and restored parts of the temple. The City of Jerusalem and Herod's Temple would be the focus of Jewish worship until 70 BC when Titus and his Roman army attacked and completely destroyed Herod's Temple and most of Jerusalem. The City of Jerusalem was eventually resettled and rebuilt, and it is a the capital of Jerusalem today. The Jews never regained control of the Temple Mount, and today it is the site of Muslim worship. There will be three major invasions of Jerusalem in the end times.

- ➢ The **first** will immediately *follow* the *beginning* of the last 3.5 years of tribulation: It will be called *The Jerusalem Campaign*
- ➢ The **second** will immediately *precede* the *end* of the last 3.5 years of tribulation: It will be called the *Armageddon Assault*
- ➢ The **third** will be the *last battle* in the 1000 year millennial kingdom: It will be called *Satan's Last Stand*

These three battles at Jerusalem are described by Ezekiel, Jeremiah and Zachariah in the Old Testament but they are fragmented and are often included in other prophecies. Ezekiel 36-39 contains the most complete description of these 3 battles, along with Zachariah 12-14. These Chapters are obscure and difficult to understand, as is evident from the diverse explanations of these prophecies among commentators. These last 3 invasions of Jerusalem frame both the last 3.5 years of Tribulation and the Millennial Kingdom.

Rightly Dividing the Word

Scriptural references to these three end-time invasions of Israel are scattered throughout the Old Testament prophets, but two stand out: The Book of Ezekiel and the Book of Daniel. Daniel and Ezekiel are both shown many visions of what will happen in the end-times. Ezekiel writes with great detail about the Millennial Kingdom and the temple where Jesus Christ will rule and reign in Chapters 40-48. The following sequence of events bracket when and how these three end time invasions of Jerusalem will take place.

- A great world leader will emerge out of the old Roman Empire who will by divine appointment be a charismatic and influential individual. He will also be a great military leader and strategist. He will arise out of an European 10 nation confederacy, and by cunning and deception manage to consolidate great military power under his leadership. He will attack and conquer 3 of the 10 world leaders. The other 7 nations will appoint him as their sovereign military leader and form a unified European army (Denial 7 : 1-28).

- By supernatural power, he will then do something which will shock the world. He will initiate a pact with Israel and place them in a position of peace and security. The wars which are now raging between Muslims, Palestine and other nations will cease. Peace will reign over Israel and many Jews will return to their homeland. However, this covenant of peace will be in reality a *Covenant with Death* (Isaiah 28 15-18). This is a covenant made with Satan and not with God.

  After many days thou shalt be visited: in the latter years thou shalt come into the land that is brought back from the sword, and is gathered out of many people, against the mountains of Israel, which have been always waste: but it is brought forth out of the nations, and they shall dwell safely all of them   Isaiah 28:8

  [**14**] *Wherefore hear the word of the LORD, ye scornful men, that rule this people which is in Jerusalem.*
  [**15**] *Because ye have said, We have made a **covenant with death**, and with hell are we at agreement; when the overflowing scourge shall pass through, it shall not come unto us: for we have made lies our refuge, and under falsehood have we hid ourselves*
  Isaiah 28: 14-15

  This great world leader, diplomat and military general will then do an astounding thing: He will manage to rebuild Herod's Temple and restore the Old Testament rituals to the Jewish people. This is made certain by II Corinthians 2:4 and Revelation 11:1.

92

[3] Let no man deceive you by any means: for that day shall not come, except there come a falling away first, and that man of sin be revealed, the son of perdition;
*[4] Who opposes and exalts himself above all that is called God, or that is worshipped; so that **he as God sits in the temple of God**, showing himself that he is God*
II Corinthians 2: 3-4

*[1] And there was given me a reed like unto a rod: and the angel stood, saying, Rise, and **measure the temple of God**, and the altar, and them that worship therein.*
*[2] But the court which is without the temple leave out, and measure it not; for it is given unto the Gentiles: and the holy city shall they tread under foot **forty and two months***
Revelation 11: 1-2

- The New Temple will be built either at the site of the current Dome of the Rock or in close proximity to the Dome of the Rock on the old temple mount. This will result in Israel exalting this world leader to the position of their long awaited deliverer. They will be deluded into thinking that this is their prophesied Messiah. The Nation of Israel will suffer a *strong delusion* until they see the truth.

[9] Even him, whose coming is after the working of Satan with all power and signs and lying wonders,
[10] And with all deceivableness of unrighteousness in them that perish; because they received not the love of the truth, that they might be saved.
*[11] And for this cause God shall send them **strong delusion**, that they should believe a lie:*   *II Thessalonians 2: 9-11*

- After the *Covenant of Death* is signed with the European coalition leader, and the Jewish temple is rebuilt, the Jews will re-institute temple worship and sacrifices. Jewish belief is that if someone would arise who could rebuild the temple must be their long awaited Messiah. The Jews will live in peace and will be protected during this time. It is likely that all of this will take place several years before an incredible event takes place. As the Jews live in peace there will be a great Heavenly war between Satan and his fallen angels, and the Archangel Michael and his Holy angels (Revelation 12). This will initiate the last half of Daniel's 70th week and will start the last 3.5 year tribulation period described in the Book of Revelation (Revelation 12: 14). Satan will be defeated and cast down to earth with 1/3 of all the created angels. Satan will be furious, and the first thing that he will do is to attack Jerusalem. His first satanic act will be to invade the Holy City of Jerusalem. This will be the *Jerusalem Campaign.* 1/2 of all the people will be killed or captured. As the other 1/2 of the people flee from the city, Satan will be in pursuit. In an act of mercy and grace God will save them by causing a great chasm to appear in the earth and swallow up the pursuing army (Revelation 12:16).

- The Satanically empowered world leader will be transformed into what we call the *Antichrist*. This is not an evolutionary process such as Judas Iscariot, but will occur at a particular appointed time. The world leader will be *wounded unto death by a sword* (Revelation 13: 1-3). As he lay in death, God will allow Satan to bring this individual back to life and Satan will assume complete control of his mind and body...He will become the *Antichrist. Why would God allow Satan to do this?* This can only be answered by understanding the real purpose of the last 3.5 years of the Church Age. God has chosen Israel as His people and although they have been set aside for almost 2000 years, His eternal plan is still to have them return to a covenant and intimate relationship with Him. The Covenant of Death will been annulled and the new Temple will be desecrated and taken over by Satan in the form of the Antichrist. Satan will still exist in his angelic body, but he will control the revived great world leader and give him supernatural powers. The Antichrist in the name of Satan will demand that all Jews worship him as lord or be martyred. The *Wrath of Satan* will then be unleashed upon *all those who dwell upon the earth*. In Zachariah 13:8 we are told that 2/3 of Israel will be slain in his assault on all Jews and Christians. This is called the *Wrath of Satan* and is unleashed during the 7 trumpet judgments. As things look hopeless, Israel and the Jews will finally turn to Jesus Christ to save them both physically and spiritually. When they do, *all Israel will be saved* (Romans 11:26). This will likely come to pass as the Holy City of Jerusalem is attacked a second time. This second assault on Jerusalem will precede the Battle of Armageddon. It will be called the *Armageddon Assault*.

- God will finally intervene, and He will pour out the *Wrath of God* upon Satan and all of the earth. The *Wrath of God* is the 7 Bowl Judgments (Revelation 16:1). Satan will assemble His followers and attack Jerusalem to destroy the city and the people a second time within 3.5 years. This will be called the *Armageddon Assault*. It will be interrupted by the 2nd coming of Jesus Christ. He will descend to the Mount of Olives.... meet Satan and his followers outside of Jerusalem..... and then fight the *Battle of Armageddon*.

- The Church age will end at the Battle of Armageddon. The *Antichrist* and the *False Prophet* will be captured and thrown into the *Lake of Burning Fire* where they will be tortured forever. Satan will be bound in chains and cast into the *Bottomless Pit* where he will remain for 1000 years.

- **** *The 1000 year Millennial Kingdom will now take place***********

- After the 1000 year Millennial Kingdom has run its course, Satan *will be loosed for a little while.* He will go to the *four corners of the earth* and gather all unbelievers to just outside of Jerusalem where he will once again (Satan never learns) march upon the City of Jerusalem and attempt to destroy the City and the Throne of Jesus Christ: This is called *Satan's Last Stand.* As Satan approaches Jerusalem, **God** himself will totally annialate Satan and all unbelievers. The battle will be swift and final: Fire will come down from Heaven and destroy them all (Revelation 20:9). Note that in this 3rd assault on Jerusalem, Satan and His forces will never actually reach the City.

- The world as we know it will then come to an end, but it will not be destroyed. The earth will be cleansed and purged by *fire* (II Peter2: 7, 12). It will be pure and free of sin just as it was in the Garden of Eden. The *New Jerusalem* will then descend from Heaven to earth and there we will live forever (Revelation 21: 1-3).
- God will also descend from Heaven and He will sit upon the Throne of His Glory with His Son Jesus Christ for all eternity (Revelation 21: 3-4).

We will now describe these three invasions of Jerusalem

The Jerusalem Campaign

An assault on the City of Jerusalem *before* the last 3.5 years of the Great Tribulation begins is demanded by the full council of scripture. We have seen that the Nation of Israel and the Jews will be living in peace *before* Satan is cast down to the earth, the Covenant of Death is in effect the Temple will be rebuilt. All of this *must* come to an end before Satan unleashes his anger and wrath upon mankind. The Satanically controlled Antichrist will sit in the temple and declare himself to be God. The Jews would never voluntarily give up temple worship, so a battle must be fought for Satan to gain complete control over the rebuilt temple.

[11] *Yea, he magnified himself even to the prince of the host, and by him the daily sacrifice was taken away, and the place of his sanctuary was cast down.*
[12] *And an host was given him against the daily sacrifice by reason of transgression, and it cast down the truth to the ground; and it practiced, and prospered*   Daniel 8: 11-12

Christ also spoke of these things in His Olivet Discourse.

[9] *Then shall they deliver you up to be afflicted, and shall kill you: and ye shall be hated of all nations for my name's sake.*
[15] ***When ye therefore shall see the abomination of desolation, spoken of by Daniel the prophet, stand in the holy place,*** *(whoso readeth, let him understand:)*
[16] *Then let them which be in Judaea flee into the mountains:*
[17] *Let him which is on the housetop not come down to take anything out of his house:*
[18] *Neither let him which is in the field return back to take his clothes.*
[19] *And woe unto them that are with child, and to them that give suck in those days!*
[20] *But pray ye that your flight be not in the winter, neither on the Sabbath day:*
[21] *For **then shall be great tribulation,** such as was not since the beginning of the world to this time, no, nor ever shall be*   Matthew 24:9, 15-21

It is interesting to note that Christ was living under the law when He spoke these words, and He knew that when this happened those who would flee Jerusalem would be Jewish people still living under the law. One of the prohibitions that every Jew must obey was that if this occurred on a Saturday (the Jewish Sabbath) no one would not be able to flee on foot more than about ½ mile without breaking the law of Moses (Acts 1:12, Exodus 16:29, Numbers 35:5). It is also noteworthy that in this warning, this event would be followed by *severe tribulation* (3.5 years).

The Jerusalem Campaign was also prophesied in the Old Testament by Isaiah and Ezekiel.

*And your **covenant with death shall be disannulled**, and your agreement with hell shall not stand; when the overflowing scourge shall pass through, then **ye shall be trodden down** by it* Isaiah 28:18

[8] ***After many days*** *thou shalt be visited: in the latter years thou shalt come into the land that is brought back from the sword, and is gathered out of many people, against the mountains of Israel, which have been always waste: but it is brought forth out of the nations, and **they shall dwell safely** all of them.*
[9] *Thou shalt ascend and come like a storm, thou shalt be like a cloud to cover the land, thou, and all thy bands, and many people with thee.*
[10] *Thus saith the Lord GOD; It shall also come to pass, that at the same time shall things come into thy mind, and thou shalt think an evil thought:*
[11] *And thou shalt say, I will go up to the land of unwalled villages; I will go to them that are at rest, that dwell safely, all of them dwelling without walls, and having neither bars nor gates,*
[12] *To take a spoil, and to take a prey; to turn thine hand upon the desolate places that are now inhabited, and upon the people that are gathered out of the nations, which have gotten cattle and goods, that dwell in the midst of the land*   Ezekiel 38: 8-12

Ezekiel 38: 9-12 *cannot* be describing the 2nd assault on Jerusalem which will take place just prior to the Battle of Armageddon. Ezekiel 38:8 and 38:11 both clearly state that the people are living in peace and safety. No one will be living in peace and safety during the Wrath of Satan and the Wrath of God. Many will actually leave their home and hide in caves (Revelation 6: 15-17). This invasion of Jerusalem is only the first of many things which will bring Israel to its knees, but a remnant will survive to enter into the Millennial Kingdom. The Archangel Michael will stand up for Israel and aid her during this time (Danial 12:1). He will not protect them from tribulation but from death. As the Antichrist rules over the entire Land of Israel, the Jews will finally realize that their only hope is to turn to Jesus Christ as their Messiah: *And so all Israel shall be saved: as it is written, There shall come out of Zion the Deliverer, and shall turn away ungodliness from Jacob* (Romans 11:26).

Satan has attacked Jerusalem and is causing death and destruction. The people must be both terrified and confused. They have been living in peace and safety and have even resumed temple worship....*what is happening*? They will realize that their Peace Treaty with the great European leader was actually a *Covenant with Death*. People will run from the city as 1/2 of all the Jewish residents are killed. As the people exit the city from the east gate, Satan and his army interrupts the direct siege of Jerusalem and pursues the fleeing remnant. Suddenly, a miracle occurs.

[**13**] *And when the dragon* (Satan) *saw that he was cast unto the earth, he persecuted the woman* (Israel) *which brought forth the man child.*
[**14**] *And to the woman were given two wings of a great eagle, that she might fly into the wilderness* (from Jerusalem)*, **into her place**, where she is nourished for a time, and times, and half a time, from the face of the serpent.*
[**15**] *And the serpent cast out of his mouth water as a flood after the woman, that he might cause her to be carried away of the flood.*
[**16**] *And **the earth helped the woman** (fleeing Jews), **and the earth opened her mouth, and swallowed up the flood which the dragon cast out of his mouth.***
[**17**] *And the dragon was wroth with the woman, and **went to make war with the remnant of her seed**, which keep the commandments of God, and have the testimony of Jesus Christ*
Revelation 12: 13-17

There are several interesting prophecies in Revelation 12: 13-17: (1) The woman (Jews from Jerusalem) flee into the wilderness where she *has a place*....Revelation 12:14. (2) She will be nourished there for 3.5 years (Revelation 12:14). This *proves* that the Jerusalem Campaign takes place before the Wrath of Satan and the Wrath of God. (3) The *serpent* Satan intends to drown them all in a flood of water (he is duplicating Noah's flood when all *unbelievers* were destroyed by a flood) (4) The earth *opened up* and *swallowed the flood* before the Jews could be killed (5) Satan is furious and he now turns to persecute and kill those who have the *testimony of Jesus Christ*. Note that this completely destroys a 7-year, mid-tribulation rapture and does serious damage to a 7-year pre-tribulation rapture. The Wrath of Satan is unleashed (7 Trumpet judgments) followed by the Wrath of God (7 Bowl judgments) over the next 3.5 years (Revelation 12:12). The *Armageddon Assault* has now arrived.

The Armageddon Assault

The *Wrath of God* is poured out upon all the earth....which are Bowls 1-7 (Revelation 15:7, Revelation 16:1). As the 7th bowl is poured out upon the earth, Satan will once again try to destroy the City of Jerusalem. He will assemble unbelievers and gather them as before outside of Jerusalem. He will then assault the Holy city and the Jews who are there. The *Armageddon Assault* at the *end* of the Tribulation is almost universally confused with the *Jerusalem Campaign* which occurs at the *beginning* of the last 3.5 years of tribulation. The following significant differences can easily be verified.

> 1.0   The motivation of both assaults on Jerusalem are different. In the *Jerusalem Campaign*, Satan is *wroth with anger* because he has been cast out of heaven and down to the earth. In the *Armageddon Assault* He knows that He must interrupt God's eternal plan and react to His Wrath.

2.0   In the *Jerusalem Campaign*, Satan is attacking only the City of Jerusalem and the Jews to gain control over the newly rebuilt temple and force all people worldwide to worship him. This will be the central point of his assault on all Jews and Christians. In the *Armageddon Assault* Satan is trying to completely destroy the Holy City of Jerusalem and all of its inhabitants.

3.0   The assault on Jerusalem is interrupted in two distinctly different ways. In the *Jerusalem Campaign* the people of Jerusalem are saved by God when the earth opens up and swallows up a great flood which Satan has unleashed out of his mouth to destroy the fleeing remnant. In the *Armageddon Assault* Christ descends from heaven to the Mount of Olives where He creates a valley through which the people will flee. Christ then fights and defeats Satan at the Battle of Armageddon.

[1] *Behold, the **Day of the LORD** cometh, and thy spoil shall be divided in the midst of thee.*
[2] *For **I will gather all nations against Jerusalem** to battle; and the city shall be taken, and the houses rifled, and the women ravished; and **half of the city shall go forth into captivity**, and the residue of the people shall not be cut off from the city.*
[3] *Then shall the LORD go forth, and fight against those nations, as when he fought in the day of battle.*
[4] *And His* (Jesus Christ) *feet shall stand in that day upon the mount of Olives, which is before Jerusalem on the east, and the **Mount of Olives shall cleave** in the midst thereof toward the east and toward the west, and there shall be **a very great valley**; and half of the mountain shall remove toward the north, and half of it toward the south.*
[5] *And ye shall flee to the valley of the mountains; for the valley of the mountains shall reach unto Azel: yea, ye shall flee, like as ye fled from before the earthquake in the days of Uzziah king of Judah: and the LORD my God shall come, and all the saints with thee.*   Zachariah 14: 1-5

Note Zachariah prophesies that: (1) *He* (Jesus Christ) will gather *all nations* to the battle. The Greek word translated as gather is *wǝ·'ā·sap̄·tî* and it can also mean *assemble*. The imagery is astounding: Just as the City and the people are being assaulted, Christ will descend from heaven and plant His feet on the Mount of Olives. The Mountain will be split into two pieces, creating a valley which will run from North to South. 50% of the people will run through this valley as they exit Jerusalem. Zachariah does not describe the Battle of Armageddon, but in Zachariah 14:9 he immediately describes Jesus Christ setting upon His new throne in the *Holy District* north of Jerusalem.

*And the LORD shall be king over all the earth: **in that day** shall there be one LORD, and his name one*   Zachariah 14:9

4.0 After the *Jerusalem Campaign*, Satan will persecute and kill Jews and Christians for almost 3.5 years. After the *Armageddon Assault*, Satan and his army immediately retreats to the Valley of Megiddo which is west of Jordan on the Plain of Jezreel where they are defeated that same day.

Following the *Armageddon Assault* on Jerusalem, the *Battle of Armageddon* will be fought. Rather than immediately describing *Satan's Last Stand* which will take place after the Millennial Kingdom we will describe the *Battle of Armageddon* which will immediately follow the *Armageddon Assault* and precede the Millennial Kingdom..

The Battle of Armageddon

The *Battle of Armageddon* is never referred to by that name in the Holy Scriptures. The word *Armageddon* comes from a Hebrew phrase *Har-Magedone*, *Har* means *hill* and *Megedone* is a *location name*. This phrase is used to refer to the battle between Satan and Christ which will end the Church Age and will be fought at a *place* called Armageddon (Revelation 16:16). Christ will return to earth to fight this epic battle with Satan, the Antichrist, the false prophet and all of their followers. The armies of the Antichrist, or at least the main body, will cross the Euphrates River which has been dried up when the sixth bowl is poured out (Revelation 16:12). They will then camp outside Jerusalem in the *Valley of Jezreel* where they will mobilize to attack Jerusalem. The most likely place that the battle is fought is on the *Plain of Megiddo*, north of Jerusalem. The people on earth who worship the antichrist will be gathered to this place by three *unclean spirits* called demons (Revelation 16:13-14). The *whole world* of antichrist's followers will be assembled by Satan (Revelation 16: 13-14). This is his last chance during the church age to destroy God's eternal plan, and he will use all of his deception to mobilize his forces and meet Christ outside of Jerusalem (Revelation 16:16).

The arrival of Christ and the total destruction of Satan and his followers are described below.

[11] *And I saw heaven opened, and behold a white horse; and he that sat upon him was called Faithful and True, and in righteousness he doth judge and make war.*
[12] *His eyes were as a flame of fire, and on his head were many crowns; and he had a name written, that no man knew, but he himself.*
[13] *And he was clothed with a vesture dipped in blood: and his name is called The Word of God.*
[14] *And the armies which were in heaven followed him upon white horses, clothed in fine linen, white and clean.*
[15] *And out of his mouth goeth a sharp sword, that with it he should smite the nations: and he shall rule them with a rod of iron: and he treadeth the winepress of the fierceness and wrath of Almighty God.*

*[**16**] And he hath on his vesture and on his thigh a name written, KING OF KINGS, AND LORD OF LORDS.*

*[**17**] And I saw an angel standing in the sun; and he cried with a loud voice, saying to all the fowls that fly in the midst of heaven, Come and gather yourselves together unto the supper of the great God;*

*[**18**] That ye may eat the flesh of kings, and the flesh of captains, and the flesh of mighty men, and the flesh of horses, and of them that sit on them, and the flesh of all men, both free and bond, both small and great.*

*[**19**] And I saw the beast, and the kings of the earth, and their armies, gathered together to make war against him that sat on the horse, and against his army.*

*[**20**] And the beast was taken, and with him the false prophet that wrought miracles before him, with which he deceived them that had received the mark of the beast, and them that worshipped his image. These both were cast alive into a lake of fire burning with brimstone.*

*[**21**] And the remnant were slain with the sword of him that sat upon the horse, which sword proceeded out of his mouth: and all the fowls were filled with their flesh.*
Revelation 19: 11-21

Christ will probably return in His 2nd advent on the *Feast of Yom Kippur* on a white horse. This is the second time that a rider was shown on a white horse. The first (Rev 6:2) was Satan riding out *conquering and to conquer*. The second is none other than Jesus Christ riding out to conquer Satan and his followers. *He is called faithful and true* for the third time (Rev 1:5, 3:7, 19:11). His eyes are like a *flame of fire*, and have not changed since John first saw Him in Rev 1:14. He has descended from heaven (Rev 19:11) with a heavenly entourage. On his head are *many crowns*. These are *diadem crowns* worn by heavenly creatures and redeemed saints, and not *stephanos crowns* worn by earthly rulers. In Rev 19: 11-13 we are told something very unusual.

*[**11**] And I saw heaven opened, and behold a white horse; and he that sat upon him was called Faithful and True, and in righteousness he doth judge and **make war**.*

*[**12**] His eyes were as a flame of fire, and on his head were many crowns; and he had a name written, that no man knew, but he himself.*

*[**13**] And he was **clothed with a vesture dipped in blood**: and his name is called The Word of God*   Revelation 19: 11-13

Who is He who Comes From Bozrah ?

Christ is descending from heaven on a white horse to fight the Battle of Armageddon, and He is clothed in a *robe dipped in blood*. Since the battle of Armageddon has not begun yet: *from where did this blood come?* The source is not explained and it is difficult to offer an explanation. There is an equally puzzling segment of scripture in Isaiah 63 which also describes Jesus in blood stained garments.

[**1**] *Who is this that cometh from Edom, with dyed garments from Bozrah? this that is glorious in his apparel, travelling in the greatness of his strength? I that speak in righteousness, mighty to save.*

[**2**] *Wherefore art thou red in thine apparel, and thy garments like him that treadeth in the winefat?*

[**3**] *I **have trodden the winepress** alone; and of the people there was none with me: for I will tread them in mine anger, and trample them in my fury; and **their blood shall be sprinkled upon my garments**, and I will stain all my raiment*   Isaiah 63: 1-3

The reference to a winepress being trodden is more than just a casual statement. In Revelation 14 John sees an angel who *harvests the earth* or gathers all those true believers who will rise to meet Christ at the rapture.

[**14**] *And I looked, and behold a white cloud, and upon the cloud one sat like unto the Son of man, having on his head a golden crown, and in his hand a sharp sickle.*

[**15**] *And another angel came out of the temple, crying with a loud voice to him that sat on the cloud, Thrust in thy sickle, and reap: for the time is come for thee to reap; for the harvest of the earth is ripe.*

[**16**] *And he that sat on the cloud thrust in his sickle on the earth; and the earth was reaped*
Revelation 14: 14-16

The *sickle* harvests the precious wheat (*believers*) which is *ripe*. This immediately *precedes* the *Wrath of God* from which the saints will be spared. The Wrath of God are the 7 bowl judgments (Revelation 16:1). The 7th bowl brings the 2nd coming of Christ and the Battle of Armageddon. After all true believers are harvested from the earth, we see another angel who appears out of the temple and upon command thrusts *another sharp sickle* into the earth and reaps. This sickle is harvesting grapes which represent all *unbelievers*.

[**17**] *And another angel came out of the temple which is in heaven, he also having a sharp sickle.*

[**18**] *And another angel came out from the altar, which had power over fire; and cried with a loud cry to him that had the sharp sickle, saying, Thrust in thy sharp sickle, and gather the clusters of the vine of the earth; for her grapes are fully ripe.*

[**19**] *And the angel thrust in his sickle into the earth, and gathered the vine of the earth, and cast it into the great winepress of the Wrath of God.*

[**20**] *And the winepress was trodden without the city, and blood came out of the winepress, even unto the horse bridles, by the space of a thousand and six hundred furlongs*
Revelation 14: 17-20

The *grapes* that are reaped are *unbelievers,* who are thrown into the *winepress of the Wrath of God*. The *Wrath of God* are the seven bowl judgments and is climaxed when the 7th bowl is poured out which immediately precedes at the Battle of Armageddon. Note again that all believers do not experience the *Wrath of God* (Romans 5:9, I Thessalonians 1:10, I Thessalonians 5:9, Romans 1:18), but there is no indication whatsoever that they are exempt from the *Wrath of Satan*. Note that that *the winepress was trampled outside the city* (Jerusalem) in the battle of Armageddon (Rev 14:20). Revelation 19:13 is without controversy describing the garments of Christ as he descends from heaven to fight the Battle of Armageddon, but Isaiah 63:3 seems to be describing how the garments of Christ will be stained *after* the Battle of Armageddon as He is returning from Bozrah. In Revelation 19:13 His garments have been *dipped* in blood, but in Isaiah 63:3 His garments are *sprinkled* with blood. Actually, the Greek word used here is *baptó* from which we derive the word *baptism*. It can be translated as both *dipped and sprinkled.* both are linked to the Battle of Armageddon Revelation. Revelation 19:13 is a direct reference to staining His garments as the battle is being fought, and but Revelation His robe is not *splattered* as one might expect in battle, but *dipped*. There is still another problem: In Revelation 19:13 the battle has not even begun yet. We can offer no sustainable interpretation of why the robe of Christ is *dipped in blood* when Christ comes down from heaven to fight the Battle of Armageddon, but he is seen wearing robes *sprinkled* in blood as He returns from Bozrah. However, a resolution of these two verses might be offered.

The Book of Revelation is full of dark and difficult prophecies which are not easily explained. One thing we do know from the full council of scripture is that when Christ came the 1st time it was as a suffering servant who would be persecuted and die a horrible sacrificial death to redeem all men and women from the curse of sin. When He will come a 2nd time it will not be as a suffering servant but as a *conquering King*.

He defeated both *death* and the *grave* when He was resurrected from the grave. When Christ returns in Revelation 19:11 the world will see him returning in triumph. When Christ was resurrected, he made a public spectacle of Satan. He revealed His power over death and Satan when He resurrected a Firstfruits of believing Jews from the grave and publicly paraded them through the streets of Jerusalem: *having spoiled principalities and powers, he made a shew of them openly, triumphing over them in it*   Colossians 2:15

When Christ returns a 2nd time (Revelation 19: 1-21), He will be seen as both a *suffering servant* and a *conquering king*. The two symbols of this duality are His *crowns* (Revelation 19:12) and his *raiment* (Revelation 19:13). He is seen wearing blood stained clothes, the blood that redeemed all mankind from death and sin. He is also seen wearing the crown of a King, the crown that He will wear as King of Kings and Lord of Lords in the Millennial Kingdom. The *result* of these two triumphs of Christ are those who follow after Him.....They are clothed in fine linen, white and clean. Their robes have been washed by the blood of Jesus Christ (Revelation 1:5, Revelation 7:14). The appearance of Jesus Christ is symbolic of His majesty, glory and victory.

It would be just as appropriate to translate Revelation 19:13 as follows.

And he was clothed with a vesture dipped in blood: and his name is called The Word of God (King James Text)

*And he was clothed with a **vesture sprinkled in blood**: and his name is called The Word of God*
(Equally Accurate translation)

If Revelation 19:13a had been translated from the Greek this way, it would have been just as descriptive and correct. This would also directly satisfy the prophetic words of Isaiah 63: 1-3.

[1] *Who is this that cometh from Edom, with dyed garments from Bozrah? this that is glorious in his apparel, travelling in the greatness of his strength? I that speak in righteousness, mighty to save.*
[2] *Wherefore art thou red in thine apparel, and thy garments like him that treadeth in the winefat?*
[3] *I have trodden the winepress alone; and of the people there was none with me: for I will tread them in mine anger, and trample them in my fury; and **their blood shall be sprinkled upon my garments**, and I will stain all my raiment*   Isaiah 63: 1-3

Carefully examining and comparing scriptural clues, it is *suggested* that Revelation 19:13 is in support of the *conjecture* that Christ will not go to Bozrah until *after* the battle of Armageddon is over. He will go to Bozrah and rescue those who have been hiding there since the *Jerusalem Campaign* and those who escaped through the valley that formed when Christ descended from Heaven and split the Mount of Olives during the *Armageddon Assault*.

Christ will fight the Battle of Armageddon with only one weapon: *a sharp sword out of His mouth.* Using this sword, *he alone will tread the winepress of the fierceness and wrath of God almighty.* He is accompanied by a heavenly host who ride white horses.

And the armies which were in heaven followed him upon white horses, clothed in fine linen, white and clean   Revelation 19:14

This is Christ's personal battle, and He *treads the winepress alone* (Isaiah 63:3). That is He needs no help in completely annihilating His foes. The battle is not protracted but is won supernaturally in a short period of time. Zachariah describes it in gory detail.

And this shall be the plague wherewith the LORD will smite all the people that have fought against Jerusalem; Their flesh shall consume away while they stand upon their feet, and their eyes shall consume away in their holes, and their tongue shall consume away in their mouth
Zechariah 14:12

The armies which are in heaven, clothed in fine linen, white and clean, followed Him on white horses. Who are those who follow Him on white horses? There are many who say that these followers are angels. There are many passages that associate Jesus Christ with His angels. They are assigned various duties but in no single passage are they said to participate in the Battle of Armageddon. It is questionable that they would ride white horses, but not out of the realm of possibility. There are, however, several passages which seem to indicate that those following

Christ on white horses are the Bride of Christ and the overcomers of Revelation 3-4. They are clothed in **white, clean, fine linen** (Revelation 19: 14). In Revelation 17:14 those with him are called *chosen and faithful*. These terms apply to those who have been redeemed by the blood of Christ and served Him. In Revelation 3:5, Christ promises those who *overcome* that they will be *clothed in white garments*. The great multitude that John saw standing before the throne in Revelation 7: 9, 13; who are identified as the raptured and resurrected saints, are wearing *white robes*. Based upon these supporting scriptures, it is reasonable to conjecture that the saints who have been with Christ at the Marriage of the Lamb now return with him to the Battle of Armageddon. There are given some identifying characteristics of Christ as He appears in His glorified state. In Revelation 19:12, Christ has *many crowns* and a name written *that no man knew, only Himself*. It is not revealed when or where this name was written. It is interesting that the overcomer (Philadelphia) is promised that he will be given the *name of My God*, and the name of the *city of my God*, and Christ will write on him *My new name* (Christ's) (Revelation 3:12). Every overcomer will also be given a *white stone* with a new name that *no one knows except him who receives it*. The average Christian understands the basic principle of a covenant relationship with Christ, but few understand what this involved in the Old Testament. When a covenant was made in the Old Testament between two people, two things happened: (1) they exchanged a portion of their garments, and (2) each was given a new name that only they knew. How revealing this custom is to our relationship with Christ! We will be given a new name and new garments of white by Jesus Christ.

The carnage from the battle of Armageddon will be unprecedented in all of history. There will probably be millions of people killed, and thousands of horses. Blood will run to the *horses' bridals* (Revelation 14:20). This is probably after being mixed with millions of melting 100-pound hailstones that have just fallen from heaven (Revelation 16:21). The carnage will obstruct the movement of people (Ezekiel 39:11) in the *Valley of Hamon Gog*, which simply means *the Valley of Gog*, or the Antichrist. It will take seven months for Israel to cleanse the land of bones and dead bodies (Ezekiel 39: 12-15), and it will take 7 years to clear the land of the implements of war (Ezekiel 39:9).

The Two Great Feasts

After the battle there will be two great feasts on the earth. The *first feast* will be on the fields of Armageddon, and the guests will be all of the birds of prey and carrion to feast upon the dead bodies.

[**17**] *And I saw an angel standing in the sun; and he cried with a loud voice, saying to all the fowls that fly in the midst of heaven, Come and gather yourselves together unto the supper of the great God;*
[**18**] *That ye may eat the flesh of kings, and the flesh of captains, and the flesh of mighty men, and the flesh of horses, and of them that sit on them, and the flesh of all men, both free and bond, both small and great*   Revelation 19: 17-18

The birds of prey feasting on dead bodies explain another mysterious statement made by Christ just prior to his crucifixion: *For wherever the carcass is, there the eagles will be gathered together* (Revelation 24:28). Christ also referred to this in His Olivet Discourse.

For wheresoever the carcass is, there will the eagles be gathered together   Matthew 24:28

The **second feast** will be the *Marriage Supper of the Lamb.* This will be a joyous occasion. Satan and all of his followers have been defeated.

[**7**] *Let us be glad and rejoice, and give honor to him: for the marriage of the Lamb is come, and his wife hath made herself ready.*
[**8**] *And to her was granted that* **she should be arrayed in fine linen, clean and white**: *for the fine linen is the righteousness of saints.*
[**9**] *And he saith unto me, Write, Blessed are they which are called unto the* **marriage supper of the Lamb**. *And he saith unto me, These are the true sayings of God*   Revelation 19: 7-9

Christ the Conquering King

Finally, the *Day of the Lord* will come to its long awaited conclusion. The Beast (Antichrist) and the False Prophet were both cast alive into the lake of fire burning with fire and brimstone.

[**19**] *And I saw the beast, and the kings of the earth, and their armies, gathered together to make war against him that sat on the horse, and against his army.*
[**20**] *And the beast was taken, and with him the false prophet that wrought miracles before him, with which he deceived them that had received the mark of the beast, and them that worshipped his image. These both were cast alive into a lake of fire burning with brimstone*
Revelation 19: 19-20

That old serpent the devil, called Satan will be cast into the *bottomless pit*, where he will be confined and bound for 1000 years.

[**1**] *And I saw an angel come down from heaven, having the key of the bottomless pit and a great chain in his hand.*
[**2**] *And he laid hold on the dragon, that old serpent, which is the Devil, and Satan, and bound him a thousand years,*
[**3**] *And cast him into the bottomless pit, and shut him up, and set a seal upon him, that he should deceive the nations no more, till the thousand years should be fulfilled: and after that he must be loosed a little season.*   Revelation 20: 1:3

All of the followers of Satan... *every one* ... are *killed with the sword which proceeded from the mouth of Him* (Christ) *who sat on the horse*. The Wrath of God is now complete..... Our Lord Jesus Christ is victorious..... and the 1000-year millennial kingdom is at hand. After the 12 tribes of Israel have each been given a section of land, they will live with Christ who will rule and reign just north of Jerusalem. The land will be transformed into a fertile, beautiful plain and Israel will flourish and repopulate the earth. After the 1000 years are over, the covenant promise that God made to Abraham will have been fulfilled. Unfortunately, not all of the Kingdom population will accept Christ as their Lord and Savior. These unbelievers must be removed and eradicated before eternity can begin. Satan will be loosed from his prison (Bottomless Pit) to assemble all unbelievers one last time. This is the battle of *Satan's Last Stand*.

Satan's Last Stand

[7] *And when the thousand years are expired, Satan shall be loosed out of his prison,*
[8] *And shall go out to deceive the nations which are in the four quarters of the earth, Gog and Magog, to gather them together to battle: the number of whom is as the sand of the sea.*
[9] *And they went up on the breadth of the earth, and compassed the camp of the saints about, and the beloved city: and fire came down from God out of heaven, and devoured them.*
[10] *And the devil that deceived them was cast into the lake of fire and brimstone, where the beast and the false prophet are, and shall be tormented day and night forever and ever*
Revelation 20:7-10

As the Millennial Kingdom comes to a close, it will be necessary to purge *all* evil and sin from the earth. Satan will be loosed from his 1000 year exile in the Bottomless Pit, and he will go out to "***deceive the nations which are in the four quarters of the earth, Gog and Magog, to gather them together for battle***". As we have previously pointed out, there is no mention here of any armies being formed from the North as there are in Ezekiel 39. This assault on Jerusalem and Christ will be led by Satan who will form his army from the *four quarters of the earth*. He will surround the "***camp of the saints***" and the "***beloved city***". The *camp of the saints* is no doubt the *Holy Oblation* in which the saints of all ages will rule and reign with Christ. The *beloved city* is Jerusalem. The reference to God and Magog in Revelation 20:8 has a straightforward explanation. Gog represents Satan, and Magog represents the lands from which they are called. These two terms are symbolic of Satan and all who will follow after him at the end of the millennial kingdom.

And (Satan) *shall go out to deceive the nations which are in the four quarters of the earth, Gog and Magog, to gather them together to battle: the number of whom is as the sand of the sea*
Revelation 20:8

This is *Satan's Last Stand*, and it is the third and last military campaign against Jerusalem. If it was not seen and written by John it would be hard to believe..... there will be as many as the *sand of the sea* that joins Satan. This is the only place in Holy Scripture that this is recorded.

In this final battle (Satan's Last Stand) the army of Gog will be gathered from the *four corners of the earth*. In the Battle of Armageddon Satan assembles his army from the *northern parts of the earth only*. Neither Ezekiel 38 or Ezekiel 39 describe this final assault. The battle is barely mentioned... it will be swift and final.

And they went up on the breadth of the earth, and compassed the camp of the saints about, and the beloved city: and fire came down from God out of heaven, and devoured them Revelation 20:9.

In the *Battle of Armageddon* **Christ** destroys Gog and Magog with a *sword that came out of his mouth* (Revelation 19: 15, 21). In this final battle **God** will destroy Satan and all of those who follow him with *fire from heaven*. Following this final battle, all those who have rejected Christ and have followed after Satan to this battle will have been destroyed. Satan is then thrown into the Burning Lake of Fire where the Antichrist and the false prophet have been tortured for 1000 years (Revelation 19:20).

The final event which will now take place is the *Great White Throne Judgment,* in which those who have died without accepting Christ as their savior will be judged. (Revelation 20: 11-15). All unbelievers at the Great White Throne will be judged *according to their works* (Revelation 20:13). The sinful nature of man inherited from Adam, This earth and its curse; the corruption, temptation and disbelief caused by Satan; and the evil that now is present will all come to an end.

The End of Sin and Sinners

[**7**] *But the heavens and the earth, which are now, by the same word are kept in store, reserved unto fire against the day of judgment and perdition of ungodly men.*
[**12**] *Looking for and hasting unto the coming of the day of God, wherein the heavens being on fire shall be dissolved, and the elements shall melt with fervent heat?*   II Peter 3:7, 12

And I saw a new heaven and a new earth: for the first heaven and the first earth were passed away; and there was no more sea   Revelation 21:1

A common misconception is that after the Church age is over and Christ returns to rule and reign over the earth, there will be no sin and no sinners during the 1000 year Millennial Kingdom. There are several biblical passages which negate this common belief.

The people who will live upon this earth during the Millennial Kingdom are real people, with real earthly bodies. Hence, they were each born with the original curse of sin that was passed down from Adam. Many will reject Jesus Christ even though He is there with them. In fact, unbelievers will be as the sand of the sea (Revelation 20:8). If this seems almost too hard to believe one only needs to remember what happened just 50 days after God had Moses lead his people from Egypt. Moses arrived at Mount Sinai on the 47th day, and went up to receive the law. When he returned, the people were engaged in adulterous acts and worshipping idols...... only 47 days after leaving Egypt!!

The intention of God has always been to establish a new heaven and a new earth, and restore man to the Edenic state. The *passport* to this new kingdom is simple: Accept His Son Jesus Christ as Lord and Savior, and receive eternal life by amazing grace. However, since sin will still be manifested all over the earth, it will need to be removed forever. The final battle of Jerusalem, *Satan's Last Stand* and the subsequent *Great White Throne Judg*ment will accomplish this goal.

[7] *And when the thousand years are expired, Satan shall be loosed out of his prison,*
[8] *And shall go out to deceive the nations which are in the four quarters of the earth, Gog and Magog, to gather them together to battle: the number of whom is as the sand of the sea.*
[9] *And they went up on the breadth of the earth, and compassed the camp of the saints about, and the beloved city: and fire came down from God out of heaven, and devoured them*
[10] *And the devil that deceived them was cast into the lake of fire and brimstone, where the beast and the false prophet are, and shall be tormented day and night forever and ever.*
[11] *And I saw a great white throne, and him that sat on it, from whose face the earth and the heaven fled away; and there was found no place for them.*
[12] *And I saw the dead, small and great, stand before God; and the books were opened: and another book was opened, which is the book of life: and the dead were judged out of those things which were written in the books, according to their works.*
[13] *And the sea gave up the dead which were in it; and death and hell delivered up the dead which were in them: and they were judged every man according to their works.*
[14] *And death and hell were cast into the lake of fire. This is the second death.*
[15] *And whosoever was not found written in the book of life was cast into the lake of fire.*
Revelation 20: 7-15

Five things are obvious from this prophecy. The *First* is that after the Battle of Armageddon and the Millennial Kingdom begins, there will be rebellion and disregard for Christ and His ordinances. *Second*, those who will not accept Jesus Christ as their Lord and Savior will be many: *as the sand of the sea*. *Third*, God Himself destroyed them all. *Fourth*, there will be a final judgment of all unbelievers. *Fifth*, Those who will *not* be cast into the Lake of Burning Fire will be those whose names are written in the Book of Life.

Every Christian can be comforted and reassured by one fundamental truth: God is in control of His creation, and His Son Jesus Christ will conquer Satan; do away with all sin; usher in a new world of peace and righteousness; banish Satan to an eternity of torture in the Lake of Burning Fire and all of those who refuse to believe in the Lord Jesus Christ will also be cast into the Lake of Burning Fire. All of these things will not take place until *after* the 1000 year millennial kingdom has come to an end (Revelation 21:1). Many interpret Revelation 21 to be what will happen at the *beginning* of the Millennial Kingdom, but it is what will take place *after* the Millennial Kingdom. God promised Noah that He would never destroy (cleanse) the world again by water. Peter prophesied that the world would one day be purged by fire.

But the heavens and the earth, which are now, by the same word are kept in store, reserved unto fire against the day of judgment and perdition of ungodly men   II Peter 3:7

The Judgment and sentencing of all ungodly men will take place at the *White Throne Judgment* (Revelation 20: 11-15). Unbelievers from all dispensations and those who have lived and died during the Millennial Kingdom will stand before the judgment seat of God. All whose names are not written in the Book of Life will be cast into the Lake of Burning Fire where they will be tormented forever (Revelation 20:10).

Gog and Magog

We would like to conclude this discussion with an examination of *Gog* and *Magog.* The names of Gog and Magog appear in only three places in the Authorized King James bible: Ezekiel 38:1-3, Ezekiel 39:1 and in Revelation 20:7-8. The relationship between these three passages of scripture has been a subject of debate for over 2000 years. All scholars agree that the reference to Gog and Magog in Rev 20:7-8 refer to participants in *Satan's Last Stand* which has previously been discussed. There are three major issues which are in debate: The *first* is exactly who or what do the nouns Gog and Magog represent? The *second* is whether or not Ezekiel 38 and Ezekiel 39 refer to the same battle or different battles? The *third* is which of the three *Jerusalem Invasions* does Ezekiel 38 and Ezekiel 39 describe?   The reader is asked at this time to read Ezekiel 38 and 39 before proceeding. These are lengthy chapters and will not be duplicated here.

Magog was a grandson of Noah and a son of Japheth. His name appears in the *table of nations* In Genesis 10-11, which detail the generations of the sons of Noah, Shem, Ham, and Japheth. From Noah and his wife the entire world was populated, so we are all direct descendents of not only Adam but Noah. We have not evolved from apes ! Magog is not referring to a reincarnated son of Japheth, but to the nations and people that he spawned out of his loins. The descendants of Magog migrated to the land north of the Caucasus Mountains in an area between the Black and Caspian Seas. Magog, Meshach and Tubal are all mentioned by Ezekiel. They spawned the Russians, Muscovites, Siberians and other people who formed modern northern Europe (Dake). Some claim that by this genealogy, Russia will be the leader of those who invade Jerusalem and will be the main force led by *Gog.* Even if Russia is included in this invasion force, it does not prove in any way that she will be the dominating force. Daniel 11:44 plainly predicts that Russia and the Northern nations will be conquered by the antichrist and his forces as the last 3.5 years of Daniel's 70th week unfolds. In conclusion, Magog is only referring to a group of countries that will be led by a person called *Gog.* There is no person called John Gog, or Paul Gog or even Gog; Gog is a title for the leader of these invading forces. In context of our previous discussion, *Gog* is the leader of the invasion described in Ezekiel 38, and he is uniquely the *chief prince* of the invasion described in Ezekiel 39. These are not the same person as we will shortly see.

The third question is the one that we will devote the most analysis: *What is the relationship between Ezekiel 38, Ezekiel 39 and Rev 20:7-8?* We believe that by carefully examining all of these scriptures that the only conclusion that satisfies the scriptural accounts is to identify the following correlations.

> ➤ Ezekiel 38 is describing the *Jerusalem Campaign*, which takes place in the first few days of the last 3.5 years of tribulation.
> ➤ Ezekiel 39 is describing the *Armageddon Assault* and the *Battle of Armageddon,* which closes the tribulation period.
> ➤ Revelation 20: 7-8 describes *Satan's last Stand,* which is the final assault of Satan against Christ, and stands independent of Ezekiel 38 and 39. The appearance of the nouns Gog and Magog in Revelation 20:8 are referring to the leader (Gog) and the lands or nations (Magog) that will be formed to encounter Christ.

It is evident from all three scriptural accounts that Gog is the leader of all three invasions. The supernatural power behind the leader in Revelation 20: 7-8 is beyond controversy *Satan*, which proves that the term *Gog* is just describing a vile and evil leader of invading armies. *Gog* is almost certainly the Satanically indwelled Antichrist in both the *Jerusalem campaign* and in the *Armageddon Assault* on Jerusalem, and it is definitely Satan in *Satan's Last stand*. As far as *Magog* is concerned, the group of unbelievers who will follow Satan into both the *Jerusalem Campaign* and the *Battle of Armageddon* come from north of Jerusalem, but those who will gather to fight *Satan's Last Stand* will be from the four corners of the earth (Revelation 20:8).

Comparing Ezekiel 38, Ezekiel 39 and Revelation 20: 1-15

The relationship between Ezekiel 38 and Ezekiel 39 is a hotly debated topic. Many expositors hold that both chapters are describing the same battle. We propose that Ezekiel 38 and Ezekiel 39 are **not** describing the same battle. The fact that Ezekiel 38 is describing a different battle from Ezekiel 39 is not unique to this exegesis. The great biblical scholar Finis Jennings Dake reaches this same conclusion and provides extensive scriptural support for this position. It was also presented as a possibility in the Ryrie Study Bible as a footnote accompanying Ezekiel 38-39. Again, recognize that there are three invasions of Jerusalem in the end times: (1) The *Jerusalem Campaign* as the tribulation period begins (2) the *Armageddon Assault* as the tribulation period ends and (3) *Satan's Last Stand* following the Millennial Kingdom.

> ➤ It is easy to resolve what Ezekiel 39 is describing. It is clearly the *Armageddon Assault* and includes a partial description of the subsequent *Battle of Armageddon*. This conclusion becomes near certainty because of two things: (1) It will take 7 months for the people slain in the Battle of Armageddon to be buried (Ezekiel 39: 12, 14) and (2) The implements of war will take 7 years to be cleaned up (Ezekiel 39:9). In both Ezekiel 39: 12, 14 and Ezekiel 39:9 there is a detailed description of a post-battle clean-up operation. This **cannot** refer to Satan's Last Stand, because after that battle a new heaven and a new earth will be formed... all of the old earth will be burned with fire. It

could refer to the Jerusalem campaign, but who would clean up the carnage? Certainly not the armies of the antichrist, and 50% of the people in Jerusalem have been killed or fled. Conjecture and conclusion becomes near certainty by considering one crucial fact: The carnage of battle will take 7 years to clean up, and there is only 3.5 years between the Jerusalem campaign and the Battle of Armageddon. This period of time can only logically apply to a period of time *following* the Battle of Armageddon.

Does Ezekiel 38 amplify Ezekiel 39 or is it describing a different invasion, either the *Jerusalem Campaign* or *Satan's Last Stand*? The following reasons seem to indicate that Ezekiel 38 is *not* describing the same battle as Ezekiel 39.

> ➤ In Ezekiel 38 and Ezekiel 39, the invading armies come from the "***remote parts of the North***"; (Ezekiel 38:15) and from the "***north parts***" (Ezekiel 39:2). This clearly indicates that both battles will involve nations from north of Israel. This is true of both the *Jerusalem Campaign* and the *Armageddon Assault*, and is consistent with the antichrist leading both invasions. This is not true at *Satan's Last Stand* in Rev 20:8. In this battle, Satan and his forces come from the "***four corners of the earth***" (Revelation 20:8) and the Antichrist has been cast into the Lake of Burning Fire 1000 years earlier.

> ➤ In Ezekiel 38:11, we are told that Israel is ***dwelling safely***. This can only be true just prior to the *Jerusalem Campaign* or at *Satan's last stand*; but *not* at the *Armageddon Assault*.

> ➤ In Ezekiel 38:12 we are told that the purpose of this invasion is to ***take a spoil*** and to turn upon the people of Israel that have been gathered ***out of the nations***. This cannot be applied to the Armageddon Assault, and is best meant to describe the *Jerusalem Campaign*. The Armageddon Assault is against the City of Jerusalem to capture the city, desecrate the rebuilt temple and establish the Antichrist as God; The Armageddon Assault is to destroy Jerusalem and all of the Jews, and is retaliation against the Wrath of God. The Battle of Satan's Last Stand is against Christ as he reigns in Jerusalem.

> ➤ In Ezekiel 39:17-20 there is a description of the ***feathered fowl*** which will come to the battleground to feast upon the dead that are laying there. In Rev 19: 17 almost the exact same words are used: After the battle of Armageddon, ***all the fowls*** are invited to eat the flesh of the slain armies of antichrist (Also see Ezekiel 39:4). This is another very strong indication that Ezekiel 39 is describing the Battle of Armageddon. There is no mention of birds of prey in either the Jerusalem Campaign or in Satan's Last Stand.

> ➤ In Ezekiel 38:20 there is an interesting description of ***mountains being thrown down*** and ***steep places falling***. At first, this would seem to indicate that this is associated with the pouring out of the 7th bowl (Rev 16:20), and would link Ezekiel 38 to Armageddon. However, this could very well explain a *mystery*. We know that when the *Jerusalem Campaign* takes place, the fleeing Children of Israel will be supernaturally saved. The *mystery of how this might happen* could possibly now be explained. In Rev 12 we are told:

[**15**] *And the serpent cast out of his mouth water as a flood after the woman, that he might cause her to be carried away of the flood.*
[**16**] *And the earth helped the woman, and the **earth opened her mouth**, and swallowed up the flood which the dragon cast out of his mouth*   Revelation 12: 15-16

The *earth opening its mouth* might have been referring to an earthquake. However, this is not conclusive. Recall the sin of Korah (Numbers 26). Korah was jealous of Moses and rebelled against his authority. The Lord was so mad at Korah and 250 of his people that He separated them from everyone else and *the earth open her mouth, and swallowed them up.*

They, and all that appertained to them, went down alive into the pit, and the earth closed upon them: and they perished from among the congregation   Numbers 16:33

There is no mention of the earth moving and shaking. It is best concluded that the people fleeing destruction and death are not saved by an earthquake but by a supernatural act of God. There is also no direct mention of an earthquake saving Jews in either the Armageddon Assault or in Satan's last Stand.

 ➢ Ezekiel 39: 25-29 provides a statement of *why* the events of Ezekiel 39 occurred, and what they accomplished. It is also records that *all* of Israel had been gathered into the land after this battle, and this was done only after "***they have borne their shame and all their trespasses, whereby they have trespassed against me".*** This **cannot be true** following the *Jerusalem Campaign*. Only after the *Battle of Armageddon*, where Israel will finally realize that Christ is their long awaited Messiah and lament their transgressions and disbelief.

There are many other scriptures in Ezekiel 38 and Ezekiel 39 that could be discussed, but those just given fully support the following conclusions

- Ezekiel 38 and Ezekiel 39 describe two separate battles. Ezekiel 38 is describing the first invasion of Jerusalem by the Antichrist and his armies *before* the last 3.5 years of Tribulation and the Wrath of Satan. This is what we have previously called the *Jerusalem Campaign*.
- Ezekiel 39 is describing the second assault on Jerusalem by the Antichrist and his armies after the last 3.5 years of Tribulation and the Wrath of Satan. This is what we have previously Called the *Armageddon Assault*.
- Neither Ezekiel 38 or Ezekiel 39 can be describing the last battle called *Satan's Last Stand* in Revelation 19: 1-21.

Chapter 7

Judgments: Rewards and Condemnation

The average Christian does not recognize or understand that there are multiple judgments

behold, I come quickly; and my reward is with me, to give every man according as his work shall be   Revelation 22:11

For we must all appear before the judgment seat of Christ; that every one may receive the things done in his body, according to that he hath done, whether it be good or bad
II Corinthians 5:10

There are three judgments which will take place that are related to the Millennial Kingdom: (1) The *Bema Seat Judgment* (2) The *Judgment of the Sheep and Goats* and (3) *The Great White Throne Judgment*. The *Bema Seat Judgment* and the *Judgment of the Sheep and Goats* both take place *after* the rapture of the saints and *before* the Millennial Kingdom begins.

The *Great White Throne Judgment* takes place *after* the Millennial Kingdom ends and *before* eternity begins. Each Judgment will be held for a distinctly different purpose. The *Bema Seat* Judgment will be for all *believers* in Christ. It is not a judgment for condemnation but for rewards. It will take place following the rapture of the *ecclesia*. Ecclesia is a Greek word which means assembly, or those identified and called out for special service. It is sometimes translated as the *church* (Cf ...I Corinthians 12:28). At the rapture, those who have died in Christ will rise to meet Him *in the air*, and then those believers who are alive will follow. This will include all Old Covenant believers who died in the faith of Abraham and all New Covenant believers who have accepted Him as Lord and Savior. The basis for this truth is rooted in the sacrificial death of Christ on the Cross of Calvary where He died and forgave all of our sins. Salvation under the New Covenant is freely offered by faith and grace. This seems almost too simple to believe, but if God was to punish all believers for their sins, His sacrificial death would be meaningless. Christ has already paid the full price for our sins and to demand any further payment or punishment based upon sins committed in the flesh would not only be unjust, but would make Him out to be a liar.

The *Bema seat Judgment* is not to forgive sin, but to *reward* those who have come to Jesus Christ for salvation. The *Great White Throne Judgment* will be to judge all *unbelievers*. Those who are Judged at the Great White Throne will all have died or are still alive in disbelief . All will be cast into the *Lake of Burning Fire* (Revelation 20:15). Many Christians fail to understand or believe how a loving and fair God could do such a thing. God did not choose the Lake of Burning Fire for all unbelievers to spend eternity; they will have made that choice themselves and they will have condemned themselves already. The Judgment of the *Sheep and Goats* will take place *after* the rapture and the Bema Seat Judgment and will follow the second advent of Christ and the Battle of Armageddon. Between the Rapture of all true believers and the Battle of Armageddon, there will be Jews and Gentiles from all over the world that have turned to Christ as their Lord and Savior. Following the Battle of Armageddon, *all* of the people from *all of the nations* will be gathered to the new throne room of Jesus Christ located just north of Jerusalem (Chapter 3) for the Sheep and Goats Judgment, sometimes called the *Judgment of the Nations* (Matthew 25: 31-46). Jesus will separate everyone into two groups: Sheep and Goats. The *Goats* will be cast off into the Bottomless Pit where they will wait for 1000 years to be judged at the Great White Throne. The *sheep* will go into the Millennial Kingdom.

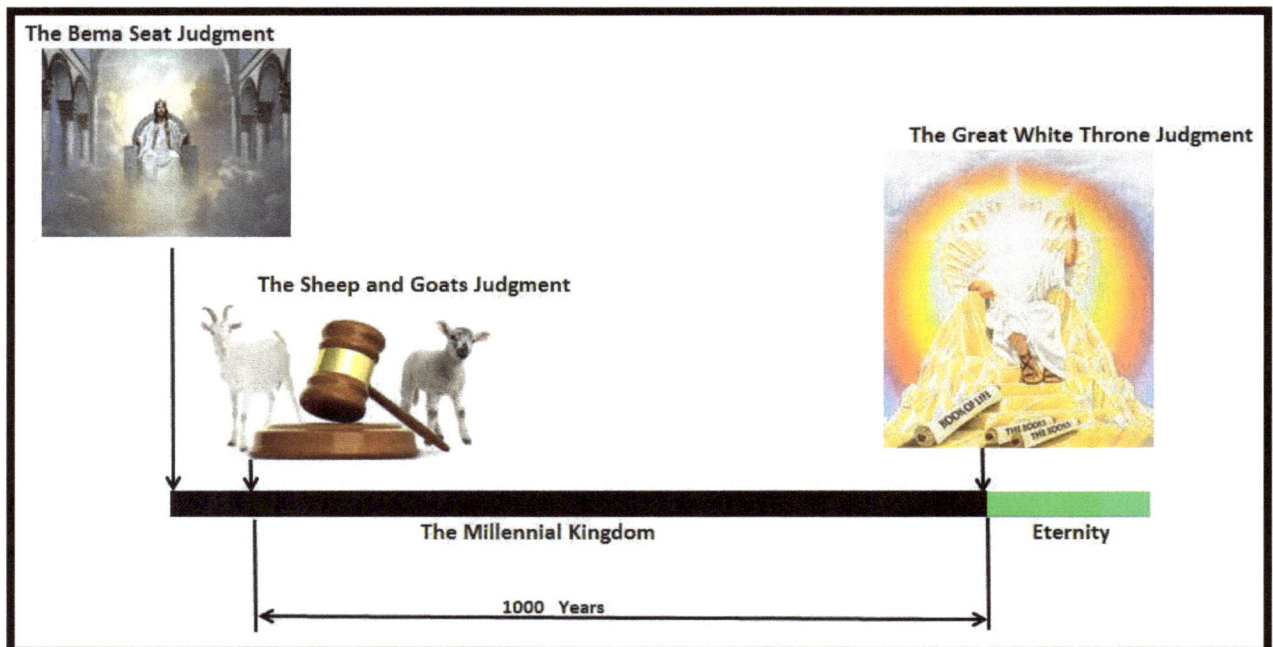

In any discussion of judgments, it should be clearly understood that every person who ever lived will be judged before God. All will be judged for their deeds in the flesh. *Good deeds* which are done by born-again Christians and please God will be rewarded. Those deeds which are done out of servitude and in the flesh will be cast away and burned like *wood, hay and stubble*.

[11] *For other foundation can no man lay than that is laid, which is Jesus Christ.*
[12] *Now if any man build upon this foundation gold, silver, precious stones, wood, hay, stubble;*
[13] *Every man's work shall be made manifest: for the day shall declare it, because it shall be revealed by fire; and the fire shall try every man's work of what sort it is.*
[14] *If any man's work abide which he hath built thereupon, he shall receive a reward.*
[15] *If any man's work shall be burned, he shall suffer loss: but he himself shall be saved; yet so as by fire*   I Corinthians 3: 11-15

Every *unbeliever* will also be judged for their works (Revelation 20:13). Because they have refused the offer of salvation and eternal life by Jesus Christ, they are condemned already. It is conjectured based upon Revelation 20: 13-14 that there will be degrees of punishment based upon good works. All will be cast into the Lake of Burning Fire. This is consistent with the judgment of works for those who are saved. A common belief is that if a person lives a good life and is kind to others that they will attain salvation. This is categorically false. The scriptures are quite clear that there is only one way to attain eternal life: *Believe upon Jesus Christ and you will be saved* (John 3:16, John 14:6). No one can be lost or saved based upon works in the flesh. Salvation and eternal happiness is an individual choice...... condemnation and punishment is an individual choice. *Which choice will you make?*

It is not necessary to be resurrected to stand in judgment. The *Sheep and Goats* judgment will concern only real, ordinary people who have survived the tribulation. When the 1000 year Millennial Kingdom comes to an end, there will be millions of believers who have accepted Jesus Christ as their Lord and savior who are still alive. *What will happen to all of the people who are still alive when the Millennial Kingdom ends?* This is a mystery not revealed in the Holy Scriptures. However, we know that they will be judged (II Corinthians 5:10). It is almost certain that those who have lived and died in the Millennial Kingdom will be judged at the *Great White Throne Judgment*. However, the primary reason for the Great White Throne Judgment is to pass sentence upon all *unbelievers* who have either previously died from all ages or who had been assembled by Satan and destroyed at the battle of *Satan's Last Stand* by God Himself (Revelation 20:12). All whose name is not written in the *Book of Life* will be cast into the *Lake of Burning Fire*. This implies that if anyone is judged that *does* have their name written in the Book of Life will be saved. Eternal punishment in the Lake of Burning Fire is called the *Second Death* (Revelation 20:14).

It is appointed unto men once to die, but after this the judgment   Hebrews 9:27

[6] *And he said unto me, It is done. I am Alpha and Omega, the beginning and the end. I will give unto him that is athirst of the fountain of the water of life freely.*
[7] *He that overcometh shall inherit all things; and I will be his God, and he shall be my son.*
[8] *But the fearful, and unbelieving, and the abominable, and murderers, and whoremongers, and sorcerers, and idolaters, and all liars, shall have their part in the lake which burns with fire and brimstone: which is the second death*   Revelation 21: 6-8

There are those who have accepted Jesus Christ as their Lord and Savior and there will be those who have not during the 1000 year Millennial Kingdom. They must be all be judged or II Corinthians 5:10 and Hebrews 9:27 make no sense. This has to happen at the Great White Throne Judgment. The ultimate goal of every Christian is to be granted eternal life and live with Jesus Christ and the Father forever. *All* who enter into eternity will be sinless and will be clothed in new, incorruptible and sinless heavenly bodies. Our miserable flesh is corrupted with sin and it must be replaced. Paul said that he had died in Christ...this was a *spiritual* transformation. Paul would later be martyred and went through a *physical* transformation. He would die to his physical body of flesh and bones and be rewarded with a new incorruptible and undefiled spiritual body. His flesh would die, but his soul would live on. This will happen to every person who will die a natural death. What will happen to those who remain alive at the rapture or at the end of the Millennial Kingdom is a *mystery* not revealed in the Holy Scriptures. All we know is that they will stand in judgment. Whether a person dies a natural death or not, it is clear that salvation will be offered in the same way that it has since time began....and that is by *faith*. Once a person becomes saved his/her name is inscribed in the *Book of Life*. What Revelation 20:15 establishes is that if *anyone* stands before God at the final judgment...saved or unsaved... If their name is inscribed in the Book of Life they will be saved. If it is not....They will be sentenced to eternity in the Lake of Burning Fire. *And whosoever was not found written in the book of life was cast into the lake of fire* Revelation 20:15

The Bema Seat Judgment

The 3.5 years of wrath by Satan upon all Jews and Christians after he has been cast down to the earth will have been completed. The rapture of all believers who are still alive and the resurrection of all believers who have died in Christ will take place *before* the Wrath of God is unleashed upon all the earth (the 7 vial or bowl judgments). Those who believe upon Jesus Christ are not destined to go through God's Wrath. This is a *Pre-Wrath rapture* position and will save all true believers from God's Wrath. This is the result of a *pre-tribulation rapture* or a rapture which will take place after the 7 trumpet judgments have occurred which are the Wrath of Satan. The real issue is: *Will the rapture rescue all believers from only the Wrath of God or from both the Wrath of Satan and the Wrath of God?* Either rapture is based upon the belief that there is never any place in scripture that promises a believer in Christ that they will be exempt from either tribulation or the Wrath of Satan. In summary, A *Pre-tribulation* rapture is based upon the belief that those who accept Christ as their Lord and Savior will be removed from the earth before the period of tribulation begins: A true pre-wrath rapture will remove all believers from the earth *before* the Wrath of God falls upon Satan and all unbelievers, but *after* the Wrath of Satan has fallen upon all earth dwellers. (See Phillips; The Book of Revelation: *Mysteries Revealed* for scriptural justification of a Pre-wrath rapture). In either case, the rapture of all believers has taken place, and the Wrath of God has fallen upon all of those who still remain.

   Note: A pre-tribulation rapture is almost always associated with a 7 year tribulation period. Hence, all true believers (living or dead) are removed before the 7 year tribulation period begins. A few have proposed that the rapture will take place at the mid-point of 7 years, or when Satan is cast out of the heavenlies. However, this appears to be an impossible position since after Satan is cast down to the earth in Revelation 12:

.....the dragon (Satan) .....went to make war with the remnant of her (the Sun clothed woman) seed, which keep the commandments of God, and have the testimony of Jesus Christ Revelation 12:17

These are obviously Christians who are alive...Where did they come from if the rapture had just taken place? After studying all possible positions, it is believed that the rapture will occur after the 7th trumpet sounds and before the Wrath of God is unleashed upon Satan and all unbelievers. Please read Revelation 11: 15-18 with an open mind and laying aside all pre-conceived notions. Those who have read almost universally been taught a Pre-tribulation rapture will cringe at the possibility of having to experience the Wrath of Satan. They would rather believe that a Christian only needs to just "hang on" and not worry about anything that is revealed in the Book of Revelation. Why worry...or why study the Book of Revelation....That would be a waste of time. If the tribulation period of time begins and Christians are not all raptured out...What a privilege and opportunity to serve our Lord Jesus Christ! There will be an opportunity to proclaim the gospel to all unbelievers and win many souls to Christ!! But wait one might say... I might be martyred...you mean just as Christ was when He died for our sins? Remember that the real reason for the entire tribulation period is to bring all Jews into eternal life through Jesus Christ. I want to be there!!! For a full scriptural justification and a presentation of a Pre-wrath rapture as the 7th trumpet sounds, see Phillips; The Book of Revelation: *Mysteries Revealed*.

Christ will hold the Bema seat Judgment in heaven and then wed His Bride. He will then take His bride to His hidden Chambers for His "honeymoon".

Come, my people, enter thou into thy chambers, and shut thy doors about thee: hide thyself as it were for a little moment, until the indignation be overpast   Isaiah 26: 10

Gather the people, sanctify the congregation, assemble the elders, gather the children, and those that suck the breasts: let the bridegroom go forth of his **chamber**, *and the bride out of her closet*   Joel 2:16

Wherefore if they shall say unto you, Behold, he is in the desert; go not forth: behold, he is in the secret chambers; believe it not   Matthew 24:26

As the Wrath of God is unleashed upon the earth, Satan in his anger will gather an army of unbelievers and once again attack the City of Jerusalem. He will have already killed 2/3 of all the people who live in Israel (Zachariah 13:8). Just as it looks as if all hope is lost, Jesus Christ will suddenly descend from heaven to the Mount of Olives just outside of Jerusalem. Satan will abandon his assault on Jerusalem to battle Jesus Christ, and he will assemble an army of unbelievers to a place called *Armageddon* just outside of Jerusalem. Christ will then move against Satan and he will totally destroy Satan and all of his forces. The Battle of Armageddon will be on the last day of the Church age.

Comment: The following verses from Chapter 20 in the Book of Revelation describe the Wrath of God.

[1] *And I heard a great voice out of the temple saying to the seven angels, Go your ways, and pour out the vials of the **wrath of God upon the earth**.*

[2] *And the first went, and poured out his vial upon the earth; and there fell a noisome and grievous sore upon the men which had the mark of the beast, and upon them which worshipped his image.*

[3] *And the second angel poured out his vial upon the sea; and it became as the blood of a dead man: and every living soul died in the sea.*

[4] *And the third angel poured out his vial upon the rivers and fountains of waters; and they became blood.*

[5] *And I heard the angel of the waters say, Thou art righteous, O Lord, which art, and wast, and shalt be, because thou hast judged thus.*

[6] *For they have shed the blood of saints and prophets, and thou hast given them blood to drink; for they are worthy.*

[7] *And I heard another out of the altar say, Even so, Lord God Almighty, true and righteous are thy judgments.*

[8] *And the fourth angel poured out his vial upon the sun; and power was given unto him to scorch men with fire.*

[9] *And men were scorched with great heat, and blasphemed the name of God, which hath power over these plagues: and they repented not to give him glory.*

[10] *And the fifth angel poured out his vial upon the seat of the beast; and his kingdom was full of darkness; and they gnawed their tongues for pain,*

[11] *And blasphemed the God of heaven because of their pains and their sores, and repented not of their deeds.*

[12] *And the sixth angel poured out his vial upon the great river Euphrates; and the water thereof was dried up, that the way of the kings of the east might be prepared.*

[13] *And I saw three unclean spirits like frogs come out of the mouth of the dragon, and out of the mouth of the beast, and out of the mouth of the false prophet.*

[14] *For they are the spirits of devils, working miracles, which go forth unto the kings of the earth and of the whole world, to gather them to the battle of that great day of God Almighty.*

[15] *Behold, I come as a thief. Blessed is he that watches, and keeps his garments, lest he walk naked, and they see his shame.*

[16] *And he gathered them together into a place called in the Hebrew tongue Armageddon.*

[17] *And the seventh angel poured out his vial into the air; and there came a great voice out of the temple of heaven, from the throne, saying, **It is done***   Revelation 20: 1-17

It has previously been stated that a *Pre-wrath rapture* is proposed as opposed to a *Pre-tribulation Rapture* which would take place before the tribulation period begins.. Please note that in Revelation 20: 1-17 there is absolutely no warning...no instruction...or no mention whatsoever of Christians. This is because they have *all* been raptured out. In fact, there is an admonition to those who watch and do not defile their garments of righteousness. They are watching and waiting to be raptured. *What about those that would accept Christ after either a Pre-tribulation or a Pre-wrath rapture?*

For we must all appear before the judgment seat of Christ; that every one may receive   the things done in his body, according to that he hath done, whether it be good or bad
        II Corinthians 5:10

Examining this verse in context, it is clear that Paul is speaking of both believers and unbelievers. All believers will be judged for rewards at the Bema Seat judgment, and all unbelievers will be judged at the Great White Throne Judgment. There is no doubt that the gift of eternal life is obtained by faith and appropriated by grace: No person can work their way into heaven. However, there are many passages of scripture which confirm that good works done in the flesh will be rewarded. This is the main purpose of the *Bema Seat Judgment*. This will include everyone (Jews and Gentiles, alive or dead)) who have accepted Christ as their redeemer and Gentiles who have believed that Jesus Christ is their Lord and savior. All have been saved by faith and grace, and all will be judged for reward of faithful service. Both Jews and Gentiles who survive the Great Tribulation will have a role to play in the 1000 year Millennial Kingdom. Those who are worthy will assume more responsibility than those who have no good works or only a few. Do not fail to recognize that those who are judged at the Bema Seat are redeemed Jews *and* gentiles. They have all just participated in the *Marriage of the Lamb* (Phillips; The Book of Revelation Mysteries Revealed, Revelation 19:7)). They are now judged for rewards and service in the Kingdom.

> At the judgment seat of Christ, believers are rewarded based on how faithfully they served Christ (1 Corinthians 9:4-27; II Timothy 2:5). Some of the things we might be judged on are how well we obeyed the Great Commission (Matthew 28:18-20), how victorious we were over sin (Romans 6:1-4), and how well we controlled our tongues (James 3:1-9). The Bible speaks of believers receiving various types of crowns based upon how faithfully they served Christ (1 Corinthians 9:4-27; II Timothy 2:5, II Timothy 4:8, James 1:12, I Peter 5:4, and Revelation 2:10).   https://www.gotquestions.org/judgment-seat-Christ.html

[10] *But why dost thou judge thy brother? or why dost thou set at nought thy brother? for we shall all stand before the judgment seat of Christ.*
[11] *For it is written, As I live, saith the Lord, every knee shall bow to me, and every tongue shall confess to God.*
[12] *So then every one of us shall give account of himself to God*   Romans 14: 10-12

Blessed is the man that endures temptation: for when he is tried, he shall receive the crown of life, which the Lord hath promised to them that love him   James 1:12

The name *Bema Seat* is not found in the Holy Scriptures. This judgment takes its common name from imagery related to the Olympic Games. In each race, a judge would sit in an elevated seat at the finish line. As the participants crossed the line, he was to determine who came in first, second, third or fourth place. Rewards were then given to those finishers commensurate with their place. Some who ran the race were not rewarded, but they were recognized as finishing the race.

Wherefore seeing we also are compassed about with so great a cloud of witnesses, let us lay aside every weight, and the sin which doth so easily beset us, and let us run with patience the race that is set before us   Hebrews 12:1

[10] *According to the grace of God which is given unto me, as a wise master builder, I have laid the foundation, and another buildeth thereon. But let every man take heed how he buildeth thereupon.*
[11] *For other foundation can no man lay than that is laid, which is Jesus Christ.*
[12] *Now if any man build upon this foundation gold, silver, precious stones, wood, hay, stubble;*
[13] *Every man's work shall be made manifest: for the day shall declare it, because it shall be revealed by fire; and the fire shall try every man's work of what sort it is.*
[14] *If any man's work abide which he hath built thereupon, he shall receive a reward.*
[15] *If any man's work shall be burned, he shall suffer loss: but he himself shall be saved; yet so as by fire*   I Corinthians 10: 11-15

There is no specific identification of this judgment as the *Bema Seat Judgment* nor exactly when it will occur. There is no doubt from the verses given above that it *will* occur. It is specifically identified in Revelation 11.

*And the nations were angry, and **thy wrath is come**, and the time of the dead, that they should be judged, and that thou shouldest give reward unto thy servants the prophets, and to the saints, and them that fear thy name, small and great; and shouldest destroy them which destroy the earth*   Revelation 11:18

Revelation 11:15 is written immediately after the 7th trumpet sounds. The 7 trumpets are the *Wrath of Satan*. The *wrath to come* is the 7 Bowl Judgments which are the *Wrath of God* (Revelation 15:1, Revelation 16:1). Revelation 11:18 clearly states that the *dead are about to be judged*. Carefully note that rewards will be given to: (1) The Old Testament prophets and (2) The Saints. This can only refer to the resurrection and snatching away of all believers at the *rapture* of Old Testament men of faith and the New Covenant believers (alive and dead). Revelation 11:15 does not imply that this judgment will take place *immediately*, but that (1) The Wrath of the Seven Bowls had come and that (2) A Judgment will take place for all believers alive and dead. The *judge* is not identified, but in his Gospel the apostle John indicates that it will be Jesus Christ.

For the Father judges no man, but hath committed all judgment unto the Son   John 5:22

The Bema Seat Judgment will take place after the rapture before the throne of God in Heaven. This conclusion is based upon the following sequence of events. The Bema Seat participants are all blood-bought believers who are raptured out to escape the Wrath of God (Romans 5:9, I Thessalonians 1:10, , I Thessalonians 5:9, Revelation 15:1,Revelation 16:1). Following the 7th Vial/Bowl judgment Satan will attack Jerusalem at the Armageddon Assault. Just as it seems that the City would be destroyed and all of the inhabitants murdered, Christ appears on the Mount of Olives and saves 1/2 of the people. When Jesus Christ appears at His 2nd advent He will not be alone. He is followed by a great army who are clothed in fine, white. linen: *And the armies which were in heaven followed him upon white horses, clothed in **fine linen, white and clean*** (Revelation 19:14). Those who are saved and enter heaven and those who are martyred for Christ will be given white robes (Revelation 3: 5,18, Revelation 6:11, Revelation 7: 9, 13-14). This army that follows Christ is the *Bride of Christ*. They are identified in Revelation 19: 7-8.

[7] *Let us be glad and rejoice, and give honor to him: for the marriage of the Lamb is come, and his wife hath made herself ready.*
[8] *And to her was granted that she should be **arrayed in fine linen, clean and white**: for the fine linen is the righteousness of saints*   Revelation 19: 7-8

The Bride of Christ has just been clothed in clean, white linen and was married to Christ following the return to heaven after the rapture. After the Battle of Armageddon, there will be a joyful marriage supper on the earth (Revelation 19:9), probably on the Feast of Tabernacles.

The Judgment of the Sheep and Goats (Judgment of the Nations)

Matthew 25: 31-46 is the only description of this unusual judgment.

[31] *When the Son of man shall come in his glory, and all the holy angels with him, then shall he sit upon the throne of his glory:*
[32] *And before him shall be gathered all nations: and he shall separate them one from another, as a shepherd divides his sheep from the goats:*
[33] *And he shall set the sheep on his right hand, but the goats on the left.*
[34] *Then shall the King say unto them on his right hand, Come, ye blessed of my Father, inherit the kingdom prepared for you from the foundation of the world:*
[35] *For I was an hungry, and ye gave me meat: I was thirsty, and ye gave me drink: I was a stranger, and ye took me in:*
[36] *Naked, and ye clothed me: I was sick, and ye visited me: I was in prison, and ye came unto me.*
[37] *Then shall the righteous answer him, saying, Lord, when saw we thee an hungry, and fed thee? or thirsty, and gave thee drink?*
[38] *When saw we thee a stranger, and took thee in? or naked, and clothed thee?*
[39] *Or when saw we thee sick, or in prison, and came unto thee?*
[40] *And the King shall answer and say unto them, Verily I say unto you, Inasmuch as ye have done it unto one of the least of these my brethren, ye have done it unto me.*
[41] *Then shall he say also unto them on the left hand, Depart from me, ye cursed, into everlasting fire, prepared for the devil and his angels:*

[42] *For I was hungry, and ye gave me no meat: I was thirsty, and ye gave me no drink:*
[43] *I was a stranger, and ye took me not in: naked, and ye clothed me not: sick, and in prison, and ye visited me not.*
[44] *Then shall they also answer him, saying, Lord, when saw we thee an hungry, or thirsty, or a stranger, or naked, or sick, or in prison, and did not minister unto thee?*
[45] *Then shall he answer them, saying, Verily I say unto you, Inasmuch as ye did it not to one of the least of these, ye did it not to me.*
[46] *And these shall go away into everlasting punishment: but the righteous into life eternal*
Matthew 25: 31-46

From Matthew 25:31 the time when this judgment will take place is revealed as *When the Son of man shall come in his glory.* This clearly says that this judgment cannot take place until Jesus Christ returns again at His 2nd advent, and Christ will not come again until the Jews have finally turned to Jesus Christ as their redeemer, the Church Age is over and the *fullness of the Gentiles* has come to pass (Romans 11:25). In Matthew 24 Christ has briefly spoken of conditions that will be happening on the earth in the latter days, which include the suddenness of His 2nd coming. In Matthew 25 He warns the Jews to be prepared in the *Parable of the Wise and Foolish Virgins* (Matthew 25: 1-13). In Matthew 25: 14-29 Christ speaks the *Parable of the Talents*, and makes it clear that there will be different rewards and responsibility in eternity for those that have done good works in the flesh. Make no mistake about it.....Salvation is not by works but by faith and grace. However: *Faith without works is dead. What does this mean if works will not save you*? It means believing in faith that Jesus Christ has forgiven our sins, and that as He was raised from the grave and conquered death is all that is required to obtain eternal life. However, when one is saved there is a *spiritual transformation* that takes place. A truly born-again Christian will *want* to serve Christ and *work* to bring others to salvation in Jesus Christ. Sincere faith should always be manifested in good works. The scriptures also teach that once one has believed in the Son of God that he/she is born again *into Christ* by the Holy Spirit (I Corinthians 6:11, I Corinthians 12:13) and their name is inscribed in the *Book of Life* (Revelation 3:5). From that point on, a true Christian should not question that they will conquer death and receive eternal life. Being eternally saved and not having any good works is much like a car without a battery. It is still a car and will always be a car, but it cannot fulfill its purpose because it has no life. There will be many Christians who will not do many good works and serve Christ, but they are still saved....they will just not get any rewards in the hereafter. The *Judgment of the Sheep and Goats,* which is also called the *Judgment of the Nations*, was revealed by Christ Himself in His great *Olivet Discourse*. The context is that it will probably take place in the early days of the 1000 year Millennial Kingdom. The Battle of Armageddon has just been fought, and Satan and His army of disbelievers have been destroyed by Christ. However, all over the world there will be people who are Jews and Christians that have refused to bow down to Satan and have not taken the *Mark of the Beast*. There will be people in the nations of the world that have been hiding in the mountains (Revelation 6:15) or shut up in their homes hearing what is happening in Israel. Some will be Christians and some will be unsaved. They will all be gathered to Christ who is now sitting upon His Throne of Glory in His Millennial

Palace: Here they will all be judged. The Judgment of the Sheep and Goats is one of the most difficult concepts in the Olivet Discourse, and it will be carefully interpreted and discussed.

The *sheep and goats* judgment will take place when Christ *arrives in glory* with His *Holy Angels* (Matthew 25:31). The only point in time when this is possible is when Jesus returns to fight the Battle of Armageddon. *The armies which were in heaven followed him upon white horses, clothed in fine linen, white and clean* (Revelation 19: 14). Most commentators say that those who follow Him are *saints* in their robes of white. This may well be true, but Jesus could also be accompanied by a heavenly host of angels based upon Matthew 25:31.

[**31**] *When the Son of man shall come in his glory, and all the holy angels with him, then shall he sit upon the throne of his glory:*
[**32**] *And before him shall be gathered all nations: and he shall separate them one from another, as a shepherd divides his sheep from the goats*   Matthew 25: 31-32

Matthew 25:32 says that *all of the nations* shall be gathered to him. The Greek word which is translated as *nations* is *ethnos*. Ethnos can mean a race, people, nation, heathen world, Gentiles. it is usually translated as *gentiles* in the New Testament but not always. The proper meaning of Ethnos should be determined by context.

Some have read this literally, and asserted that entire nations will be separated one from another. This cannot be true: Nations do not feed people, give them clothes or are cast into everlasting punishment. This is the fate of individuals. The angels will gather all the people from all nations to Him for judgment. It is more than interesting that Jesus Christ immediately separates one individual from another. He knows by sight whether any one person is to be classified as a *sheep* or a *goat*. Jesus said: *I am the good shepherd, and know my sheep, and am known of mine* (John 10:14). There is no mention of faith, grace or salvation. Those who are the *sheep* are placed on His right and those who are Goats are placed on His left. The sheep will enter His Kingdom and inherit life eternal, but the goats will be cast into everlasting punishment. In order to understand what is happening, suppose we discuss what is happening in relevant groups of scripture.

[**31**] *When the **Son of man shall come in his glory**, and all the holy angels with him, then shall he **sit upon the throne of his glory**:*
[**32**] *And before him shall be gathered all nations: and **he shall separate them** one from another, as a shepherd divides his sheep from the goats:*
[**33**] *And he shall set the sheep on his right hand, but the goats on the left.*
[**34**] *Then shall the King say unto them on his right hand, Come, ye blessed of my Father, inherit the kingdom prepared for you from the foundation of the world*   Matthew 25: 31-34

Looking at Matthew 25: 31-34 several things are evident: (1) When Christ *comes* He is going to Judge the nations from His *earthly throne*. His throne of Glory will be just north of Jerusalem at the site where Shiloh once stood. This was prophesied almost 6,000 years ago.

The scepter shall not depart from Judah, nor a lawgiver from between his feet, until Shiloh come; and unto him shall the gathering of the people be   Genesis 49:10

In the Hebrew language *Shiloh* means *peace*. It is there that the *Prince of Peace* will rule and reign during the 1000 year Millennial Kingdom (2) People from *All nations* will be brought before Christ. The rapture has occurred and the Battle of Armageddon has been fought. Many people in Israel (2/3) have been killed during the tribulation period of 3.5 years but 1/3 still remain. In addition, there are people all over the world who have survived this time of persecution. Many have not taken the Mark of the Beast and they have held firm in the faith, but there will also be many who have never believed in Jesus Christ. These people may not really know what is going on before their very eyes. Those who have become Christians and those that are unsaved will be both Jews and gentiles, and they will be scattered around the world. In 2018 there were over 7 million Jews in the United States alone. (2) Christ will immediately divide the people from all nations into two groups: *Sheep* and *Goats* (Matthew 25:32). Notice that Christ does not initially mention *why* or on what basis. He declares that those on His right (Sheep) will go into the *Kingdom* and into eternal life (See Matthew 25:46) and those on His left (Goats) into the Burning Lake of Fire where they will be tormented forever. Surely there should be no doubt as to why one person is a *sheep* and the other is a *Goat*. These people are all *alive* and no one can inherit eternal life unless they accept Jesus Christ as their Lord and Savior, not as a group but as individuals. It is their eternal choice. No man or woman will ever enter into the Kingdom or into eternal life unless they have been saved in Christ: There is no other way. Christ said: *I am the way, the truth and the life. No man cometh unto the Father except by me.* If this was all there was to this discourse, no one would be confused and all true believers would understand exactly what is happening. However, Christ now continues.

[**35**] *For I was an hungry, and ye gave me meat: I was thirsty, and ye gave me drink: I was a stranger, and ye took me in:*
[**36**] *Naked, and ye clothed me: I was sick, and ye visited me: I was in prison, and ye came unto me*   Matthew 25: 35-36

Christ has been dead for almost 2000 years, but He now proclaims that he was hungry..... He was thirsty..... He needed clothes..... He was in prison. *How can this be*? We recall that when Christ met Saul of Tarsus on the Road to Damascus after He had ascended to Heaven He said:

Saul, Saul, why persecutest thou me?   Acts 9:4

Amazing!! Christ had died and was buried, but He declares that Saul has been persecuting *Him* !! This is an astounding statement. Anytime that a Christian is suffering and being persecuted, he or she is not alone. Christ said that: *I will never leave thee, nor forsake thee* (Hebrews 13:5). What a glorious promise. He will use the Holy Spirit to bring others to your rescue and provide aid and comfort if it is in His eternal plan to do so.

[**37**] *Then shall the righteous answer him, saying, Lord, when saw we thee hungry, and fed thee? or thirsty, and gave thee drink?*
[**38**] *When saw we thee a stranger, and took thee in? or naked, and clothed thee?*
[**39**] *Or when saw we thee sick, or in prison, and came unto thee?*   Matthew 25: 37-39
Those who are righteous (Sheep) are stunned and confused. *When did they feed Him, or give Him a drink or give Him clothes?*
[**40**] *And the King shall answer and say unto them, Verily I say unto you, Inasmuch as ye have done it unto one of the least of these my brethren, ye have done it unto me.*
Matthew 25: 37-40

Just as when Christ spoke to Saul, He tells them that if they have done these things to help His *brethren*, then they have done them to Him. *Who is His* **brethren**? This has been a highly debated topic. The Greek word translated *brethren* is *adelphos*, which is used 21 times in the New Testament and it is always translated in the King James Bible as either *brethren* or *brother*. According to the *Strong's Concordance* it means "a member of the same religious community or another Christian, or a brother". In fact, *adelphos* is almost universally translated as "brother" in subsequent versions of the Holy Bible. Considering the context, it is believed that Jesus is talking about both Jews and Gentiles that have been aided by others and have survived the tribulation. They are all *in Christ* and are all sons or daughters.

[**44**] *Then shall they also answer him, saying, Lord, when saw we thee an hungry, or thirsty, or a stranger, or naked, or sick, or in prison, and did not minister unto thee?*
[**45**] *Then shall he answer them, saying, Verily I say unto you, Inasmuch as ye* **did it not** *to one of the least of these, ye did it not to me*   Matthew 25: 44-45

They also is referring to the Goats on His left. They also failed to understand. They asked Him: "When did we see you hungry or thirsty or downtrodden and *did not* help you?" Then Christ answered to the goats: "If you saw any of my brethren suffering and needing help and did nothing, you were doing nothing for Me personally". This is serious business.....eternal joy or eternal suffering is at stake.

[**41**] *Then shall he say also unto them on the left hand, Depart from me, ye cursed, into everlasting fire, prepared for the devil and his angels:*
[**42**] *For I was hungry, and ye gave me no meat: I was thirsty, and ye gave me no drink:*
[**43**] *I was a stranger, and ye took me not in: naked, and ye clothed me not: sick, and in prison, and ye visited me not.*

There is nothing that can be said and done by either the Sheep or the Goats as they are separated by Christ. Those who will placed on His right (Sheep) have been saved by faith and grace, and those that had been placed upon His left (Goats) would be sentenced to eternal damnation.

And these (the goats) *shall go away into everlasting punishment: but the righteous* (the sheep) *into life eternal*   Matthew 25:46

Each individual had been offered salvation and eternal life, but sadly only those on His right accepted the gift. The confusing part is that the separation of the saved from the lost seem to be based upon *works* and not *faith*. This can never be true. *What then does it mean that those on His right had helped his brethren and that those on His left had not?* Here we must use spiritual discernment. Those who have been saved by grace and faith will help their brethren not because it will earn them salvation, but because *that is who they are*. We are to conform to the spiritual image of Christ and just as He loved all people we are to do the same. We are *blessed to be a blessing*, and we are given riches in this world not to store them up but to use them to help others. This is how a true Christian can be recognized, and not by how loudly or how often he or she prays. Those on His right hand have shared what they had and helped others even as the wrath of the tribulation was all around them. They will be allowed to enter into the Millennial Kingdom by *faith* and *grace* and they will be rewarded for their good deeds during this special period of time. Note that those who have accepted Jesus Christ as their redeemer, Lord and savior have all done so since the rapture.

After the *Wedding Supper of the Lamb* takes place (Revelation 19:7), The *Millennial Kingdom* will begin.

The Great White Throne Judgment

After a thousand years have passed the Millennial Kingdom will come to an end. It is incredible and hard to believe, but sinful man will apostatize and reject Jesus Christ as Lord of Lord and King of Kings, even as he rules and reigns amongst them. They have:

....changed the truth of God into a lie, and worshipped and served the creature more than the Creator, who is blessed for ever   Romans 1:25

God has always had only one plan for mankind. He created Adam and Eve to live forever and He wanted to walk among them as a friend. When Adam and Eve both sinned, this plan was interrupted. But God will yet fulfill His original plan. He chose Abraham to be a Father of many nations, and chose Israel to be His own people. He promised them that they would be a *peculiar people among all nations*, and that they would be given a land of promise to inherit as their own. In the fullness of time God sent His only Son who lived a sinless life, and then offered Himself as the perfect sacrificial Lamb of God. *He who knew no sin became sin for us* and died on the cross of Calvary for the sins of the whole world..... Jews and Gentiles alike. He defeated death when he rose from the dead after 3 full days and 3 full nights, and then sent the Holy Spirit as a guarantee to all who would accept Him as Lord and Savior that they would also defeat death and be raised from the grave.

God will someday dwell upon this earth and rule and reign with His Son Jesus Christ, but not until He has finished His Covenant with Abraham, and sin and death are completely destroyed. This will be fulfilled in the Millennial Kingdom. One of the attributes of God is that He is Holy and cannot live or exist in the presence of sin. Although the Millennial Kingdom started sinless, it would not remain so. Although Satan will be bound for 1000 years in the Bottomless Pit, the sin nature inherited from Adam will still be in everyone who would live in an earthly body during the Kingdom. It must be understood that before God can fulfill His eternal plan four things must come to pass: (1) All unbelievers must be removed from the Earth (2) All sin must be removed from the earth (3) Satan and all of his fallen angels must be cast into the Lake of Burning Fire (4) The earth, which was cursed by God when Adam and Eve were cast out of the Garden of Eden, must be cleansed and renovated with fire. All unbelievers will be judged and cast into the Burning Lake of Fire at the Great White Throne Judgment.

[7] *And when the thousand years are expired, Satan shall be loosed out of his prison,*
[8] *And shall go out to deceive the nations which are in the four quarters of the earth, Gog and Magog, to gather them together to battle: the number of whom is as the sand of the sea.*
[9] *And they went up on the breadth of the earth, and compassed the camp of the saints about, and the beloved city: and fire came down from God out of heaven, and devoured them.*
[10] *And the devil that deceived them was cast into the lake of fire and brimstone, where the beast and the false prophet are, and shall be tormented day and night forever and ever.*
[11] *And I saw a great white throne, and him that sat on it, from whose face the earth and the heaven fled away; and there was found no place for them.*
[12] *And I saw the dead, small and great, stand before God; and the books were opened: and another book was opened, which is the book of life: and the dead were judged out of those things which were written in the books, according to their works.*
[13] *And the sea gave up the dead which were in it; and death and hell delivered up the dead which were in them: and they were judged every man according to their works.*
[14] *And death and hell were cast into the lake of fire. This is the second death.*
[15] *And whosoever was not found written in the book of life was cast into the lake of fire*
Revelation 20: 7-15

At the end of the Millennial Kingdom unbelievers from all ages will be judged at the *White Throne Judgment.* During the 1000 year Millennial Kingdom people that have been born will be scattered all over the planet. There will be a mixture of unbelievers and believers just as there is today. Satan has been bound in the bottomless pit for 1000 years, and when he is loosed *out of his prison* (Revelation 20:7) he will go forth across the 4 corners of the earth (Revelation 20:8) to gather all unbelievers to Jerusalem, where he will attack the sanctuary of Jesus Christ and the Holy City. There will be so many unbelievers who have repopulated the earth that : *their number will be as the sand of the sea.*

[7] *And when the thousand years are expired, Satan shall be loosed out of his prison,*
[8] *And shall go out to deceive the nations which are in the four quarters of the earth, Gog and Magog, to gather them together to battle: the number of whom is as the sand of the sea.*

[9] *And they went up on the breadth of the earth, and compassed the camp of the saints about, and the beloved city:* **and fire came down from God out of heaven,** *and devoured* them
Revelation 20: 7-9

Satan and his army will march upon Jerusalem in an assault called *Satan's Last Stand*. This time they will not enter the city, but **God** *Will devour them all with fire.* This time there is no mention of Jesus Christ nor of a heavenly army. God created Lucifer and God will remove him. After this final encounter, Satan will be cast into the *Lake of Burning Fire* where he will be tortured forever. Those who have been slain at this battle and all of the unbelievers from ages past will be assembled before *God* where they will all be judged at the *Great White Throne Judgment*: Not for salvation but for eternal punishment in the Lake of Fire. They will all be judged for *their works* (Revelation 20:13). The decision as to whether anyone will spend eternity in the Lake of Burning Fire or be with Jesus in the New Jerusalem (Chapter 8) is simple and does not involve any deeds or works done in the flesh. It is based upon only one thing that is so simple a child can understand....*What did you do with my Son*? Believe in faith that He died for your sins and that He was the Son of the living God or did you refuse to believe?

Hell is a place where all of the dead unbelievers will reside until they are called to the *White Throne Judgment*. Hell is composed of two compartments: *Paradise* and a *Place of Torments*. Unbelievers from all ages will remain in the Place of Torments until they are called to judgment (Phillips: *Life After Death*). We are told that there are angels in heaven who are responsible for keeping *books* which contain the deeds (good and bad)which every person has done while here on earth. There is one special book called the *Book of Life*. Once a person has been born again and become a blood-bought Christian, his or her name is inscribed in the Book of Life. There is a great deal of debate over whether or not a Christian can lose their salvation and have their name erased from the Book of Life. In Revelation 3:5 Jesus Christ assures the Church at Sardis that once one's name is written in the Book of Life it can *never* be erased.

He that overcometh, the same shall be clothed in white raiment; and I will not blot out his name out of the Book of Life, but I will confess his name before my Father, and before his angels
Revelation 3:5

> The promise in Revelation 3:5 *that I will not erase his name from the book of life* does not necessarily imply that some *do* have their names erased. It simply says, to the one who has *overcome* and is in the book, and who conquers in faith: Their name will never be blotted out. In other words, being erased is a fearful prospect, which cannot happen to those who believe and persevere.   John Piper   https://www.desiringgod.org/

At the Great White Throne Judgment the sea will gave up their dead (There will be no sea in eternity, Revelation 21:1), and all unbelievers in Hell (Place of Torments) will give up their prisoners.....and all who were *not found written in the book of life was cast into the lake of fire.*

And the sea gave up the dead which were in it; and death and hell delivered up the dead which were in them: and they were judged every man according to their works Revelation 20:13

The last enemy that shall be destroyed is death I Corinthians 15:26

There is no flesh and blood left on the planet earth. All of God's enemies have been *put under His feet* (I Corinthians 15:25), all sin has been removed from the planet earth and Satan has finally met his final destiny.

[**21**] *For since by man came death, by man came also the resurrection of the dead.*
[**22**] *For as in Adam all die, even so in Christ shall all be made alive.*
[**23**] *But every man in his own order: Christ the firstfruits; afterward they that are Christ's at his coming.*
[**24**] **Then cometh the end, when he shall have delivered up the kingdom to God, even the Father; when he shall have put down all rule and all authority and power.**
[**25**] *For he must reign,* ***till he hath put all enemies under his feet****.*
[**26**] *The last enemy that shall be destroyed is death.*
[**27**] *For he hath put all things under his feet. But when he saith, all things are put under him, it is manifest that he is excepted, which did put all things under him.*
[**28**] *And when all things shall be subdued unto him, then shall the Son also himself be subject unto him that put all things under him, that God may be all in all* I Corinthians 15: 21-28

Sin and the Man of Sin (II Thessalonians 3:10) have both been destroyed, and It is now time to purify the *earth* with *fire* (II Peter 3:7, 10-12) and to begin eternity.

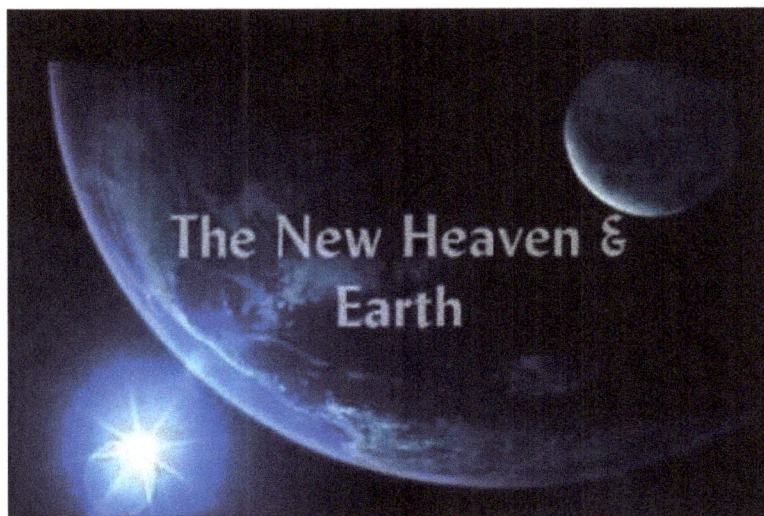

The New Heaven & Earth

Chapter 8

The New Jerusalem and Eternity

A proper understanding of the New Jerusalem and the role that it will play in eternity is important to understanding the eternal plan of God. The New Jerusalem is identified in the Holy Scriptures in only two places: Revelation 21:2 and Revelation 3:1.

[**1**] *And I saw a new heaven and a new earth: for the first heaven and the first earth were passed away; and there was no more sea.*

[**2**] *And I John saw the holy city, New Jerusalem, coming down from God out of heaven, prepared as a bride adorned for her husband*   Revelation 21: 1-2

Revelation 21: 3-27 provides a detailed description of the New Jerusalem.

God created the heavens and the earth, and He said: *it was good* (Genesis 1: 1-10). He created the animal kingdom, fish and birds and then He created Adam and Eve to live in a paradise called *Eden*. Adam and Eve were to *replenish the earth* and have *dominion over all that God had created* (Genesis 1:28). There were trees in the garden with all manners of fruit to feed Adam and Eve. God walked with them in the cool of the evening and they communed every day. In the midst of the Garden stood a tree with beautiful fruit which was called the tree of the *Knowledge of Good and Evil* and Adam and Eve could do anything that they wanted to do but eat of this forbidden fruit. God said that the day that they eat this fruit; *they would surely die.* We all know the terrible story. Satan appeared to Eve as a beautiful serpent and both Adam and Eve ate of the fruit. Man had sinned, and since God cannot stand in the presence of sin both Adam and Eve were cast out of the Garden and they both began to die that very day. Adam did not immediately die, but he began to die when he sinned. He lived 930 years after he was banned from the Garden of Eden. Man and God had been separated and alienated because of sin. *The wages of sin is death....*and spiritual death is separation from God. But God in His mercy sent His only Son Jesus Christ to redeem all men from sin and death.

Wherefore, as by one man sin entered into the world, and death by sin; and so death passed upon all men, for that all have sinned   Romans 5:10

For the wages of sin is death; but the gift of God is eternal life through Jesus Christ our Lord
Romans 6:23

God not only expunged Adam and Eve from the Garden of Eden, but He also put a curse on the earth.

And unto Adam he said, Because thou hast hearkened unto the voice of thy wife, and hast eaten of the tree, of which I commanded thee, saying, Thou shalt not eat of it: cursed is the ground for thy sake; in sorrow shalt thou eat of it all the days of thy life   Genesis 3:17

God always had one plan for man. He desired to live among His creation and walk and talk with man just as He did in the garden of Eden, but Adam fell and imputed his sin to every person who ever lived upon the earth. Before He would restore man and dwell among them, every man would need to be redeemed and cleansed of all sin.... and the earth had to be purified and the curse removed.   All sin will be removed from this earth and the earth will be cleansed and purified by fire at the end of the *Millennial Kingdom*. The 1000 year Millennial Kingdom will be populated by real people in real earthly bodies. The Sheep in the Judgment of the nations and 144,000 Jews from 12 tribes of Israel. The *Age of Grace* or the *Church Age* began when Jesus Christ shed His precious blood on the Cross of Calvary and established a New Covenant by which anyone could be saved simply by placing their faith in Jesus Christ who died for our sins. The *ecclesia* are those who have been called: They are destined to a *heavenly calling* (Ephesians 1:3, Philippians 3:20) to rule and reign with Christ during the 1000 years Millennial Kingdom. Israel has an *earthly calling* to live in the land promised to them by God in the Abramic Covenant (Genesis 15: 1-19, Genesis 26: 4-5). The Jews through Abraham were promised land that they would someday live upon in peace and prosperity. Jesus Christ is the way, the truth and the life for all "Sons of Abraham"....Old and New testament.   The main purpose of the 1000 year millennial Kingdom is to fulfill the covenant Promises to Abraham, Moses and King David concerning their inheritance of the "promised land".

After God has fulfilled His covenant promises of land to Israel, the eternal plan of God to dwell with men which was interrupted when Adam and Eve fell from the Garden of Eden will then be fulfilled (Revelation 21:3, Revelation 22:3). Christ redeemed all men from sin when He shed His blood on the cross, but sin would still reign in man until every sinner is removed from this earth. The earth will remain cursed until the earth is renovated and cleansed by God.

The Sin Issue

Satan was captured, bound and cast into the *Bottomless Pit* after he was defeated at the *Battle of Armageddo*n. The Antichrist and the false Prophet were then cast into the *Lake of Burning Fir*e (Revelation 19:20, Revelation 20: 1-3). At the end of year 1000 Millennial Kingdom Satan will be *loosed* for a little season (Revelation 20:3). Satan will then go forth to deceive the nations into thinking that man can defeat God and be like Him, just as Satan deceived Eve in the

Garden of Eden (Genesis 3: 1-6). He will assemble all unbelievers, who are as numerous as *the sand of the sea* outside of Jerusalem for *Satan's Last Stand.* This time there will hardly be a battle at all: *God* will destroy all who have gathered there with *fire from heaven.*

[**8**] *And shall go out to deceive the nations which are in the four quarters of the earth, Gog and Magog, to gather them together to battle: the number of whom is as the sand of the sea.*
[**9**] *And they went up on the breadth of the earth, and compassed the camp of the saints about, and the beloved city: and* ***fire came down from God out of heaven, and devoured them****.*
[**10**] *And the devil that deceived them was cast into the lake of fire and brimstone, where the beast and the false prophet are, and shall be tormented day and night forever and ever* Revelation 20: 8-10

Satan and all of His followers will march (again) on Jerusalem to kill everyone there and to destroy the Holy City. This is called *Satan's Last Stand.* Christ will not take place in this final battle. God who created Satan and man will destroy all who have gathered there (Revelation 20: 9b), and Satan will be cast into the Lake of Burning Fire (Revelation 20:10) where he will be tortured forever along with the Antichrist and the False Prophet (Revelation 19:20). The *Great White Throne Judgment* will then take place (Revelation 20:11). Where this judgment will be held is not revealed in scripture, but it is likely to be held in the throne room of Jesus Christ north of Jerusalem. *Every* person who did not die in faith will be judged by God at the Great White Throne. Those who were with Satan and were slain at the Battle of Armageddon and at Satan's Last Stand will be raised from the dead and *judged for their works* (Revelation 20:12). While not clearly stated, it is obvious that two other classes of people will also be judged at this

time: (1) Anyone who is still alive and remain from the Millennial Kingdom (2) Anyone who has died during the Millennial Kingdom. Once these people have all stood before the Great White Throne there will be no more humans left on the earth. The earth will then be consumed and renovated by *fire. Everyone* whose name is not written in the Book of Life (Revelation 20:15) will be cast into the *Lake of Burning Fire.*

 [**11**] *And I saw a great white throne, and him that sat on it, from whose face the earth and the heaven fled away; and there was found no place for them.*
[**12**] *And I saw the dead, small and great, stand before God; and the books were opened: and another book was opened, which is the book of life: and the dead were judged out of those things which were written in the books, according to their works.*
[**13**] *And the sea gave up the dead which were in it; and death and hell delivered up the dead which were in them: and they were judged every man according to their works.*

[**14**] *And death and hell were cast into the lake of fire. This is the second death.*

[**15**] *And whosoever was not found written in the book of life was cast into the lake of fire*
Revelation 20: 11-15

This fulfills the words of John the Baptist when he was baptizing in the wilderness.

John answered, saying unto them all, I indeed baptize you with water; but one mightier than I cometh, the latchet of whose shoes I am not worthy to unloose: he shall baptize you with the Holy Ghost and with fire   Luke 3:16

Peter also spoke of this purification.

[**7**] *But the heavens and the earth, which are now, by the same word are kept in store, reserved unto fire against the day of judgment and perdition of ungodly men.*

[**12**] *Looking for and hasting unto the coming of the day of God, wherein the heavens being on fire shall be dissolved, and the elements shall melt with fervent heat?*   I Peter 3: 7,12

Eternity Begins: God Descends to Earth

And I saw a new heaven and a new earth: for the first heaven and the first earth were passed away; and there was no more sea   Revelation 21: 1

The Millennial Kingdom will come to an end. The entire earth has been purged with fire and is without the presence of sin.....Eternity begins. The entire earth has been restored to as it was before Satan fell from heaven before time began, and it is as it was before Adam and Eve left the Garden of Eden. God in his sinless character can once again walk upon the earth as He did in the Garden of Eden. The palace and throne from which Jesus Christ ruled and reigned for 1000 years will be where God will rule and reign for all eternity with His beloved Son

*And I heard a great voice out of heaven saying, Behold, the tabernacle of God is with men, **and he will dwell with them, and they shall be his people, and God himself shall be with them**, and be their God*   Revelation 21:3

All of the tribulation suffered by man...all sickness......all pain......and all sorrow, will exist no longer.

*The **last enemy** that shall be destroyed is death*   I Corinthians 15:26

And God shall wipe away all tears from their eyes; and there shall be no more death, neither sorrow, nor crying, neither shall there be any more pain: for the former things are passed away Revelation 21:4

All things have been made new.

[**5**] *And he that sat upon the throne said, Behold, I make all things new. And he said unto me, Write: for these words are true and faithful.*
[**6**] *And he said unto me, It is done. I am Alpha and Omega, the beginning and the end. I will give unto him that is athirst of the fountain of the water of life freely*
[**7**] **He that overcometh shall inherit all things**; *and I will be his God, and he shall be my son* Revelation 22: 5-7

There are many who want to change portions of the Holy Bible. They want to do the things that the scriptures say are a sin, and they cannot accept anything that changes their lifestyle. Many modern churches accept pedophiles into the pulpit, let homosexuals teach children's church and appoint adulterers to leadership positions. Many theologians teach in bible colleges and deny the virgin birth. Amillennialists and Postmillennialists both deny the clear and literal interpretation of the Book of Revelation and what it says concerning the 1000 year Millennial Kingdom. In Revelation 22:5 God tells the Apostle John to: *Write: for these words are true and faithful.* Those who choose to pervert, change and ignore what is taught and revealed in the Holy scriptures are in danger.

Be not deceived; God is not **mocked**: *for whatsoever a man soweth, that shall he also reap* Galatians 6:7

[**18**] *For I testify unto every man that hear the words of the prophecy of this book, If any man shall add unto these things, God shall add unto him the plagues that are written in this book:*
[**19**] *And if any man shall take away from the words of the book of this prophecy, God shall take away his part out of the book of life, and out of the holy city, and from the things which are written in this book*   Revelation 22: 18-19

The consequences of mocking God, ignoring His commandments and changing the words of God cannot be articulated or known, but Paul had strong words against such behavior when he wrote to backsliding Christians in Rome.

[**18**] *For the wrath of God is revealed from heaven against all ungodliness and unrighteousness of men, who hold the truth in unrighteousness;*
[**19**] *Because that which may be known of God is manifest in them; for God hath showed it unto them.*
[**20**] *For the invisible things of him from the creation of the world are clearly seen, being understood by the things that are made, even his eternal power and Godhead; so that they are without excuse:*
[**21**] *Because that, when they knew God, they glorified him not as God, neither were thankful; but became vain in their imaginations, and their foolish heart was darkened.*
[**22**] *Professing themselves to be wise, they became fools,*
[**23**] *And changed the glory of the incorruptible God into an image made like to corruptible man,*

and to birds, and four-footed beasts, and creeping things.
[24] Wherefore God also gave them up to uncleanness through the lusts of their own hearts, to dishonor their own bodies between themselves:
[25] Who changed the truth of God into a lie, and worshipped and served the creature more than the Creator, who is blessed forever. Amen.   Romans 1: 18-25

In Revelation Chapters 2 and 3 the Apostle John is told by Christ to write a letter to each of 7 churches in Asia. In each of these churches there are those who are called *overcomers* to whom special promises are made about their journey through eternity. As this world comes to an end, God again speaks to those who have become *overcomers* and have been saved by faith and grace are told two things:

> (1) They will drink of the *water of life*.
> (2) They will serve the Lord forever

[1] *And he showed me a pure **river of water of life**, clear as crystal, proceeding out of the throne of God and of the Lamb.*
[2] In the midst of the street of it, and on either side of the river, was there the tree of life, which bare twelve manner of fruits, and yielded her fruit every month: and the leaves of the tree were for the healing of the nations.
[3] And there shall be no more curse: but the throne of God and of the Lamb shall be in it; and **his servants shall serve him**   Revelation 22: 1-3

During the Millennial Kingdom a river came up out of the earth beneath the Throne of Jesus. This river split into two pieces, one ran into the Dead Sea and one ran into the Mediterranean Sea. These waters caused fish and marine life to grow in abundance. Throughout eternity, the same river will come up out of the earth beneath the Throne of God (Revelation 22:1) The *Tree of Life* which God planted in the Garden of Eden will be growing on both sides of the river, and it will bear 12 types of fruit (Revelation 22:2). The fruit will evidently be to sustain all people, and the leaves will contain something unique and special for the *healing of the nations*.

In Revelation 7:17 one of the 24 elders (Revelation 4:10) spoke to John and revealed to Him that God would provide *living fountains of waters* to sustain the innumerable heavenly multitude that was seen standing before the throne of God. Revelation 22:1 is a fulfillment of that promise. There will be a *River of Life* in eternity but there will be no more sea.

*And I saw a new heaven and a new earth: for the first heaven and the first earth were passed away; and there was **no more sea***   Revelation 21:1

Not only will the earth be renovated (not destroyed), but the absence of any curse on the land and the presence of God and His Son Jesus Christ sitting on their throne of glory will magnify the restoration of the earth. No one who will spend eternity with Jesus Christ will be under the crushing weight of the law or under the curse of Satan. There is no doubt that all who have been called to Jesus Christ will be his *servants*....Revelation 22:3 (*doulai* which is the plural of doulas in the Greek). Paul was not ashamed to include himself in this group when he declared that he had died to Christ (Romans 6:7, II Timothy 2: 11-12) and in the flesh that remained he was a *doulas*, a slave or more correctly a *bondslave* to Christ. The KJV consistently translates doulas as a servant, but this is a poor translation from the Greek. A servant is like a modern butler. It is someone who is hired for wages and is a free person, as opposed to a slave who has been bought and purchased and belongs to someone. Paul said that He was a *bondservant* to Christ. A bondservant is someone who sets aside all of his own wants and needs to serve someone else and they are generally bought with a price. Praise God forever, we who live in Christ have been bought with a great price and we belong to Him. We will serve Him and worship Him forever for saving our sinful souls and offering us eternal life.   It is conjecture, but other servants may be those who were martyred for Christ. It is certain that they will all hold a special place in the Millennial Kingdom and throughout eternity. All servants to God the Father and to God the Son will experience an intimate and personal relationship.

And they shall see his face; and his name shall be in their foreheads   Revelation 22:4

There will be a name in every redeemed saint's forehead. This was a promise to those that had *overcome the world* in the Church of Sardis (Revelation 3:12).

Everyone who will enter into eternity will *see His* (God's) *face*. When Adam and Eve sinned in the Garden of Eden, they hid their face from God (Genesis 3:8). Moses was not allowed to see God's face (Exodus 33:20), but Jesus said that *Blessed are the pure in heart: for they shall see God* (Matthew 5:8). We cannot see God's face now but when we do see Him we know that we will be like Him.

[1] *Behold, what manner of love the Father hath bestowed upon us, that we should be called the sons of God: therefore the world knoweth us not, because it knew him not.*
[2] *Beloved, now are we the sons of God, and it doth not yet appear what we shall be: but we know that, when he shall appear, we shall be like him; for we shall see him as he* is
I John 2: 1-2

The glory and radiance of God as He sits upon His throne of glory is almost indescribable.

And there shall be no night there; and they need no candle, neither light of the sun; for the Lord God giveth them light: and they shall reign forever and ever   Revelation 22:5

Revelation 22:5 says that there will be no light **there**. *Where is **there**?* In Revelation 21: 11-27 a description of the New Jerusalem was given. This was continued in Revelation 22: 1-3. This does not mean that the sun will no longer give its light, but that in the brightness of His appearance there will be no reason to have any other light in the Lord's presence (II Thessalonians 2:8).

King David in the Book of Psalms wrote that the sun would give its light as long as the name of Jesus Christ is spoken.

His name shall endure for ever: his name shall be continued as long as the **sun***: and men shall be blessed in him: all nations shall call him blessed*   Psalms 72:17

> The fact that God is light sets up a natural contrast with darkness. If light is a metaphor for righteousness and goodness, then darkness signifies evil and sin. I John 1:6 says that "if we claim to have fellowship with him and yet walk in the darkness, we lie and do not live out the truth." Verse 5 says, "God is light; in him there is no darkness at all." Note that we are not told that God is a light but that He is light. Light is part of His essence, as is love (1 John 4:8). The message is that God is completely, unreservedly, absolutely holy, with no admixture of sin, no taint of iniquity, and no hint of injustice.
>   https://www.gotquestions.org/God-is-light.html

The New Jerusalem

The New Jerusalem is described in great detail in Revelation 21: 1-27. This world cannot conceive the beauty and size of this heavenly city. Abraham lived by faith and He longed to see this city.

For he looked for a city which hath foundations, whose builder and maker is God.
Hebrews 11:10

Jesus Christ has been building this great city in heaven for almost 2000 years.

In my Father's house are many mansions: if it were not so, I would have told you. I go to prepare a place for you.   John 14:2

But as it is written, Eye hath not seen, nor ear heard, neither have entered into the heart of man, the things which God hath prepared for them that love him   I Corinthians 2:9

And the city lieth foursquare, and the length is as large as the breadth: and he measured the city with the reed, twelve thousand furlongs. The length and the breadth and the height of it are equal   Revelation 21:16

And I John saw the holy city, new Jerusalem, coming down from God out of heaven, prepared as a bride adorned for her husband   Revelation 21:2

Revelation Chapter 21 has been interpreted by many biblical scholars to describe things which will happen *in the Millennial Kingdom* and not after. Since the city is descending (to the earth) from *God out of heaven*, this is often declared as happening as the Millennial Kingdom *begins* its 1000 year duration. The reason for this theological belief is an objection concerning heavenly bodies (resurrected and Raptured saints) co-existing with real people who will live upon this earth during this period of time. This does not seem like a reasonable objection since Christ walked, taught and ate with His disciples over a 40 day period of time after His crucifixion. Those who take this position further teach that the New Jerusalem will be the dwelling place of all redeemed believers for 1000 years, hovering over Jerusalem. They also literally interpret Revelation 21:2 as revealing that the New Jerusalem is the *Bride of Christ*. Of course, this is not what Revelation 21:2 says at all. John clearly wrote that he saw the New Jerusalem ***prepared as a Bride*** for a new husband. John is so overwhelmed by this magnificent city that it could not be described except by a literary construction called a *simile* (the comparison of one thing to another that is seemingly unrelated but is descriptive). For example, people often say that "life is a bowl of cherries" or "he is stubborn as a mule".

The *New Jerusalem* will be the largest structure ever built. This massive complex could be a *cube* of 1500 miles or it could be a pyramid with a 1500 square mile base and an apex of 1500 miles high (Revelation 21:16). This means that the base is about as large as an area in the United States which would be bounded by the Atlantic Ocean on the east; the Mississippi River on the west; the border of Canada on the North; and the Gulf of Mexico on the south. An area this large would completely cover *all* of the land of Israel. If it was hovering directly above Jerusalem the entire country would be in darkness. Trees, grass and grain cannot grow without light .

Revelation 21:1 says that: *And I* (John) *saw a new heaven and a new earth: for the first heaven and the first earth were passed away; and there was no more sea.* The 1st assertion that there was a New Heaven and a New Earth is twisted to mean that Israel would be completely changed and that the heaven above it will also be changed. *How could this be believed in light of other scriptural records*? Perhaps even more damning to this position is that there will be no more sea. This cannot possibly be true during the Millennial Kingdom since a river will flow from beneath the throne of Jesus Christ and then split into both the Mediterranean and Dead Seas.

Details and wonders of the New Jerusalem are given in Revelation 21: 10-27 and Revelation 22: 1-6. These will not be discussed in detail but include the following.

- It glowed with light like a Jasper stone, clear as crystal (Revelation 21:11)
- It had a high wall surrounding the city with 12 gates, 3 on each side.
- Each gate was made of a gigantic pearl and each had a name of one of the 12 tribes of Israel (Revelation 21: 12-13, 21)
- The city streets were made of pure gold and the walls were made from Jasper stone (Revelation 21:18)
- Each wall was 144 cubits high or about 216 feet high (Revelation 21:11)

- Each wall was adorned with all kinds of precious stones: The 1st was Jasper, the 2nd Sapphire, the 3rd Chalcedon, the 3rd was Chalcedony and the 4th was Emerald. The 5th was Sardonyx, the 6th was Sardius, the 7th was Chrysolite and the 8th was Beryl. The 9th was Topaz, the 10th was Chrysoprase, the 11th was Jacinth and the 12th was Amethyst. It is interesting that an *ephod* was worn by the High Priest when he performed his duties in the ancient tabernacle. The ephod was adorned with 12 precious stones, one for each of the 12 tribes of Israel. The stones in the ephod were not the same as those found on the 12 foundations of the New Jerusalem, and the 144,000 which were sealed (12,000 from each of the 12 tribes of Israel) do not correspond with either the tribal names written on the 12 foundations nor the precious stone on each foundation. This is a mystery not revealed to us.

- Underneath each wall were 12 foundations. Each had a name of one of the 12 disciples (Revelation 21:14)
- The 12 gates were never shut (Revelation 21:25a)
- There was no night in the city (Revelation 21:25b) because the glory of God and the light of Jesus Christ illuminated the whole city (Revelation 21: 23). Note that this is proof that Revelation 21 is *after* the Millennial Kingdom since *both* God and Jesus Christ will both live in the City with the saints.

Revelation 21:24 in the King James bible demands an explanation.

And the nations of them which are saved shall walk in the light of it: and the kings of the earth do bring their glory and honor into it   Revelation 21:24

In researching Revelation 21:24, it was discovered that all respected Greek scholars agree that the phrase *of them which are saved* is not in the original Greek manuscript. The following is a direct transliteration of Greek to English.

24 καὶ	περιπατήσουσιν	τὰ	ἔθνη	διὰ	τοῦ	φωτὸς	αὐτῆς ,	καὶ	οἱ	βασιλεῖς	τῆς
And	will walk	the	nations	by	the	light	of it	and	the	kings	of the

γῆς	φέρουσιν	τὴν	δόξαν	⟨καὶ	τιμὴν	τῶν	ἐθνῶν⟩ .	αὐτῶν	εἰς	αὐτήν .
earth	bring	the	glory	and	honor	of the	nations	of them	into	it

It is suggested that a more accurate translation of the Greek might be:

The nations will walk in the light of the New Jerusalem and all kings of the earth will bring praises of glory and honor to all who live there

Former kings of the earth from every nation...Jews and Gentiles......White, black or brown, who have had their names written into the Book of Life will be welcome in the New Jerusalem. They shall see all their prior honor and glory swallowed up in the glory and honor of that magnificent city. The heavenly crowns which will be given to all true believers will exceed the glory of any earthly crown which earthly kings wear, and their robes of righteousness will be white and glorious.

Henceforth there is laid up for me a crown of righteousness, which the Lord, the righteous judge, shall give me at that day: and not to me only, but unto all them also that love his appearing.
II Timothy 4:8

And there shall in no wise enter into it anything that defiles, neither whatsoever works abomination, or makes a lie: but they which are written in the Lamb's book of life
Revelation 21: 27

Revelation 21:27 is *not* speaking of two classes of eternal inhabitants which will exist in eternity with God: (1) Those who defile and work *abomination* and (2) Those who have their name written in the *Book of Life*. John is accurately telling us who will enter into eternity and live in the New Jerusalem and who will not. To read into this verse that those who have rejected Christ and engage in sinful practices live outside the city, and those that have become overcomers live in the city, is simply in conflict with too many other scriptures. This verse is just a warning to those who hope to live in the *New Jerusalem* and have had their name written in the *Book of Life* must not be willingly to persist in abominable and sinful practices. People who accept that Christ is the Son of God who died for their sins will die in Christ and be born again spiritually. Those who choose to live in sin and oppose the commands of God will be denied eternal life and residency in the New Jerusalem: *they whose names are NOT written in the Lamb's book of life.*

The New Jerusalem will be far more than an improved version of either ancient or modern Jerusalem. It will be a holy city that will rest upon a renovated earth below a new heaven (Revelation 21:1). The Lord Himself will leave His current home in the 3rd heaven and will live in the New Jerusalem with those who have been redeemed from the earth. Both God and Jesus Christ will live in the New Jerusalem with its inhabitants. It should be noted that there is no mention of where the original 2/3 of all angels who did not follow Satan after he rebelled against God will spend eternity. Perhaps they too will have a special place in the New Jerusalem..... We can only speculate.

To Him that overcometh will I make a pillar in the temple of my God, and he shall go no more out: and I will write upon him the name of my God, and the name of the city of my God, which is new Jerusalem, which cometh down out of heaven from my God: and I will write upon him my new name   Revelation 3:1

But as it is written, Eye hath not seen, nor ear heard, neither have entered into the heart of man, the things which God hath prepared for them that love him.   I Corinthians 2:9

Bibliography

Phillips, Don T., The Book of Revelation: *Mysteries Revealed*, 2nd Edition,
    Virtual Bookworm. com, PO Box 9949, College Station, Texas 7784.

Phillips, Don T., The Book of Ruth: *Historical and Prophetic Truths* ,
    Virtual Bookworm. com, PO Box 9949, College Station, Texas 7784.

Phillips, Don T., Life After Death: *Mysteries Revealed*,
    Virtual Bookworm. com, PO Box 9949, College Station, Texas 7784.

Phillips, Don T., The Eternal Plan of God: *Dispensations, Covenant Promises, Salvation*,
    Virtual Bookworm. com, PO Box 9949, College Station, Texas 7784.

Phillips, Don T., The Birth and Death of Christ,
    Virtual Bookworm. com, PO Box 9949, College Station, Texas 7784.

Phillips, Don T., The Book of Exodus: *Historical and Prophetic Truths*
    Virtual Bookworm. com, PO Box 9949, College Station, Texas 7784.

Phillips, Don T., A Biblical Chronology From Adam to Christ,
    Virtual Bookworm. com, PO Box 9949, College Station, Texas 7784.

Finegan, Jack, Handbook of Biblical Chronology, Hendrickson Publishing Company, Peabody, Ma.

Larkin, Clarence, Dispensational Truth, P.O. Box 334, Glenside, Pa., 1920

Logos apostolic Church of God and Bible College, Interlinear Greek and Hebrew Translation, Logos apostolic.org, United Kingdom, Logos apostolic.org

Ryrie, Charles C., The Ryrie Study Bible, King James Version, Moody Press, Chicago

Dake, Finis J., Dake's Annotated Reference Bible, Dake Bible Sales, P.O. Box 1050, Lawrenceville, Ga., 30246

Walvoord, John F. , The Millennial Kingdom, Academic Books, Zondervan Publishing Company, 1415 Lake Drive S.E., Grand Rapids, Michigan 49506

Salerno, Donald A., Revelation Unsealed, Virtual Bookworm.Com, P.O. Box 9949, College Station,Texas, 77842

Thomas, Robert L., Revelation 1-7, An Exegetical Commentary, Moody Press, Chicago, Illinois

Thomas, Robert L., Revelation 8-22, An Exegetical Commentary, Moody Press, Chicago, Illinois

Nee, Watchman, Come Lord Jesus, Christian Fellowship Publishers, Inc. New York, N.Y., 1976

Footnote: This manuscript has drawn upon several excellent websites found by GOOGLE search. It is my intention to recognize every biblical scholar and source of information from those *giants that walked before me*. This information was sometimes not made available. In other cases information was marked open source or not marked at all. If any author(s) sees any material that they want referenced, please contact me and will acknowledge their previous research and scholarly work. In any case, I am extremely grateful for previous investigations o or conclusions that may (or may not) support this work. God will know them and He will know the source.

Don T. Phillips
Senior Author
phillipsdon60@gmail.com

Spring, 2020

www.ingramcontent.com/pod-product-compliance
Lightning Source LLC
Chambersburg PA
CBHW040858100426
42813CB00015B/2843